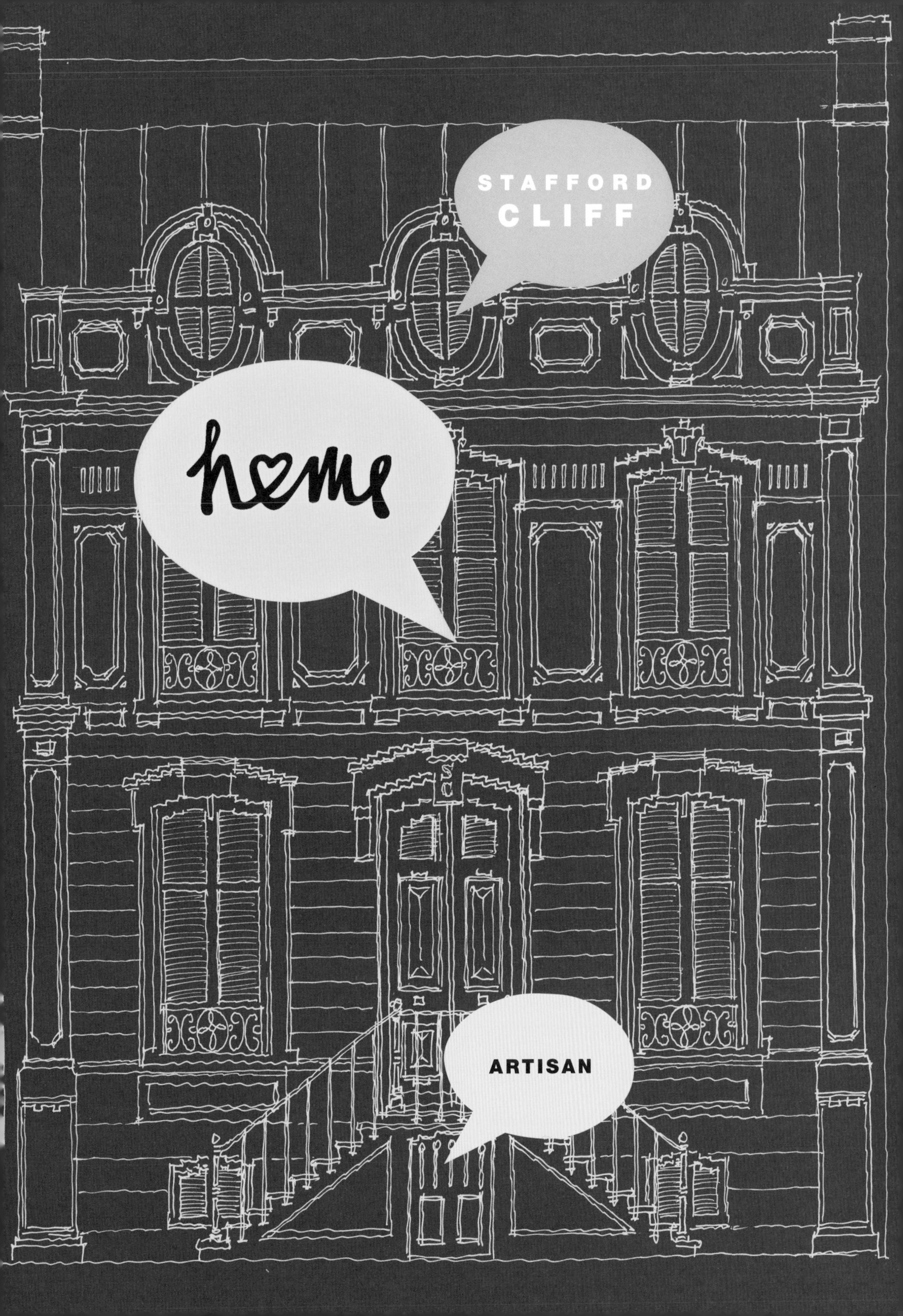
STAFFORD
CLIFF
home
ARTISAN

20
JASPER CONRAN
Fashion Designer

34
PAUL SMITH
Fashion Designer

44
SHERRI DONGHIA
Creative Director Donghia Inc.

30
CELIA BIRTWELL
Fabric Designer

26
DONATELLA VERSACE
Fashion Designer

70
DONNA HAY
Author

14
LI EDELKOORT
Trend Forecaster

48
NICK ASHLEY
Fashion Designer

62
ANDREE PUTMAN
Interior Designer

58
VLADIMIR KAGAN
Furniture Designer

38
NATE BERKUS
Designer

52
BARBARA HULANICKI
Designer

68
ARLENE HIRST
Journalist

78
FERGUS HENDERSON
Chef

74
MICHAEL GRAVES
Architect

88
MIRANDA RICHARDSON
Actor

94
JONATHAN ADLER
Designer

82
KIT KEMP
Design Director

100
SUE TIMNEY
Fabric Designer

106
LULU GUINNESS
Purse and Accessories Designer

114
TIMOTHY HILL
Architect

136
JANE NORTHUMBERLAND
Duchess of Northumberland

120
RICHARD WEST
Cultural Activist

110
PIET HEIN EEK
Furniture Designer

124
DAVID ROCKWELL
Designer

That was the day we came to the village, in the summer of the last year of the First World War. To a cottage that stood in a half-acre of garden on a steep bank above a lake; a cottage with three floors and a cellar and a treasure in the walls, with a pump and apple trees, syringa and strawberries, rooks in the chimneys, frogs in the cellar, mushrooms on the ceiling, and all for three and sixpence a week.

I don't know where I lived before then. My life began on the carrier's cart which brought me up the long slow hills to the village, and dumped me in the high grass, and lost me. I had ridden wrapped up in a Union Jack to protect me from sun, and when I rolled out of it, and stood piping loud among the buzzing jungle of that summer bank, then, I feel, was I born. And to all the rest of us, the whole family of eight, it was the beginning of a life.

But on that first day we were all lost. Chaos was come in cartloads of furniture, and I crawled the kitchen floor through forests of upturned chairlegs and crystal fields of glass. We were washed up in a new land, and began to spread out searching its springs and treasures. The sisters spent the light of that first day stripping the fruit bushes in the garden. The currants were at their prime, clusters of red, black and yellow berries all tangled up with wild roses. Here was bounty the girls had never known before, and they darted squawking from bush to bush, clawing the fruit like sparrows.

Our Mother too was distracted from duty, seduced by the rich wilderness of the garden so long abandoned. All day she trotted to and fro, flushed and garrulous, pouring flowers into every pot and jug she could find on the kitchen floor. Flowers from the garden, daisies from the bank, cow-parsley, grasses, ferns and leaves—they flowed in armfuls through the cottage door until its dim interior seemed entirely possessed by the world outside—a still green pool flooding with honeyed tides of summer.

The long day crowed and chirped and rang. Nobody did any work, and there was nothing to eat save berries and bread. I crawled about among the ornaments on the unfamiliar floor—the glass fishes, china dogs, shepherds and shepherdesses, bronze horsemen, stopped clocks, barometers and photographs of bearded men. I called on them each in turn, for they were the shrines and faces of a half-remembered landscape. But as I watched the sun move around the walls, drawing rainbows from the cut-glass jars in the corner, I longed for a return of order.

Then, suddenly, the day was at an end, and the house was furnished. Each stick and cup and picture was nailed immovably in place; the beds were sheeted, the windows curtained, the straw mats laid, and the house was home. I don't remember seeing it happen, but suddenly the inexorable tradition of the house, with its smell, chaos and complete logic, occurred as though it had never been otherwise. The furnishing and founding of the house came like the nightfall of that first day. From that uneasy loneliness of objects strewn on the kitchen floor, everything flew to its place and was never again questioned.

And from that day we grew up. The domestic arrangement of the house was shaken many times, like a snow-storm toy, so that beds and chairs and ornaments swirled from room to room, pursued by the gusty energies of Mother and the girls. But always these things resettled within the pattern of the walls, nothing escaped or changed, and so it remained for twenty years.

"That people could come into the world in a place they could not at first even name and had never known before; and that out of a nameless and unknown place they could grow and move around in it until its name they knew and called with love, and call it HOME, and put roots there and love others there; so that whenever they left this place they would sing homesick songs about it and write poems of yearning for it, like a lover;..."

My fascination for houses goes back to my childhood in South Australia, when I would visit as many of the elegant old homesteads that I could find, ticking them off from a list provided by the National Trust. Creeping up the drive, I would perch at a safe distance and paint or draw or photograph them, trying to absorb their atmosphere and their character, trying to imagine what sort of life went on in there, without ever daring to knock on the door or ask to look inside. At that stage the ones that fascinated me were the grand European style buildings, not the indigenous wide, ornately embellished verandah and corrugated-iron roof style that attracts me nowadays.

My first job in Adelaide was as a junior commercial artist in a small advertising agency that produced those black-and-white ads in the Sunday papers that advertise three-piece suites in stain-resistant covers at spring sale / summer sale / autumn sale prices.

Arriving in London in the mid 1960s, I joined Sir Terence Conran's design company, and helped create the first Habitat catalogs. One of the innovations I introduced was to take the furniture out of the photo studio and put it into real houses, in the UK, in France, and in America, and to mix antiques and family treasures with the store products to create a more personal impression, and to show that a room depends on old things as well as new. Right away, we began to get requests from customers wanting to buy the old pieces too, and as time went by, I introduced more and more decorating tips and furnishing solutions. It became clear that people were looking for ideas and answers when it came to their homes, and soon we

published "The House Book," a giant compendium of advice and inspiration that became the best-selling home book of all time.

Without knowing it I had found my home ground, or it had found me, and my passion and fascination for homes was to grow and grow, creeping across the globe as, with my friends Suzanne Slesin and Daniel Rozensztroch, we developed the Country-by-Country Style Book series in the '80s. Exploring Japan and Greece and the Caribbean and India, we really did knock on doors and ask to look inside, and the more remote the home, the more delighted they were to show us around and let us take pictures, creating a unique record of what, up until that time, had not been considered relevant to home-furnishing publications. These homes were more about culture, tradition, and family values than about decorating trends, and as such they told a story that spanned the generations and had a resonance that crossed every boundary, and transcended languages. But they were still essentially picture books, destined—as reviewers patronizingly labeled them—for the coffee table. All together, I've done more than 60 books about design or the home, so when my publishers said, "I think it might be interesting to find out more about what people really think of their home—why don't you ask them?," I thought, that sounds pretty simple, doesn't it? Most people have one (some have several) and surely most of them are happy to talk about it. In fact, I was surprised to find out that some people very definitely are not. Of the two or three hundred on my initial list, some of the people had a house that is an extension of their working life—their public image—and it is photographed and redecorated as often as the rest of us buy a new automobile. But as I began to talk to folk, I realized that hardly any of them had been asked about the sort of things that I wanted to know. When we got started, we both realized how very clear their memories were of even their very first experiences of home, and in many cases, how powerful those early influences have been in contributing to who they are today. If our homes are what we make them, then the most interesting, the most comfortable, and the most personal ones are those that, at the same time, reflect the things that made us.

What about you? Do you remember the house you lived in as a child? Did you play beneath the legs of a seemingly enormous table, and can you perhaps even remember the smell of the floor polish? Was your home one that had a special room set aside for "best," or was it full of dogs and cats, muddy shoes, unfinished jigsaw puzzles, and abandoned chickens hatching on the Aga cooker beside the damp tea towels? You see—you've already started to remember things that I bet you've never pondered on before. Perhaps, like me, you grew up in a house that had belonged to your grandparents, or did your family move about every few years, even to different countries? Maybe your early years were spent at boarding school—itself the shell of what was once a grand country house.

From the outset, I wanted to talk not to decorators—who've written or talked about interiors, and whose views we already know—but to those whose work in some other way affects all of our homes, and who might offer a pointer to help the rest of us. Then, as the interviews progressed, I became fascinated by how many people mentioned the same things, and how people living thousands of miles apart had memories that intersected each other, like a marvelous spider's web. I won't tell you what they were; I'll let you find them for yourself, in the same way that you will discover that one person's passionate point of view is contradicted a few pages later by being dismissed as totally unimportant. Quite often, I wanted to jump in and say, yes, yes—that happened to me too; you'll see what I mean. Even those who began by saying that they had no interest in the home whatsoever, turned out to have remarkably firm views on furniture or decor, even preferring to stay in the exact same room of a hotel they often visited. Most interestingly, though we all see many houses in our lives, and find inspiration on house tours or real estate hunting, nobody wanted to switch their own home for someone else's. Most of us live in homes that evolve and grow as we do, changing as our life changes rather than as fashions do. But we should not underestimate the effect that fashion and trends and new technology have on our lives, even the way we use the spaces in the home. Nevertheless it is reassuring to know that when I spoke to some of the most innovative designers and experimental architects, and said, how do you start to work with a new client?, most of them said, "I ask them lots of questions, and get my ideas and inspiration from what they tell me."

I'm not a designer, I'm not a couturier, I'm not an illustrator; I'm a forecaster. Therefore, I always know what fashion has to be, or what style should be, or what lifestyle will be. I've never had the ambition to have my own store or brand, because my fantasy is so great that I've already envisioned it in my mind. Once I've had an idea, I don't need to necessarily see it. I can just imagine it. In fact I am often disappointed when it is finally there, because it's not as good as I imagined. My advice is meant to be used as inspiration and guidance but I'm not waiting and thinking, where is it? Most people who do my job, at some point want to do something solid and three-dimensional, to make a hotel or a shop or a brand, or whatever. I've very rarely had that urge, although I do see opportunities. I think, if I do this now, I can make some money, but I'm not so keen on being pulled out from behind the curtain. One exception is a restaurant called Laurier I've created in Paris; I had already imagined it, even before we began. Then of course it took so much time to get the whole thing together.

As a child I was already living in my imagination: painting, drawing, making things; I made everything out of cardboard—a record player and records, full size. I wanted to be an adult and have adult things. In our living room I had one corner that was my doll's area, with kid-sized furniture. There was a shop and a kitchen with a flame to keep tea hot, and one Sunday I decided to boil milk on it. It took me from ten in the morning till four, when the milk finally began to bubble, and then my parents said, "Put out that thing, we're going for a walk." I protested but they forced me to go and I deeply hated them. When I was born, in the 1950s, we lived in Wageningen in the middle of a beautiful forest hill in Holland. It's the only mountain in the Netherlands and the houses were temporary bungalows given by the Canadians after the war. Yet they're still there; I went back to see them recently. It looks a bit like an artists' community—completely "Bloomsbury," if you want. We were really lucky because it was all young families living around a circular street. My father was the only one with an automobile—he had an Austin Morris—and when there was snow he would tow all our sledges around and around with us on them, my sister and me and all our neighbors' kids. It was an amazing place to grow up. When I was three, we moved to a bigger house, very beautiful with three stories. We didn't have a lot of money, so the house was quite simply furnished, and my mother was developing a modest modernistic taste so we had daybeds in there. I remember they were called "Cleopatra beds." There were rattan chairs and 1960s modern design, and we had fabrics from an artists' community called de Ploeg. In fact, I recently found an old piece of one of those fabrics at my sister's house; it's spooky because your childhood comes back through the print, and it's quite emotional.

My mother had a dressmaker who would make her own clothes and many of ours too, so sewing was something that was highlighted in our house, but often she gave me things to wear that were either too old or too new, discards of her own life: platform shoes, black-and-white fake furs, and very bizarre dress prints. She also gave me some very artistic clothes like handwoven dresses, which I would like to still have now; today they would be 100 percent Prada. When we went to dance parties, all my friends would be wearing synthetic petticoats in pastel colors, while I would have a sleeveless shift dress made from a curtain fabric, exactly what is in fashion now. By the time I was 17, I was anxious to leave home, to have my own universe. I was so desperate to go that I accepted to live in a basement room. When my mother brought me there, she was in tears, saying, "How can you leave our home to live in a place like this?" It smelt of apples. I didn't stay there long, as I soon started to live with a boyfriend. This was the beginning of a wild period; I was at art school in Arnhem and a house was not very important to us. It was all about work and fun. I studied fashion and textiles and we had to work very, very hard, so our environment was not very important, not the way it is today; it was make-do living. You would have maybe a bed and a table, you would find things at flea markets and paint them, but there was not much emphasis on decor. A lot of us were smoking joints with the best Afghanistani stuff, so you had to have places for a lot of people to sit, a lot of cushions on the floor, things from India; the "hippy trail" came in, so I remember there was a lot of Hindu imagery around. The first place that I really established as my own was in Amsterdam, when I got my first job as a forecaster of fashion trends for a department store. I was 21, incredibly young to do such a thing, and at first I had problems with my credibility. I remember that the second week I was wearing a beautiful black crepe dress that I found for one guilder in the Arnhem flea market, and I was told not to dress this way. They really wanted to mold me, so I had to buy commercial clothes and wear horrible things so that I would fit in. A year later, however, I was dressed in all-in-ones from the Korean War and pilot outfits. After a few years, I put on the black crepe dress again and everyone said, "How beautiful!" I traveled to Paris, London, and New York: it was fantastic, it was the Biba period, so decor and fashion were becoming equally important for the first time, and so was food. The whole idea of the concept store was Barbara Hulanicki's invention. Visiting Biba was like going to the Holy Grail; I remember buying reptile papers and my then boyfriend covered our whole bedroom in them. So we had a sort of art deco interior, with a lot of chrome furniture, black lacquer, palm trees, and all those ingredients, which in a way are coming back again, I think. In our store was a woman called Annie Apol who was forecasting interiors. She was a much older woman and we got on very well. I learned a lot from her, about life, about interiors, and decoration. The whole idea of what today we call "well-being" is what she spoon-fed me.

Eventually I wanted to leave my country; it is too small and it doesn't allow you to excel, because once you excel then people start to spit at you. You cannot put your head above the poppy field and I didn't like that. I went to Paris because some boy fell in love with me, so it was very easy. That love didn't last so long, but then I got my own first home, in the 14th arrondisement: a very nice apartment in a courtyard with cats and two big trees. It was very small—a living room, a bedroom, and a kitchen/bathroom—but it was very cute and very Parisienne. There were a lot of writers and special people living in the courtyard and we had a crazy Russian woman who'd climb into the trees. It was just like you imagine Paris would be and I was very happy. I remember I bought a daybed covered in a beautiful pattern of big flowers on a tomato-red background, very opulent and crazy. I then also did a pattern collection for a textile manufacturer so I guess it was a pattern moment again. From there I needed more space, so I moved to another apartment, which was a mistake. It was not as beautiful and it was a big lesson that you cannot change the proportions or the atmosphere of a place with decoration. In terms of housing, I'd rather have a small house with a very beautiful layout and nice light; I'm very conscious about light. In a beautiful building, you don't have to do a lot of decor. Often I have gone from minimal to decorative and back again, inspired by my Protestant upbringing and taste for the new and exotic. Therefore, my quest in life is now to seamlessly blend the contrasts of old and new or severe and seductive. I see a lot of places where I could live very easily. That's a requirement when you travel a lot; I live in hotel rooms and hotel bungalows for a quarter of the year at *least*. Now I have an apartment in Eindoven where I direct the Design Academy, and one in Amsterdam with my partner Anthon Beeke, and a house in Normandy and in Paris, and a loft in New York. The secret is to be able to adapt, because not all of those spaces are the way I want them. I don't have the time or the energy or the focus to make one place *perfectly* the way I want it. I'm not there enough, but I do prefer to be in my own space rather than a hotel, though hotels are better than they once were; the boutique hotel has become a motor for young people to change the way they live, to see design as part of life and not just as an inspiration. Kitchens, bathrooms, and bedrooms are the most important rooms in a house, that's all you need. Today people focus on these three places so much that the others are completely obsolete. It's very strange to see; people will

sacrifice their salon to make a bigger kitchen. Flowers too have become important in my life. I think we've seen an enormous change in flowers now, even the bouquets you get at a railroad station have become much better, although I think England is far behind the rest. In Holland it's got really trendy, whereas in England they still have carnations. The carnation is a very beautiful flower if you study it, like an Issey Miyake design, really, and they have a very nice smell. It's been associated for too long with deep bourgeoisie, so one is not able to look at it fresh anymore. The horticultural industry is now modifying flowers—the scale, the scent, the character, or the color—so you can look at them with a new eye. Sometimes I give them advice as a consultant and of course we show a lot of ideas in my magazine *Bloom*, which has been going for several years now, and I think it's had a big impact. It's interesting to see flowers being sold in fashion stores now. The introduction of them into an otherwise stale environment makes everything come alive; like baking bread in a supermarket, you see that even the plastic-wrapped cookies start to speak—they trigger our senses. I believe that our interior comes to life through living things—cats, birds, fish, plants—and I think that in future we might have a pet plant that we like so much that we take it on holiday with us. Our relationship with living things is very, very strong.

I also believe that creativity is life's insurance, because if you instill creativity even in the smallest children, they will have no fear, because they can improvise. I see it as a solution for all the problems we face today. Creativity is not about a nice interior or a nice wardrobe, or a sense of design. It's about a very subtle way to think and to realize, if this doesn't work, then I can solve things in another way; confidence and flexibility. This century will see the maturing of consumption, so you can make your own choices in terms of transportation, vacations, interiors, everything. I think that creativity is the key, particularly for Europe, and it's something we must build upon. But it must be taught from day one. Then I think we will have more resourceful people. Better bank managers, better travel agents, and even better cab drivers.

PREVIOUS PAGES, OVERLEAF LEFT AND RIGHT
My Paris home consists of three floors in two separated living quarters; here, the main floor leads to a dining/sitting area and a mezzanine. The dining area is furnished with pieces from Paris and abroad: a French industrial table with Senufo stools and furniture from the Paris flea market. The stairs lead to a guest bedroom, while a balcony overlooks my courtyard garden.
FOLLOWING PAGES
My kitchen was created with architect Stephen O'Reily and features reclaimed wood benchtops found in Paris.

When I'm looking for an apartment or a house, I usually have a clear picture in my mind. I've definitely had enough of the five-story house without an elevator, I can tell you—that's for sure. My apartment now is just three ballrooms really—they're big second-floor rooms, but not that many of them. Light is very important. There's lots of light. I knew what I was looking for; I didn't know I was going to find it. There's a target and there's a process of knowing what I don't want. A lot of my memories of childhood are about homes. I remember that my nursery was painted tomato red. I lived with my grandmother at Portsmouth for a while, and I remember looking out at gray aircraft carriers on gray sea. Then my father bought a little house in Suffolk. It had a very old-fashioned English country atmosphere—almost magical. Then when I was seven or eight I went off to boarding school in Shaftsbury. That was definitely not home. Bare light bulbs are not my idea of homely. It was a Tudorbethan house built originally for the Grosvenor family and—understandably—abandoned soon after. Then I went to Bryanston school, which is as ugly as sin in my book. We used to have our classes in ballrooms. I wouldn't say these houses were atmospheric, these houses, they'd been stripped of adornment; their use had been changed.

My mother, Shirley, kept on moving throughout our childhood, so that also became quite a difficult scenario, inasmuch as we really didn't know where we'd be ending up when Sebastian and I got back from boarding school. We'd suddenly find that she'd sold up and bought a new house. We were being moved further and further away from central London. It was hideous, because it underlined how we felt. We never had our own rooms in any of these houses and our things would be in packing cases. I think that's why home means so much to me now. Sometimes we used to be taken by my mother to stay at Longleat; that had quite an impression on me. It was nice, not overwhelming at all, lovely. I liked those proportions. I responded very, very well to big houses— I wanted one. I also liked the countryside, unless I was locked up in it.

As a child, I grew up in my father Terence's houses too. He married Caroline when I was two, and they lived in a very beautiful house in St. Andrew's Place, London. I was very aware that it was special. But I remember them more as Caroline's houses. I felt that she had more influence, she would buy things. It was a combination of the two of them really; I would never say that they were Terence's houses because that wouldn't be true. They were a melding of different influences: very modern furniture juxtaposed with antiques and interesting objects. We were never prevented from touching things. Caroline didn't want that kind of house at all. I think we broke quite a lot of things. Then I went to live in New York, and when I came back my father had left St. Andrew's Place, so my brother and I took it over. I had my own room and a room in the attic, and he was immersed in The Clash punk pop group scene. That was an interesting juxtaposition. But I was still not settled; I was longing to get my own apartment.

For our 21st birthday my father bought us each an apartment. Mine was a very nice maisonette in Chalcott Road, which cost 39 thousand pounds. For the first time, I had somewhere that was mine, an opportunity to use my own design voice. Growing up I had done paintings, but everyone saw Sebastian as the one who was creative. I was just in my own bubble. The apartment was all white, with wooden floorboards, wooden blinds, quite sort-of Colonial, with two big Indian portraits and banana trees. I completely redid the kitchen, and just as they were finishing it I sold the apartment and bought a house, in Regent's Park Terrace. This was the 1980s. At the same time, I had a little house in France, which I'd been doing up over the years. I'm certainly not a do-it-yourself person. It was extremely rundown, so I did it bit by bit: the roof, then the interior, then the electricity, and the plumbing. I think there are certain types of agony that one wants to avoid, but I didn't think, never again. My life, as far as I can see, has been spent buying buildings. But now I've found the right builder.

I never thought that I could be a decorator back then. Interiors were so much my father's domain, or so I thought, so it didn't occur to me. It has now. It occurred to me that I have my own viewpoint. I recognize the validity of the Bauhaus, but I don't need it, and I no longer see it as a modern concept. But what pisses me off is when people rehash it and call it new. A Charles

Eames chair is not new, and it's not modern. What is modern, I wonder? I would say that there is a correlation between fashion and interiors, but I wouldn't say that they are specifically linked within me. If I have a brief to design a range of ceramics or whatever, I just design it. I don't try to make it fashionable. When people are buying their lofts, they need to fill them with furniture that goes with that idea, so then you get the chandelier, and a different proportion of furniture. I would say that there are fashions in interiors—otherwise nobody would be buying furniture, would they? It can be situation-led as well. If you have dogs in the countryside, forget interiors—it's all over. Which is a kind of good thing, because it keeps you free. That's what the countryside is all about.

Having sold my house in France, I wanted something that was in the countryside but easier to get to. For me, a home has got to be attached to a garden—I think that's fundamental to what I think about home. I would say that I'm far more country than urban. I was looking all over the place but a lot of the houses were near roads; I didn't want the sound of traffic. Then a friend of mine sent me a picture of "Flemings," so I went down and I bought it. It had the air of a lost domain. Built in 1240, it is a medieval "hall" house with Elizabethan additions—like a mad ship, all slightly wonky, with wonderful wide, undulating oak floorboards. There is a moat and a big garden. The same family, the Beddingfields, had lived there for 500 years, but recently the owners had tried to turn it into a grand Surrey mansion. I had to begin by unraveling all the stuff that had been put on top: removing the festoon drapes and the nylon carpet, and the textured paneling all over the house; everything gold. The building is heavily listed (which means any alterations have to be approved), but that didn't put me off, because nothing I was going to do would not be right. I wanted to be faithful to it, to reveal it. But it's got very fast rules about what it does and doesn't like, which is fascinating because it's not something that I'm altogether in control of. I can recognize what is right and not right. Modern things don't suit it—radiators for a start. A nightmare. They just look wrong. I don't yet know what kind of light fitting it likes. Added to that, it had plenty of ghosts—benign ones that turn on the radio or the hair dryer in the middle of the night; things like that happen all the time. This house is the hardest thing I've ever done. I like to belong to it, and I realize that I'm basically just looking after it for the duration: I enjoy it, but I don't own it. I just pay for it.

I've always had this idea, this intrigue, for those 1930s couture salons in Paris, like Madame Viollet, that existed in hotel particulair—but the idea was more in my head rather than in actuality. It sat there for years, and then the time came for my business to look at retail, and I thought how boring: those windows; those fittings. I wanted to have a store that was very, very personal to me. I had done so many different products that the idea of the home came to mind as a place to bring everything together and to show my intent—to contextualize. Also a lot of what I do and why I do it doesn't come from a "school," it comes from my Britishness. I like the idea of using heritage, reexamined and reapplied through my head, and this Georgian townhouse just off Piccadilly, London, is a focus for that. Maybe I'm house obsessed: I love them.

OVERLEAF AND FOLLOWING PAGES
I've done so much work on the house in Suffolk, but one of the first jobs was to strip out all of the horrible '80s and '90s finishes, replaster the whole house, and restore and repolish all of the old floors. The effect makes it look curiously modern. This is one of the seven bedrooms and five bathrooms, for which I've gradually been finding furnishings. By contrast, in the drawing room, most of the furniture I've had for years. Unexpectedly, the kitchen was one of the easiest rooms to do; tiled floors, open shelves, Aga stoves, butlers sinks, and rustic finishes are all things that fit my aesthetic and work perfectly in this house.

POSTSCRIPT
Since talking about Flemings Hall, my obsession for houses has struck again, and I have decided to sell it and move on. No doubt I will shortly be in the midst of yet another challenging new home project.

I always maintain that a home reflects the owner's personality. I feel totally at ease within my house. Culture, feeling, color. This is the way I summarize my home. I chose vivid colors, courageous but harmonious, and diffused by a warm sunlight. Sentiments are translated into warmth: the elegance of the furniture, the spectacular internal prospectives, the richness of the objects, in my opinion do not cancel the ever-present personalization of the whole. Culture: references, quotations, similitudes.

From the smallest details to the atmosphere as a whole, everything is positioned to stimulate interest and lightness. For example, my dining room combines Imperial consoles with spectacular Chinese vases, at my request also painted on the walls in a trompe l'oeil effect, creating an atmosphere suspended between dream and reality. I've been searching for a long time for this home. I wanted to have a home that I also loved from the outside.

When I first saw the building in which I now live, distinguished by time and covered with ivy, I was really fascinated and I immediately understood it was the right place. This home—in the center of Milan—at the beginning did not reflect the needs of myself and my family. Initially two apartments on the same floor were united, and more recently a further apartment situated on the third floor has been added.

The most symbolic anecdote I have about my home is one referring to my bathroom, a room in my house very important to me. Despite all the work, it never appeared to be large enough and at the conclusion of the renovation, despite already being considerably large, I chose all the same to include a mirrored wall to add to the effect of space. Now I'm satisfied.

How do you identify who you are, and what you're going to be? Sometimes I think that possibly, had I been given the opportunity, I should have done more things for the home rather than for fashion. My parents had three daughters and we lived in a semidetached "sunshine house" in a suburb of Manchester (England). This tiny, funny house had a dining room that went right through from front to back, so the sunshine would always hit it depending on the time of day. My father was a very bookish man. We had these very nice "minty" bookshelves that had sliding glass doors. As a kid I recall going to junk shops, and I once got this ridiculous vase with a parrot as a handle. Whenever my friends were coming around, I'd wait till the others had all gone out, and then I'd revamp the sunshine room to accommodate my friends. When it came to buying my parents' three-piece suite, I went with my mother and chose this 1950s lime-green wool fabric—hideous now, of course. She was very practical. I'd take her to a Manchester store called Kendal Milne & Co. and say, I want a dress like this. Then we'd go off to Liberty's and buy some fabric and she'd make patterns out of newspaper. She worked as a dressmaker, so she was very good at children's clothes— they were flat and simple to make. We had her tied to the sewing machine almost all of the time. Home was always quite a big part of me. I'd say, let's go and get some wallpaper to put above the fireplace. I remember Heal's (in London) did a range of rather avantgarde papers with seascapes and things. She took me to these stores.

My father was a keen gardener, so I've got that from him, but I'm not bookish like he was. He couldn't wait to get us away so that he could just sit and read. I regret it, though, because if you like books as a child you're bound to be brighter than if you're visual and a bit of a dreamer. I've always been attracted to people who read a lot. At art school in Salford I thought, what on earth am I going to do? I'd trained as a textile designer but there was no fashion course there. Then they gave me a job two days a week teaching home economics students how to make cake decorations. That was quite amusing, but I had no idea really. Fate plays a big part in one's life. Around this time, I came down to London for a summer vacation. A girlfriend had a room in Ladbroke Grove, so I came to stay with her for six weeks, and I never went back. In London I met this extraordinary man called John Manesseh. It was 1964, and he had a double-fronted house in Allison Road W3, where lots of artists had rooms. Peter Blake, Derek Boshier, and Pauline Boty were all there. I had a room with a little kitchen in one corner, but the brilliant thing about it was that John was an antique dealer of a very strange breed. He had fabulous taste, and his home was quite extraordinary. There were two huge rooms on the first floor that were filled with wonderful furniture, and I could just go and borrow whatever I wanted to furnish my place. He would take me to auctions and country house sales in an old Harrods van he'd bought. Eventually, he got very grand ideas to upgrade the house and make it smart, so he threw us all out. Then I met Ossie Clark —just by chance—and my life changed. Thinking of rooms from that period, I remember we always had to have a black-and-white check floor in the kitchen, even if it was only linoleum. I still have one in a little extension I've just built in my current house. Tongue and groove walls, usually varnished in a dreadful yellow pine color; there was a table made from the metal base of a sewing machine with a marble top, and everyone had a paper lantern. These were characteristics of the 1960s in London.

Property is the only thing I've ever really made money on. For a while I lived in a four-story house across the road from the shop in Westbourne Park Road. I've always lived in the Portobello Road area; I'm not a flyaround, I'm a creature of habit. A home in the country would be my dream, but I've never been able to afford it. For the past seven or eight years, I've lived in a three-story house, still in this area. I like my house very much now; it has a very nice feel to it. But when I first moved, I remember feeling quite ill. It was a sort of panic, I felt as if it was never going to be right. The boxes had to stay unpacked until I could decide what to do. The sofa was too big and had to be thrown out. I love second-floor sitting rooms, and I like traditional rooms, with fireplaces, cornices, and traditional features. I like light, but you can often *make* light by using mirrors and color in a certain way. At the same time, in my old house, I painted the main hallway a navy blue. I thought, there's no point in pretending this is ever going to be anything but a gloomy room, so I made a feature of it. I've often had a red room too. I've got quite a lot of nice pictures, and they sit well on red. In the winter it's gorgeous, but not so good in the summer, when I think, God, I hate this room. Lighting is very, very important in rooms; in fact, I sort of collect chandeliers.

Though I have the shop, I've always worked from home. I get up and just go straight to my drawing board and fiddle about. Designing is quite personal, and at home you can be "as you are." I am a bit of a magpie— I have some nice things; they're not expensive but they give me a certain amount of joy. Clutter is OK if it's restrained. I do go to garage sales and buy endless "tosh," but I also give lots of it away. I put little stories together, little vignettes. A room evolves over time, doesn't it? Things emerge that you might never have imagined had you not lived there for an amount of time. If you change your pictures, you can change a lot of the room—it's a good way of making it look quite different. People remember that when I was younger I was always moving rooms around and rearranging things, but I don't do it so much now. It can become a bit of an illness, can't it—a sort of neurosis?

RIGHT
The striped fabric that I've used on these sofas is called Seraglio from my collection, and the cushions in front of the mirror are a collage of my designs, made by Kay Dimbleby.
OVERLEAF LEFT AND RIGHT
The wire sculpture is by David Graves. I also love the display-top coffee table (left) from Andrew Palmer.

I've always been attracted to houses. When I was 21 my wife Pauline, who was teaching fashion design at Nottingham School of Art, would take a selection of her students (and me) twice a year to see the couture shows in Paris. In those days, unlike now, there would be perhaps 30 people in the audience, so we saw Chanel when she was still alive; the famous Yves Saint Laurent show when he did the homage to the Vietnam War; Patou; Courrège. They were always held in these beautiful houses and I thought one day it would be my dream to open a shop in a house. My shop in Notting Hill Gate, London, is in a house and now, after many, many years of searching, I've just managed to open a menswear shop in Nottingham in a beautiful house called Willoughby House, which was built in 1738. It has a 150-foot garden and it's right in the middle of the city. When we opened, it caused such a stir—people looked on it as a kind of museum, they were so proud of it; they went in almost with tears in their eyes. When we open a new Paul Smith shop, we start by looking for a building that we hope has character. With two colleagues, I now design all our shops around the world.

I was born in a small town just outside Nottingham called Beeston. My parents bought the land and had the house built. It was just a simple provincial house with a nice garden, an apple tree, and a toy house. I don't really know about the design, I guess my father just hired a builder. My father did everything; I think his business was really modest, so he not only repaired the automobile, he would also repaint and decorate the house. He would lay new carpet or if there was electrical work, he would do it. It was very of its time (1958) with patterned wallpaper—people were doing all the things we now hate: covering up a lovely door with hardboard; taking down the picture rail, and hanging wallpaper right up to the ceiling; filling in the banisters of the staircase. It was the trend of the time to add something to your home; my parents built a little porch at the front door. They were fairly aware of what new things were happening. My father met lots of people every day; he was something that doesn't exist today—a credit draper. He sold household linen and clothes to people from his automobile, and they paid him so much a month. It was a little business that he'd built up from his previous experience as an insurance salesman. He had a "round," a selection of people in the town. They'd say, "I need a shirt, Dad"; he was a father figure to so many people, because everybody used to discuss their worries with him. My mom was a mom. Our house was always full of aunties and relations; it was a happy house. Neighbors kept popping in. My father had a very strong personality—very happy, always coming up with jokes, making things, inventing things. Even on the beach, he would pick up a pebble and draw a picture on it with his pencil. There was always creativity around me, but we never discussed art, or my going to art school.

My memory of my childhood is very strange; it doesn't really start until I was 11, when I got my first racing bicycle and became hooked on cycling. I kept my beautiful bike in my bedroom, so I could look at it at night. I became very interested in how things were made, the beauty of engineering. I could build a bike and take it apart. I started to race as a schoolboy and eventually as a junior, going on club runs. So suddenly I was going away from my family; I was independent. That was a punctuation mark. Then when I got to 15, my father said, "What do you want to do?" I just wanted to cycle—to be a professional rally cyclist—that was my dream. But he said, "That's not a real job" (which it would be nowadays); so I left school on a Friday, and on the following Monday I started work at Cree and Fletcher, one of the wholesalers where he used to buy some of his dry goods and shirts and things, in Nottingham's Lace Market. I never had an interview, he just rang up Mr. Fletcher. I remember I had to arrive with a gray overall, a pencil, and an eraser, and I got paid three pounds five shillings a week. I was just a runaround boy, but I learned a lot from that job, because it was a very thrifty company, run on old-fashioned terms. In the meantime I was still cycling, and when I was 17, I had a bad crash and ended up in hospital for three months. When I came out, that was when my life changed and the reason I'm sitting here now. Some of the other patients arranged to meet up in a pub called the Bell Inn in Nottingham and, unknown to me, it was the pub where a lot of the local art students met. I began to hear about the Bauhaus and Kandinsky and Andy Warhol and pop art and swinging London, which was then related to fashion and Carnaby Street, and suddenly I thought—this sounds really good! I recognized that fashion was probably a nice way to earn a living.

In 1967 I met Pauline, who continues to be my wife, and we got our first apartment together. It was a fantastic place in a beautiful Georgian street in Nottingham called Park Terrace. The owner told us later that the reason he let it to us was because of Pauline's smile. Frankly we couldn't really afford it, but we fell in love with it. It had high ceilings, big entrance hall with a magnificent door, but the main feature was the living room, which had a big window overlooking

"the park," and beyond to Nottingham Castle. We had one 11-foot-long couch made and covered in pale gray velvet—that was our big expense. There was a brass bed, but otherwise it was very sparsely furnished. We came to London once or twice a month; there was such an explosion of energy—Habitat had just opened. Around this time, with Pauline's encouragement, I opened my own little shop. Up until then I had been in partnership with a friend buying menswear for her shop, but with Pauline's support I started designing menswear. She never taught me physically, but I learned from her: the importance of scale; of proportion; the pitch of a sleeve; the qualities of hand stitching. I think that's the real reason I've managed to have some longevity in my business: the practical training of my father and the warehouse, but also, the importance of beautiful quality and the understanding that simplicity can still be special. Eventually, we bought a modern house in the same area. We missed the large proportions, but the idea of owning your own home is a very British idea. And that's when we went for a whole modern look: leather couch by Tobia Scarpa; a couple of Andy Warhol Marilyn prints; dark brown carpet.

Finally we moved down to London; Pauline, who'd gone to the Royal College of Art with David Hockney and Ossie Clark and all that lot, couldn't keep away any longer. At first we lived in a tiny one-room bed-sitter. Then later we got a little house in Notting Hill Gate, but we pretended it was Byzantine and painted it all white with a turquoise front door, and put down parquet floors. We loved to travel and wherever we went, I'd take an extra bag to bring back little things from markets to sell in my London shop: rag rugs from Greece, pen knives, nice old notebooks. I was one of the pioneers of selling things other than clothes in a clothes shop. When we could afford it, we bought art. I remember going to Hockney's first-ever show at the Whitechapel Gallery in 1970. They had produced a limited-edition print called "Pretty Tulips," which cost 42 pounds. I decided we either had to pay the gas bill or buy one of these prints. They came to switch off the gas, but fortunately Pauline's smile came to the rescue again and we managed to get by. We now live in a beautiful square in London and we're very settled. But we've always loved Italy—the people are very, very nice and they really have a love of life. We have two houses there, one in the Tuscan countryside and one by the sea in Sardinia. The Sardinia house was built the year we met (1967) by an Italian architect from Turin; but he'd died and his family never wanted to go back, so they just closed the door and sold it, complete with all the contents from that era: Joe Colombo chairs, Flos lights, tin trays from Habitat. I could hear echoes of those days back at the Bell Inn —hearing about a man called Le Corbusier and his technique of shutterboard concrete construction. This house was made in exactly the same way. It was a must-have. I also spend a lot of time here in my office, where I have lots of books, antique textiles, tin robots, advertising things. But my real indulgence is art, and it's not any specific sort of art. It can be by a student or a very famous person. I have so much piled up and more downstairs; it's like an addiction. I change them around from month to month. My latest project is a little "home" shop in Albemarle Street in London, where we sell some of the housewares I've designed—rugs and ceramics and fabrics—along with some of the huge collection of "stuff" I've acquired: tables, chairs, ceramics; things that are interesting without being classics. It's a bit of fun and a bit of self indulgence.

Apart from that I still travel for seven months of the year. To be honest, I love my homes, but I don't spend a lot of time in them. So when I'm away, I don't miss home. I'm totally where I am at the time. But I do always stay in the same room in the same hotel—in Tokyo or Paris, even Nottingham. I'm a creature of habit.

PREVIOUS PAGE

My office is on the top floor of our London headquarters, a brick-built warehouse from the 1900s. This, as you can see, is where I work and where I keep most of my books and my purchases. The desk at the far end was made by Gordon Russell Ltd in 1978 and, underneath the top, there is the original label crediting AT Harvey.

RIGHT

In the room next door, I have covered all three walls with what is only a fraction of my art collection. The rest is in storage. The table and the two chairs are from the 1960s by the Danish designer Yens Kiskard, and on the Danish sideboard, also from the same period, is a contemporary (Blue Cross) medicine chest by Paul Kelly.

When I began to do residential projects, the most enjoyable thing was finally arriving at a level of experience and self awareness, knowing that I was able to help people make decisions about their home that they felt good about. When people are paying for your opinion you have to know yourself very well and that is one of the things that has shifted the notion of decorating private homes for me. It was developing a degree of honesty with my clients and allowing them to feel comfortable enough to truly tell me how they live. I don't really work very well with people who aren't comfortable in their own skin. I don't want to create an interior that someone won't be able to appreciate—I mean really love living in. That applies to the projects we do for my company, as well as the makeovers I do for television. I need to understand peoples' motivation behind their decorating. Is it for them and their children; are they decorating to impress other people; are they open to collecting things they truly have a passion for, or because they just want a wall of books? I sort of react viscerally to peoples' personalities, and one of my most rewarding projects was for a couple who were getting married a bit late in life and who had collected outsider art and created this sort of manic collection, and they had no idea how to create a shell to house it and to live gracefully with those things. That to me was a challenge that I could sink my teeth into. They were surrounded by things that they loved, and came to me to find out how to make it enjoyable. We also get a lot of projects where we collaborate with the builder and the architect before the ground has been broken. I find that the most talented people in my business are really not ego-based. As long as you have the capacity to communicate clearly, the more the merrier. We all steal ideas from every-where. There are very few people who have truly original ideas outside of sculptors and painters, so design is based on inspiration and the interpretation of that inspiration. I've never closed myself off to the opinions of others.

I was raised in a family where the home was very important. We lived in Minneapolis and my mother was a decorator. She did do some commercial work, but it was primarily residential. Some of my earliest memories are of coming home from elementary school to find a completely different environment from the one I'd left that morning. It wasn't discussed beforehand. For instance, the entire living room would have been changed and furniture from storage or from another area in the house would have been brought in, and the seating configuration would be different. Things would be waiting to be sent out to be re-covered. That

happened often, very often. It was just a fun environment to grow up in. Sometimes my bedroom was moved to a different room in the house. My mum solicited my opinions: "What do you think? Do you think we should move this back? I was thinking of having this piece painted." It was very much an open dialogue. My dad didn't have much of an opinion regarding these things. Then when I was 13, I was given my own room and I remember being so heavily involved in the decorating process. I would race home to find out what progress had been made and I would ask all the contractors working on the job—the wallpaper hanger, the plumber, the painter—a thousand questions. At the same time, I would go to friends' homes and push their furniture around as well. I would tell their parents that the room would be better a certain way and they might say, "Well, fine, go ahead and try it." Most often it was met with success, but I would always have ideas at the end that required them to buy some other things. That's when it got a little strange, and I was asked to go back to my own house. My grandparents were in Philadelphia and we would go visit them, and I remember that in their house everything that they did, they did once. I think that my mother felt very constrained by that. She knew that when we walked into someone else's home I would immediately be thinking of the decisions that they'd made in creating a home for them-selves. But for me, it didn't really translate into a career. I thought that I would work in fashion or around furniture in some way. My mother and I would go antiquing together and I remember that feeling when you walk into a really large antique shop on four levels, and you're 12 or 13 years old, and you know you're going to be there for the next four hours, because it's major. That is something I still like to do today. My mother's decorating style was French Country, which couldn't be farther from my own design aesthetic. But it was pleasing to her. We traveled a lot as a family. But wherever we went—it could be a day trip to somewhere in the Midwest, or it could be France—furniture and decorative arts were always a part of the itinerary, always. On biking trips through France, there was a family joke that she would pretend to be going to cycle with us but would end up riding in the van with all the things for the home that she'd bought.

When I graduated from college, I took an internship with an auction house in Chicago. That's when my fascination for furniture became all-encompassing. I remember the first day that I worked there being in such awe of the specialists in the different departments and thinking, how does anyone retain that much information? It became a goal for me to be

a generalist. I really wanted the bigger picture. My goal was to be able to walk through an estate and get 75 percent of the things correct as far as their period and value, and what they were made of and their stories. Again I asked a thousand questions, and I worked 60 hours a week. Regional auction houses, if they want to get one or two fine paintings that somebody might have, are often obliged to take the entire estate, which might be 7,500 square feet of decorative objects and furniture that they might not normally want. After a while I was given a series of monthly auctions to run myself, selling the less expensive items. I was 23 years old. I would set up the sale room for each exhibition in a series of separate room settings or vignettes. I was obsessed. The items sold very well because they were shown in a way that people could relate to. I was the only person in the company who got upset when something that was hideously upholstered came in, because I knew it would throw out my displays. I was left trying to sell what other decorators had convinced people to buy. Nobody in the company wanted to speak to me because I caused them so much extra work. I was also tempted into buying a lot of things for myself every month, and when I left the auction house I owed them so much money. It took me two years to pay it back. During this time my boss, a woman called Leslie Hindman, was asked to host a television show based on the auctions on the newly launched Home and Garden Channel, and she asked me firstly to art-direct the show, and later I began to appear on the shows as a guest, giving tips on how to use different items in different settings, etc. At this point I had two goals: I wanted to have my own business, though I didn't know what that should be; and I wanted to be independent so that I could travel, which I still love to do. And so I brainstormed with some friends and we decided collectively that I should go into design and decoration. At the time I was living in a really tiny, charming apartment in Chicago that I had sort-of filled with all the things that I'd bought from the auctions. From then on I got business cards printed and just started getting clients. My work was well received in the local press, but for me the most difficult part of starting up was finding craftsmen and suppliers who could create what I wanted to do. I remember walking through someone's home and them suggesting they'd like a wall of woodwork and thinking, yes that would be great, but I have no idea who can build it. I think I made a lot of mistakes in the beginning.

I'm an ideas person. I was constantly being told that many of the ideas I had couldn't be done. Later, when I gained more experience, I found that many of my ideas and plans could absolutely be done. That's one of the things that was so appealing to me when I started working on "The Oprah Winfrey Show." Having worked on design projects that took a year or two to complete, the opportunity of being able to finish something top-to-bottom in just a few days, sometimes with people working around the clock, was amazing. Creatively it was fantastic. I was just so taken with the notion that I could have an idea and then see that vision come to life instantly, often with items being located and delivered within a matter of hours. It is an incredible acceleration of the design process. I was completely unaware of the camera. I wasn't really connected to the fact that millions of others were seeing it too, until I started writing my book. That was when I really became aware of the many questions that people wanted and needed to have answered, so they could live better in their own homes. Whether it's the pages of a book or a television makeover, I think it is important to share two things. The first being to educate and empower. People should feel confident in their decisions and their ability to implement certain ideas themselves. And two, pleasing the homeowner. On every project, I spend quite a bit of time asking them about their likes and dislikes. My main concern is that they absolutely love the way they live.

PREVIOUS PAGE

Part of my library, the room I spend most of my time in. Oriental limed oak panels designed by Samuel Marx in the 1950s are a perfect backdrop for my modern furniture.

RIGHT

This is a corner of my favorite room in my home, in a 1918 building on Chicago's north side. The mirror I designed, and hanging next to it is an old Hermès seat found in the junk shops of the 16th arrondissement in Paris, that I carried around all day like a lunatic. The table is Italian chrome with an inset onyx top from the 1970s, and the lamp I'd say is mid-century American. On the table is a little folk art frame.

OVERLEAF

I think every home needs a wall of memories; this is a view of my bedroom that includes an 18th-century drawing by Gonse, a Parisian architect who designed much of the wrought iron in the city, a Christopher Makos portrait of a camel, which I think I resemble early in the morning, a song board given to me by James Taylor, and photography I love, as well as a houndstooth child's wool coat from the '20s.

For me, fashion and interiors are totally inter-connected—totally, totally. They feed off each other. I definitely think fashion people get a lot of inspiration from home furnishings. Things start with the fabric. I am having garments made for myself out of our Donghia Furnishing fabrics. You can't get that kind of fabric in the fashion industry. The life-span of a fabric at Donghia is eight to ten years. Fashion is for one season, and there are four to six seasons a year. Our kind of fabrics would be between the highest ready-to-wear and couture. People don't realize that, but they're really special. If we really move fast we can get a new fabric on the market in six months, the average is two years, but I think in future we'll be able to speed that process up. The things we do are not trendy, they're timely and timeless. We have a knack of taking whatever everyone is being inspired by and doing the ultimate versions of that. A look that is going to become like a design classic. I like doing designs that are chameleon enough that they look different to different eyes. To me, a pattern might look Ottoman; to someone else it's Far Eastern or Indian. We're selling these fabrics to go on anyone's furniture— beautiful vintage pieces, as well as drapes, as well as duvets on the bed. I remember my mother had different bedspreads for different times of the year. The bed clothing was all the things that were made for her wedding trousseau. There was one quilted satin piece that she had on her bed in the winter that I still remember; I always thought it was so elegant. Whether it was dressing herself or dressing the house, it was the same, she was into all that stuff—and still is.

We lived in Vandergrift, western Pennsylvania, a small town of ten thousand people that was designed by Frederick Law Olmsted, who designed Central Park in New York. It was meant to be the perfect blue-collar working-man's town. My parents built their house in 1957 when I was ten and my brother was six. I don't remember the architect, but my parents did a lot of the drawings themselves; it had these beautiful bay windows and columns in the front. My mother always loved design and their house was something they worked on together. It wasn't huge, there was a terraced backyard and an alleyway in the back. All the houses had amazing gardens, with tomatoes and special dandelion greens from Italy—a lot of Italian families lived in this area. Even then, I was such a fabric person that I remember the man from Pittsburgh, who came with all these amazing fabric samples for the Austrian shades and the draperies. My mother never changed the draperies and they're still like brand new. At 85, she still lives on all three floors and keeps the house like a shrine. Everything was of a really good quality and you'd never think it was old; the oven and the cook top are still like brand new. She could head up the house in that film "The Remains of the Day." She is totally into knowing how to maintain a house. She had a special attachment in the furnace to filter the air. I could go on and on. The den had a stone fish-pond in the corner of the room, a little tiled area with a fountain, and actual goldfish that we used to have to take out with a net to clean the fountain once a month. One of the fish was called Whale.

I always wanted to be a fashion co-ordinator, even though I didn't totally know what that meant. I loved those big stores in Pittsburgh. It was really elegant then, to go into the city—you got dressed up. My parents would go in every week and my father—he was a doctor—would have a manicure, and we'd go to a really nice restaurant. In college, my desire was to get out and move to New York City. To me, that was the mecca for fashion clothing, and all of that was my passion. I married shortly after I started my career. Roger and I met while we were both working at Bloomingdales. We had a one-bedroom apartment on 66th Street, and that was the beginning of who I am. It was really terrific. This was the early '70s, when Angelo Donghia (my cousin) was just beginning to become the superstar decorator. I don't really remember him when we were growing up, because there was such an age difference. All I remember was going swimming with him during the summer.

Since I've been in New York, I've lived in three spaces: the one-bedroom apartment, the two-bedroom apartment, and the three-bedroom loft where we are now. The first apartment was great, it was like a little box of chocolates. We painted the bedroom dark green, and I know that I had real grosgrain ribbon trim on the draperies—pattern on pattern; it was definitely about what was happening in fashion, reflected in the home, but that's what Angelo was doing in his interiors about then also. Then we moved to the two-bedroom apartment, which had this fabulous view of New York City, and a curved wall; that was really something. I had this amazing shearling coat that I'd bought in Paris. It was a beautiful geometric design with shades of

camel, gray, and taupe with black leather, and I thought, this is what I want my living room to look like. I saw it in terms of color and texture. The whole apartment was about creating a very calm setting for this amazing view. I had these huge pillows on a banquette that we had built because we couldn't afford the Donghia furniture. We always liked to entertain; my husband likes to cook. He and I always had similar tastes so there was never an argument. We stayed there —I hate to tell you—too many years. In the end, it had three makeovers. That's when I learned that a few pieces of oversized furniture work so well in a smallish apartment. It also became a laboratory for the work, because Angelo passed away in 1985, and I went from the fashion business into the furnishing world. The man who was running the Donghia product company and the furniture company wanted someone from the fashion world as a partner. I kept sending him my friends because I was doing really well with my own design-consulting business by this time; but in the end, he said, "I think you should consider joining me."

We've been in my dream apartment in Tribeca for seven years. It was about two things, the luxuries that you can't ever have enough of: light and space. Initially I didn't want to make any major statement, I wanted to live there for a year first, so we brought all the furniture with us. I didn't want to go in and have it finished in a month, I wanted it to evolve. I wanted to figure out if I wanted two fabulous sofas, or just this huge expanse of seating that floats in the middle of the room. I wanted the fabric on the big pieces of furniture to be really comfortable against naked skin. Your environment is a blank canvas and you paint and texture and furnish it with your bits and pieces—it's a collage and you put it together. You should use every inch of space, and not save space for a special occasion. The formal dining room, that's long gone. We had this white "floating" wall between the living space and the kitchen and I decided that it couldn't remain white, it had to anchor the space. So I found this amazing artist who does stucco Veneziano, and I said to him, crushed olives and capers, and he did this gorgeous job using plaster, marble dust, wax, and paint. That wall makes such a difference to the space.

I love old fabric mixed with new fabric, and I collect vintage fabric from everywhere, and I collect old boxes and trunks. My home is a collection of all the things I really like, that are meaningful to me; so I can see that, in another life, I could be a 21st-century nomad, or a Bedouin. I could pack everything into the trunks and take it all with me.

PREVIOUS PAGE
This is the living room, looking from the entryway, of my previous Midtown apartment. There is handmade Donghia wall covering on both the walls, and the bulletin board (which is really a screen) displays anything that I find inspirational, such as a number of Romeo Gigli fashion illustrations by Mats Gustafson, notes from friends, and postcards from exotic places. There is wool sisal carpeting throughout the place and in terms of furniture, the picture shows a vintage Donghia faux-ivory coffee table and a selection of our upholstery pieces, including, in the back, one of my favorite pieces ever: the Plaza Suite chair, which is 50/50 upholstered in gold and silver Donghia Palazzo fabric.

RIGHT
This is a view of the living area in my current Tribeca loft, as seen from the long hallway. I had the mirror made (which can also be seen in the previous picture), after I had seen a similar piece at the American Academy in Rome. It reflects a shelving unit, which displays some of my collections of coral, mercury glass, and red lacquer boxes. You can also see the Supper Table (a design by Joe D'Urso for Donghia), the Donghia Studio X dining chairs in our Onde fabric and a beautiful window treatment with a pelmet, using zari (metal thread) embroidery that is done in India.

I've always been obsessed with clothes. Probably I was influenced by my mother; in fact, I'd had a subscription to *Vogue* magazine from age seven. I also had a subscription to *Autocar* magazine, so that balanced it out. It's the same to this day. After going to the fashion school at St. Martin's College of Art in London, I got a couple of short jobs and then went to work for my parents. I went straight in at the top—design director—and began to build up a team of people who were doing fashion and home, it was equal. We were not modern, we were Renaissance. As my mother said, one of her guiding principles in design terms was that you should always look behind before you go forward. So basically it was about evolution. If we were designing a cup and saucer, then why start from scratch? With a design that's evolved over the years, it's only really a question of applied decoration, and as Laura Ashley was a print house there was no shortage of that. I think that she was trying to uphold good old-fashioned values basically, which were about more than the product. It was about the way you lived within your home as well. All her dreams and inspirations were instilled in her by her mother's mother, whom she called "Grandmother Wales" and who had high standards but low income. My mother pushed them into us.

I had an older sister and brother and when I was born we lived in a small rented cottage on an estate in southern England. They weren't allowed to do a lot to it, maybe paint it. My mother grew vegetables out the back, and we had a goat for milk. I was raised on goat's milk till I was three. I can remember spending an awful lot of time outdoors and apparently we would just run about with no clothes on the whole time. There was an ashes dump from the fire, and one of our favorite things was to roll in the ashes and go round looking like little black chimney-sweeps or something. My parents were both a couple of suburban kids from Croydon who had gone off to the Second World War, and when they came back, I think they wanted a life that was a little more interesting than the humdrum expectations of suburbia. Then my mother said, "Let's bring our kids up in Wales!" That's where she was brought up. So we moved to what was basically a tent, where we lived for a year, till the first winter came. Having started making products on the kitchen table in an apartment in Pimlico, London, by this stage they were pouring all their money into building a factory with the help of government grants and things. So accommodation got second place in terms of priority. From there, we moved to a caravan in a trailer park—so we upgraded to trailer trash; it was 1964 in wildest Wales.

Children love small houses, don't they? There's no creepy upstairs bedroom to have to go to at night. I think my parents' friends were amused by "the eccentric Ashleys." I remember when I was seven I rode my bike seven miles to school. My mother could see some creative potential in me, I guess. Once she took me clothes shopping at Kids in Gear in Carnaby Street. When I got back to our Welsh village, they were very confused by my clothes. They thought I was a girl. I was wearing white jumbo-cord flares with a black patent-leather belt on the hips, and a psychedelic-colored paisley Jimi Hendrix-style shirt. I had hair down to my shoulders. They were all pudding-basin haircuts, donkey jackets, and wellies. Luckily I was good at sport. My vacations were spent in the factory, cleaning machinery or packing stuff into boxes. It took them 20 years before they finally cracked it and got their first shop in London (1971). They didn't have a vision. My mother was just interested in product and my father liked big business and occasionally those two things kind of gelled together. If one of them had an idea, the other one would encourage it, at the expense of everything. They both trusted each other, and would gamble their whole house on the other's idea. That's very unusual.

In the early 1970s the money started to come in and they managed to buy a large country house in Wales, which we still have now as a family home. We'd grown up by then, so my brother and sister and I weren't so interested in the family house, we just wanted to get the fuck out of it and start doing our own thing. My parents didn't mind, it got us out of the way so they could get on with the business. At first, we all stayed in the family apartment just off the King's Road, London, but I remember when I got my own first tiny apartment my mother and father took me to furniture shops and explained why I should have decent things—they were guiding principles. My mom gave me a really nice 18th-century wooden bed, and my father a nice modern desk and chair and lamp and table. I had a really cool place. I only just realize it now, but they set me up really well, because quite a lot of that stuff I still have today. The glass table got broken, but I wish I still had that, too.

In the early 1980s the Laura Ashley style was all chintz country house look for peanuts; champagne taste for beer pockets. It was flying out, we were in the candy box at that stage. Everything we touched turned to gold. So I was having to live the actual formula—the baby country house in London look. I found a fantastic "grown-up" place in Kensington: an apartment on the second floor of an old German embassy building, which had been the ballroom. It had 16-foot ceilings and balconies you could walk out onto from all the windows. In fact we stayed there for quite a while, till Ari and I started having children. I like shopping, but a lot of the things we had were bought by stylists for our catalog photography. We had an army of people who would go to auctions and early-morning markets. This was the first time I'd opened my doors to publicity and it was redone almost every year. My mother had bought a chateau in France which she restored; that was one of her dreams realized. We had five hundred shops worldwide and the business was just about to go public. Then my mother died.

That was the end of it all, really. It was always very nice to work with my mother, but once she died it was time to move on, to start my own business. So the first thing I had to do was downscale. Like my mother, I ran back to Wales to plan and to regroup. We bought a tiny stone cottage and we spent a year doing the place up, without spending much money. We didn't care any more about how the house looked; in fact, we'd been so force-fed on this over-the-top room-set look that now we didn't give a toss, and we still don't. We don't do showcase homes. We like to have small bomb-proof houses, so if the children run around and have an accident, no-one's crying. In the end, Wales was too extreme for the children but we've kept the house and we can go back any time we want, but 13-year-old girls need more of a social life.

Now we've just moved down to a house in the New Forest in Hampshire. I'd describe it as a crap house in a fantastic location, but we plan to add on about 30 percent to it laterally. It's a challenging project, it doesn't have good bones. I've already blasted through three rooms to make one enormous kitchen and we need to do the same in the sitting room. We also need a wetroom for saddles and cycles and outdoor stuff. All the interior walls will be just one color: soft white. Then when you spring-clean, you can go around with a paintbrush and touch up as well. We don't want to spend too much on posh furniture; a nice big Aga cooker, a big piano, good horsehair beds, quite lean on the electrical side, we're kind of reassessing the possessions we own. We want to put our money into the fabric of the building. It won't make for a very photogenic home because it's very simply done, but that can be nice. The really important things are clean (spring-fed) water, wood from our own land, food from our own garden. I make my own cider. My idea of heaven is to pick my own food, cook it, eat it, sit by the fire, and then go to bed on a wonderful mattress. I mean, come on, you can't argue with that.

PREVIOUS PAGE AND RIGHT
One of the first rooms to get sorted out in our cottage was the kitchen, which opens onto the yard where the Shetland ponies wander about. The floor is still the original 1960s marble tiles, and the table we bought in an antique shop in Brighton when we were furnishing our first house. Even though the girls are growing up, there's still a lot of rough and tumble. We have cats and dogs, and I once came back to find a horse in the kitchen being given my last beer.

My father was not really a collector, but I always remember that he had the most amazing carpets from all over the Middle East. He just loved beautiful, intricate tapestries. He had been the Polish Consul General, and he had been given an incredible collection of sabres by all the various nomads and people he was visiting in the desert. My mother hated them and banned them from all except one room. We spent the war in Jerusalem. In our home there was so much of my mother's influence; she was an amazing homemaker. She made the drapes, the pillows, our clothes ... she would have been a wonderful designer. She had no training, except that she had been brought up by nuns, so the sewing and embroidery bit was incredibly strong. There was nothing to buy. This was all being done out of parachutes given by the Polish army. I had two sisters and I remember hating having to all wear the same matching clothes—panties too. My mother was Polish but she was brought up in England. She was very ... European, and she really didn't like that Eastern way of living. I remember that my father had furniture made, sideboards, etc; it was a very steady home life.

But then my father was killed in 1948 just as we were preparing to come to England. London was an incredible shock. My aunt Sophie was living at the Ritz and she looked after us. She was a fantastic grand lady. For a while we lived in Chesham Place and I remember that we had a nanny who took us around to see all the exhibitions. I recall spending a lot of time in the Peter Jones store—I don't know why. Then, when my aunt couldn't afford the Ritz any longer, she moved all of us down to Brighton where she took a whole floor at the Metropole Hotel. It was a bit of a gin palace at the time. She had been married to an Austrian who had estates in Yugoslavia and, after he died, she moved back to England. At the Metropole she made them open up all the storage rooms and get out all this incredible furniture. In the daytime, she would be wearing quiet jewelry—wonderful art deco pieces—and then at about five o'clock she would change into something else, and then the *real* jewels would come out. She really didn't like children, so we were regimented like little soldiers. I was in a boarding school in nearby Worthing that backed onto the Downs, like a sort of summer house.

But it was falling apart, there were big holes in the floors and half of the staircases were missing. There were only three of us with one teacher, and I had the most wonderful time. I loved the decaying grandeur of it, but every weekend we'd have to go to Sunday lunch with my aunt. We had to walk in the front door at 12.30 pm—it couldn't be before or after. We were terrified of her; we didn't know what mood she was going to be in. There was this wonderful smell about her that I used to think was scent. Of course, later on I discovered that she was boozing like mad—gin and tonic. Every so often she would go off and be fitted out at Norman Hartnell. During the 1950s and '60s she was having huge soirées in the Metropole and people would come down from London to stay with her. I don't know who they were. Our homes were always immaculate—my mother's strict Polish upbringing. It would drive me crazy. It was horror if there was anything in the waste-paper basket. I remember that once the kitchen caught fire—we got the fire brigade in—and all she was doing was screaming, "Be careful of the carpets."

I left home when I was about 17 or 18. I couldn't take it any more. I'd been to art school in Brighton, and all I wanted was to get a job. I worked in a London studio doing drawings for newspapers and so on. Most publications didn't use photographs very much at that time. I met my husband Stephen Fitz-Simon in 1962 and got my first apartment, which I furnished with Victorian and Edwardian junk. It became a complete passion—junking every Saturday. My husband encouraged me to work freelance from home, and I began illustrating fashion for magazines: *Harpers and Queen*, etc. I got tons of work. I went to see the shows in Paris—incredible. The journalist would say, "I want this and this and this," and then you booked a model and she would stand for me to draw the clothes. That was an amazing experience, but being my age—20 or 21—I thought that stuff was so awful; it was all clothes for the ladies who lunch. Terribly formal. That's really when the urge for Biba started. Fitz worked in advertising, so he knew about mail order. He said, "Do a dress and we'll see if we can sell any." It wasn't advertising; it was editorial. Then we found someone to make it. After a while, we got one huge hit from Felicity Green; she gave a whole

page to one dress. We got 17 thousand replies in money orders. Oh my god! It's amazing how in ignorance you get things done. The most difficult thing was to get the bank to accept the money orders. Then we moved to an incredible apartment by the park—Princes Gate. These were not homes any more, they were work places. It was only after we opened the first shop, in 1964, that one was able to divorce work and home.

That first shop was a huge success. I've always rented wonderful historical premises; this one was an old pharmacist's. The V&A Museum had taken the interior and we were left with these wonderful huge windows. Then the next shop was an old grocery, with this amazing old wooden shelving. I was trying to find a home to put the clothes into. There were sofas for the men to sit on while their girlfriends shopped. A lot of our customers lived in bed-sitters around the area; they liked to have somewhere to go. There was no meeting point where they could listen to music during the day. There had been coffee shops in the 1950s but by then they had become extinct. I'm talking about young people.

I always wanted a house with a studio and we found a house that was built by Lord Leighton, a huge studio with two or three rooms underneath. I love living in the best room, rather than saving it for "best." This time everything was in the one room, including the bed. Chocolate-brown walls, lots of leopardskin; we had crossed over into art deco, and so we had deco lamps and figures. We had moved on from Edwardian. But by then we had the first shop in High Street Kensington. That became our home. We went home exhausted. For the first time, financially, I was able to do exactly what I wanted to our home, but I was always so upset when I'd finished it. I like a thing that's moving forward all the time, ongoing. I work for people now where they want everything finished before they move in and I don't understand that at all. It needs to be evolving. After that, we took over the big old Derry and Toms department store. My whole idea was to preserve the old building, because the English really didn't like or understand deco. It had wonderful elevators, mirrors, and of course the roof garden.

From there to Miami is a long reach. After Biba closed in 1975 we went to Paris, then Italy, moving then to Brazil for a while to do manufacturing. Then back to England, where someone came in and said, "Would you like to design a hotel in Miami Beach?" Fifteen years later, I'm still here. It hadn't occurred to me that I had been doing interiors all along. It was just after *Miami Vice*; we arrived in this amazing dilapidated art deco beachfront—incredible. Full of old people. Like a preserved time warp. A huge underworld too; scary. That first hotel building is worth millions now; it's been redone about a hundred times. After that, every time I went onto the beach, someone would ask me to do a new job. It was fabulous. I did a lot of restaurants. Then Chris Blackwell gave me a corridor to do in this hotel, The Marlin. The building was full of apartments and I've been redesigning them one by one. As I finish one apartment, I move into it and start on the next one. The joy of being able to move every eight months. I'm working my way down to the best apartments on the mezzanine floor, where they have incredible windows. It's taking a while. My husband died eight years ago and I just thought, whatever plans one makes—just forget them. Just go with whatever comes up.

PREVIOUS PAGE AND RIGHT
Where I live at the moment is just a studio, but it has an old Florida pinewood ceiling and curved windows. Most of the furniture is block-shaped metal pieces that I've had made. I try to be very abstemious and not collect too many things, but I do like 1960s chrome lamps, and 1950s orange glass objects—quite weird and futuristic. When I see them, I buy them.

OVERLEAF
This was our studio when it was photographed by James Mortimer for *Vogue* in 1975. Filled with art deco from floor to ceiling, the walls were all painted a series of rich matte browns that varied in hue to define the different areas. A brown-painted spiral staircase led to the dressing rooms on the gallery, and below—hidden behind a screen—was the kitchen, with a sink and a cooker. The caption for the photograph read, "Everywhere lamps, small fringed or mushroom topped on long slender stems; everywhere figures, ferns, flowers; everywhere an intricate arrangement of colour, pattern and space."

Recently I've been visiting the homes of some of the people who are the collectors of my furniture. They have a new name for them: metrosexuals they're called. People who are totally enamored with their home—that's where all their passions go. I've walked in and seen a piece of vintage Kagan furniture and I'm absolutely staggered. I'm talking about a multimillion-dollar environment, and there's a piece of furniture that I made 50 years ago—sitting there like it's on a pedestal. It's also nice to come into an old home that hasn't changed for 50 years, and to see the furniture still respected and loved and still functioning with the same grace. The funny thing is that I remember almost every piece I've made. They're all family to me, all part of my life. I remember when I was working with my father in the 1940s, we had a client who was a dentist. I designed the entire living room for these people, with wonderful pieces of furniture. A year or two ago, a second-hand dealer called me up and told me he'd just bought some furniture, and would I mind authenticating it. He pulled up in front of our Park Avenue apartment in a truck with all this wonderful furniture he'd bought from that dentist's estate—and there it was.

When I first moved away from home—in the 1950s—I got a one-room apartment on East 78th Street in New York. That was a challenge because I had to make one room into an elegant space—a bedroom, a dining room and a living room—but it functioned very well. Curiously those challenges are the same that are facing young people today, with real estate at a premium and prices spiraling. We still have some of those early pieces in our apartment today. Erica, my wife, and I have lived here for 36 years and for the first 30 nobody ever gave a damn what it looked like or took a picture of it. Now it's become the most photographed place you can imagine. My apartment today is my museum. Visitors are overwhelmed because it's not what they expect. This is a warm, eclectic, lived-in home, full of accumulation—as opposed to the minimalism that I expound and design for my clients. There's not a trip that I've taken, even today, that something doesn't come back as an unnecessary addition to my collection. I don't try to build collections, I just buy things that amuse me. I also have some pieces of my father's sculpture. He was supposed to become a rabbi, but he ran away from his home in a small village in Russia and apprenticed himself—at the age of 14—to a cabinetmaker. He really wanted to be a sculptor, but to do images of man was against the Jewish religion. Cabinetmaking was as close as he could get. I was born in Worms in Germany, and I

remember when I was seven or eight, we lived above my father's shop in the market square. In fact I still have some drawings I did of the rooms at that time. My father was a wonderfully skilled cabinetmaker and a modernist in his own time, much influenced by the Bauhaus philosophy of clean lines. In the store, he sold art objects and fabrics as well as furniture. He was also a great connoisseur of oriental rugs and collected Impressionist art, and became friends with Joseph Hoffmann and people like that. We lived there for about ten years during the rise of Nazi Germany. Eventually, the store was taken over by the employees—Jews were not allowed to own shops. Dad kept the workshop in the back of the courtyard and made a living building "lifts," the wooden containers that families used to transport all of their belongings to America. The boxes were lined with waterproof wax paper: you shoved everything in and then you hoped that all your possessions would come out undamaged. Eventually, being Russian citizens, we were kicked out of Germany and were able to take everything we owned, including all of my father's tools and his art collection, but hardly any money. So for the first few years in America we lived off that art collection, which he sold to museums and art dealers. Ironically, he also supplemented his furniture-making by restoring people's damaged pieces after they unpacked their "lifts."

From an early age, my father recognized that I could draw. He could not. For him to express himself on paper was painful and he would labor at it. So he insisted that I learn to draw representationally. I had this illusion that I wanted to be an artist. Now I could wish that my son—who is an artist—had come into my business. I would have had much more continuity. My learning to draw became, for me, the most important tool in my profession, because I could visualize a finished product. At that time, to present something with realism was the key to being successful. I started to work with my father in his factory after school. Later, he would take me along to visit a customer and I would make sketches of what they wanted, and what my father needed to make. Very early on, he gave me my own head in developing design and creativity. People came to him for his modern furniture, but to me it was very boxy and style-less. I was fascinated by organic shapes; human anatomy also fascinated me. I looked at the way things grew: the way that branches come out of the trunk of a tree—never two from the same point; the way a branch comes out thick from the stem and then thins out. I didn't study engineering, but the things I designed came from natural engineering.

Combined with an interest in pottery, I developed vessels to support the human anatomy, and those became chairs. That was the essence of my early furniture. In 1947/8 we opened our first store. And just as my father had in Germany, I wanted to have a modern store that incorporated the arts. A showcase for creative artists, but showing them in a house setting, not in a gallery. I had access to some magnificent artwork that I wish I owned today: Modigliani sculpture, Louise Nevelson ceramics. Louise would come to our factory every week and take all the trash pieces of wood, which then became the foundation of many of her wood sculptures. If you look carefully at some of those black-painted Nevelson pieces you can see the negative shapes of my chairs. The store became very successful and people began asking us to design their homes. We had a wonderful ability to be totally vertical. I could go into a home, design it, make it in my own factory, and then install it. Then I brought upholstery into our company, which we didn't have. That gave me the added element of sculpture. But the technical capabilities and the materials I needed to create my shapes didn't come into play until 30 years later. I was motivated by elegant lines and I thought, why do we need furniture with lots of cushions that need to be puffed up? That's old-fashioned. Why can't we make tight seat upholstery and tight seat backs? That philosophy became my serpentine sofas, and the most significant one has just sold at Christie's in New York for 195 thousand dollars. I had clients—young people—who were in awe of my things and would press their noses to the shop windows at night. They would save up to buy things. I guess they were braver then, inasmuch as they were out of the mainstream. Today "modern" is a much bigger audience. In those days it was a very small group that appreciated my furniture.

My early designs lived by hugging the walls, but then my clients started to collect major artworks, like Jackson Pollock and Hans Hoffmann—wall-to-wall paintings—and all of a sudden there was a need to move the furniture away from the perimeter of the room into the center. In order to make people sit within the cubicle of the room and focus on the artwork, I developed a concept of interior landscaping. That changed the whole philosophy of how a room functions. From there, the idea of modular furniture started to develop, so that you could actually take the furniture apart and reconfigure it to the needs of the room. At the same time, 1950s architecture became much more about open space. The first thermopane glass windows arrived, so architects created these huge window/walls and we became more and more constrained as to where we could put the client's art collection—and the furniture. Usually directly opposite the window was the fireplace; that also wanted attention. Then there was perhaps a piano, or the television. Traditional thinking no longer worked, and I had to come up with more creative ideas. That's when I really blossomed. Unfortunately, there were some things I designed in those days that bombed. They were too expensive and the people who liked what I did couldn't afford them, but today they are best-sellers. I was too far ahead of myself. Now I am riding the crest of a retro phase. Modern architecture, which back in the 1950s was a rare occasion for a singular client, today is much more common. Those Richard Meier buildings down on the Hudson river are full of glass boxes that just cry out for my furniture. I love it. I think of myself as a fashion designer in furniture. The fashion world is quite capable of making a product in China or Taiwan for the mass market and still retain the joy of doing the one-off dress that costs 10 thousand dollars. I'm at that threshold now with my work. I can also produce things in a medium where the technology allows me to do them at an affordable price. There is a cute saying that I've always adopted: you work for the classes and eat with the masses; you work for the masses and eat with the classes.

Predictions are always very difficult to make. Human nature and the human spirit has always had the same urge, whether it was two hundred years ago, or in two hundred years time. You will still have to deposit your ass on something that is reasonably comfortable and has got a good support for your back, no matter what style it is.

OVERLEAF

Two worlds meet in my Manhattan apartment. The clean lines of my modern furniture are contrasted with textures in fabrics, sculpture, paintings, and antiques. The Omnibus sofa in the living room was a complete breakthrough in the 1960s; until then, sofas were traditionally set against the wall. Omnibus could be arranged any way you want. Shown here, it encircles my stainless steel and glass Infinity table, leaving the wall free for our Frank Stella painting. The naïve paintings were collected on visits to Haiti, and the cushions on the sofa were made by my wife, Erica Wilson, from layers of shaded gauze and colored velvets.

People think that to be modern means that everything you own has to be manufactured recently and be simple and chic, with a tendency to be expensive. But to be modern doesn't mean that you have nothing in common with people who lived centuries before you. It's much easier for people now to do their home. When I see these very avant-garde little girls of 20 or 22, whether they will marry or not marry, when they open their life to people, invite their friends to their new apartment, I think probably there will be something their grandmother left them, and maybe something from the flea market, and they will decorate the table with some bizarre little object that is fun and frivolous. This to me is very modern. But it seems that most people, if they are "modern," cannot own something from before the year of their birth. I don't think it's good, this explosion of interest in the home. Too many of the objects are expensive and there is something ambiguous about interior design; ways to do something that can look very dramatic—repetitions of the same idea for instance—and you think that it's art. But it's not art. There is a lot of cheating, I think, with money. Money has become too important in the world of design. Art schools are full of people who want to be designers and you rapidly find out it has to do with the money they expect to make, and they want it immediately.

A home project depends enormously on the personality of the client I'm working for, and some of them depress me very much. They want to intimidate, to clearly announce to the world that they've achieved what they wanted to, and they use their apartment like a kind of power. There is a snobbishness about who owns what, and it provokes envy in others; it can kill a curiosity that they have when they're young for art and design. When they see the sadness of many things around design, it can make them reluctant to explore. It doesn't have anything to do with those people I met when I was young, who were full of doubt and enormously lonely and not accepted. They were all very tormented.

When I was born, we lived in a beautiful old abbey from the 12th century called L'Abbaye de Fontenay, in Bourgogne. That has since been listed as a World Heritage Site by UNESCO. As a child of four or five, it was almost too much. I was in the cloisters of the abbey thinking that I was becoming an angel and I was going to the sky. Although my parents wouldn't take me to church or push me, I felt the intensity of religion, the feeling that I was called somewhere. The house was the part of the abbey that over one hundred monks had lived in until they were expelled by the French Revolution, so there was a lot of space. The place was owned and organized by my grandfather, Edouard Aynard, who was quite famous for his taste, but he had very classical ideas.

Both my parents were quite gifted, and beauty appealed to them. My father was from that very famous school of École Normale and my mother was a very good pianist. She wanted us—my brothers and sisters from two marriages (very complicated)—to be pianists too, so we studied music until we were 18 or 20. I had enormous respect for my adored parents, but they became so interested in objects that they ruined the lines of the architecture with too many objects. They had beautiful furniture and things and I had an exposure to beauty that was like too much sun: it burns you. They had so much but they never spoke about it. It's a habit; to have too many things is like a nightmare. Something that invades your home like a poison. When I was 18 I went to my mother and asked her, can I empty my room, I can't breathe any more. I wanted her to be nervous about my state of mind and maybe let me do anything to improve my head. She said, "I understand very well what you mean; what would you put out?"

By this time we had moved to Paris and were living on Saint-Germain-des-Prés in front of the church—at the time one of the most interesting districts in Paris. So once my room was empty I added just a few things so that I could live there. One of those metal camp beds from the Napoleonic wars; I loved that kind of utility style, it was so clean and full of energy. On the wall I had a very beautiful poster of Miro, and I had a Barcelona chair (by Mies van der Rohe) from a little shop nearby called Knoll, which sold only five or six pieces. It was so strong; after I saw that shop, I started to look at modern furniture and I realized that it was going to be very important. But it was looked on as strange and cold. One member of our family looked at my beautiful Florence Knoll couch and said, "How come they make couches for kitchens now"! She said it was more suitable for a clinic or a hospital. It made me so furious, but I hope I was polite. At the same time I thought that most things from the end of the 19th century were so much junk. But I did discover the beauty of modest objects.

Being in Paris changed my life because, secretly, I started going to Le Café de Flore, and I would see Samuel Beckett and Alberto Giacometti and Picasso. The waiters would introduce me and I immediately realized that they were very strange people, as you would say, and I was interested in strange people. I was still only 16 or 17. Beckett lived like a student of 20 years old, in a room with no furniture; two chairs maybe. But I noticed that in his closet he had smoking jackets. It was so funny to see evening clothes, because in my family if you had a smoking jacket you were a very conventional person, and if you were rich you had a rich house and if you were poor you looked very unhappy. But Beckett was full of contradictions, and I discovered the power of contrasts. I became very interested in things that live together in a very violent contrast. People who look like saints but who are monsters; people who look full of taste, but who are in the end ridiculous. Later I introduced it into my work, because I love poor materials that are incredibly pure and naïve and touching, and at the same time not costly. Wood, concrete, and a certain kind of flooring called "American olean" that is used in kitchens and bathrooms. It is very matte and comes in odd colors that, when combined with other colors, can become absolutely wonderful. So I started to do many things where I used only opposites. I had velvet with a contradictory material such as lacquer; a very rough wood wall and a silk tapestry on it. I was trying to reconcile things to make you rediscover something that had been hidden.

When I got my own place at last, I edited things a lot. I used very plain and wonderful antiques that were not fashionable at all, like a Spanish table from the 17th century, combined with a piece of new sculpture or maybe an abstract painting. The room was quite big and there was a mixture of rather precious things that were not appealing or famous. It was a time when a set of chairs by Jean-Michel Frank didn't cost much. Now the prices are not to be believed: two zeros, not one.

I've lived in the same building for 45 years and in this apartment for nearly 30. At first I was living with my husband in a very wealthy-looking apartment with five-meter-high ceilings and great art on the walls, and I used to sit at the window and say to him, I don't know what I'm doing here when I was born to be there, pointing to the adjacent loft space. I was the first person in Paris to live like people lived in a New York loft. I'd never been to New York at the time, but I was drawn to the feeling of light and space. That was in 1975.

I owe my career to a very good friend called Michel Guy who was like my beloved brother. I designed seven apartments for him, as if I were his wife. He became the French Minister of Culture and was responsible for introducing American and English ballet to France. I did a house for him in St. Tropez in 1964 and he said, "You have some very odd ideas which are sometimes a bit shocking or provocative, but I think you should become a designer." He helped me in the sense that, through his apartments, he gave me the feeling of being wonderful. But I wouldn't do it. I said no. Then Karl Lagerfeld told me, "You must absolutely open your own studio; you are the only person today (that was in 1970) who is not like all the others—believe me—do it!" I had a kind of stage fright. I was afraid that I would maybe not be understood. It's true that when I worked as a consultant for the Prisunic Store Group, I would hear them say, "No, no, Madame Putman, don't ask us to do that, our customers won't

understand—it's a question of education." But I thought, what do you mean, not understand? Do they have a heart; does it function normally like yours or mine?

Sometimes I think that I am fighting a war for less received ideas, less aggression between people who like or do not like something. At the same time, I think design has been used for a lot of bad reasons, and I regret that very much. I've never used my ideas as recipes. Many designers have one good solution, which they're comfortable with, and it's good and it's been proved to work. I'm not doing that at all. If it's a client's own home I would have to talk to them a lot. I'm not a shrink, but there's so many things you need to know. I need to know what time the sun hits their wall and things like that. It's like doing a portrait of them. For me, the kitchen and the bathroom are the most important rooms in the house, especially the kitchen table, because maybe you save someone's life by being wonderful and keeping them for dinner when they don't expect it.

I'm designing an enormous number of objects for the home —linen, textiles, furniture, rugs, lighting, silver, etc—and I enjoy that, but I'm very keen to protect them from being too expensive. Some good friends once said to me, "Andrée, you know we love you and we speak about you very often. How come you never came to our place to dinner? Oh yes, we wanted to invite you, but my wife and I said to each other, we don't have the right silver!" I said to them, you have no idea how incredibly cruel that is to me, because I would *never* judge your silver. Please don't do this to your other friends because it's very painful.

People think that I see everything and I judge things, but I am never mean.

OVERLEAF
This 23rd- and 24th-floor penthouse for gallery owner Pearl Lam is a recently completed project in the former French quarter of Shanghai. At one end of the 20 meter-long and 5 meter-wide salon, two Croissants de Lune sofas face each other across a lacquered table that was designed in 1978 for Ecart International.
FOLLOWING PAGES
The full-height laminated glass wall of the staircase leads to the bedrooms. In the smaller of two bathrooms, the tub rests on huge marble balls. Throughout the apartment, beiges and grays are mixed with white and brown, and poor materials are given equal importance to precious ones. In this way, luxury frees itself from the hierarchy of representation.

During the week, I live on a very beautiful "landmark" street on New York's Upper East Side in a small one-bedroom apartment, and on the weekends in our house on Fire Island, which is about an hour's drive from the city. That is where I feel totally at home and happy, even in the winter —perhaps especially in the winter, when there's no one else about. I love the peacefulness and the smell of the sea. The house is on the first street of the island's westernmost town, Kismet, and it has a fantastic view of the ocean, Great South Bay, and Fire Island Lighthouse a half mile away.

The house was built in 1959; the first A frame on the island. We bought it from the woman who had designed and built it; she had lived there with her family until the family got too large (she has six children and this house only had two bedrooms plus a wall of bunk beds). She built another house for them across the street and rented this house out for many years. When we took possession it was a perfectly simple A frame with Masonite panels of primary-colored hues on the front of the house and a tiny balcony off the master bedroom at the house's peak. There was only one bathroom. We bought it because of its location; the fact that it bordered the national seashore and that there would never be additional construction behind us.

We lived there for a year, then took the plunge with a major renovation, enlarging the back half of the house from an A shape to a W, adding another upstairs bedroom and bath and a large deck that lets us enjoy the spectacular view. Our contractor was a son of the woman from whom we bought the house. The renovation was traumatic and took an agonizingly long time—about two years in all. We installed a brand new kitchen, new bathrooms, new floor-to-ceiling glass windows, and even added a foot to the length of the house. It was a time filled with money worries and free-floating anxieties, mostly about all the design choices that had to be made: decisions about everything from sofas to door knobs. When you live with someone, the interior is never a total reflection of your own personality. It's very hard. Bobby is not in the design business but he has very strong opinions. We were frequently at an impasse. What evolved was that neither of us was allowed to buy anything for the house unless we both agreed on it. No exceptions. To this day, I cannot buy anything without consulting him (and vice versa). I'm basically happy with the way the interior looks now. But because I work in the business, I'm constantly thinking about changing things. I get invited to every design show, trade fair, and new store opening. I look at books and magazines all the time. I am always bombarded with newness: new design ideas and new products. Whatever I saw last is what I want. I'm constantly tempted to change things. But then I remember how hard it was to reach any consensus the first time around and that usually stops me in my tracks. I also have a hard enough time on my own to make changes. I can be very weak and indecisive. I trust my own judgment, but I am very strongly influenced by my designer friends. I value their judgment, perhaps too much.

I don't have many fond memories of where I grew up. We lived in a row of brownstone apartments in downtown Philadelphia—four joined buildings that had 12 tenants. A very large, well cared for garden spanned the length of all four buildings. Since I was the only child in the building, I thought of the garden as all mine and spent quite a bit of time there. We lived there until I was about ten. My mother hated antiques: she desperately wanted to be modern, so our apartment was furnished in a contemporary way, not with good mid-century modern pieces, but with lower priced facsimiles. Since I rebelled so strongly against my parents, I'm amazed that I never rebelled against this predilection of hers. Instead I wound up embracing it and making it my career.

We later moved to a more suburban neighborhood (still in the city) so that I could be around children my own age. It was similarly furnished by my mother with pseudo-Scandinavian style designs. (My parents lived there long after I left home.) I think I became aware of design only after I graduated from college and started to work at a department store. That's when my interest became focused.

We never had lived in a house. I think that's why I always wanted one. Bobby and I bought the house at the beach in 1986, and that's where we've always been. When I'm away, that's where I long to get back to—the house and my cat Miss Kitty. I do prefer the house to be neat and tidy, but the reality is quite different. I respond to light rather than color. The size of the space is not as important to me; it's what is in the space, and what you see from it. The sense of space. I could live in open-plan or multilevel, it wouldn't matter, but it would need to have lots of daylight and storage space.

RIGHT

The view from the upstairs bathroom at our Fire Island house looks out toward the lighthouse and the Atlantic. Originally Bobby wanted a colored bath but I wanted white, so we compromised by adding small multicolored squares between the white tiles.

During the building of my new house all my colleagues kept asking, "What's the kitchen going to be like?" I felt very pressured. It's terrifying making decisions about the details of a room. You can be easily swayed from your choices into something you don't really want. I don't know how people cope. I'm used to working on a brief for an article for my magazine or one of my cookery books—you think of a concept and you stick to it. So you know what fits. When I went to look for taps for the house I said to the guy, where are the taps—taps that are taps? I don't want taps that want to be hi-fi systems. Just let them be taps—where are they? "Oh," he said, "they're called English taps"! I thought good on the English for not changing. I say to my architect all the time, that's not a light, it's a *feature*. This room just needs a light. I can't have things in the house that are faddish; I get bored really quickly, I'd be continually ripping stuff out. Things that are fashionable go *out* of fashion very quickly. When I was growing up, interiors weren't like fashion, though talking to my builders recently we were recalling how in the 1970s our kitchens matched the color of our automobiles. We had a bright green kitchen and a green automobile. It was my parent's first house after they got married. In fact, in their photo album, pictures of my father helping the builders come right after their wedding photos. It was a kind of suburban house—not small but not huge—in a new part of Sydney that was just opening up, near the beach.

I was a very outdoor child; the things I remember are the front and back yards. I had two older sisters, and my father made us a swing set and a cubby (play) house and a sandbox with a cover, which were the envy of the street. He was always making things, but I don't think my mother let him make anything for inside. I remember when we got a new television, it was like furniture; it had big speakers on the sides covered in gold fabric. And then I remember my mother got our lounge recovered; it was a very big event. I remember the deliberation over it. It had been purple, and she changed it to a neutral color. Then we got new carpet. Deciding on those things would have been really big for her. I remember there were swatchbooks coming home, and she would have got advice from her girlfriends. We weren't a wealthy family, so those purchases were more considered; it

wasn't like you could change them in two years' time. They were a lifetime purchase. I was drawn to the kitchen even then. We had a table in there for casual meals, but for dinner parties my mother would use the dining room. She would dust, and put out matching sets of beautiful doilies that she'd made as a child, or my grandmother had made. She had a really beautiful garden so she'd always have beautiful cut flowers in the house, but these dinner parties would put her into an absolute tizzy for days beforehand, so then I began to help her cook for them, and eventually—with her encouragement—I took over.

I moved out when I was 18. I needed to get out of the suburbs and move closer to the city. That's where all the cool places were. I finished college and started getting freelance work as an assistant food stylist, as well as writing recipes for different magazines. Looking for an apartment was exciting at first, but then I remember spending so many Saturdays at open-house inspections; that was quite tedious. The ones within my price range were all pretty awful. I wanted to find something that had a good structure that I could maybe change, knock down a few walls, and hopefully add value to. With those apartments, you're not going to spend your whole life there, so you try and make enough money when you sell it at a good price. At 24 I guess I was pretty shrewd, wasn't I?

When I had dinner parties, I would jam so many people in there (12 at one stage) that I'd have to move the furniture. I always found enough chairs, or boxes sometimes. My girlfriends were all stylists, some interiors and some fashion, so we all saved up to buy the overseas magazines: *The World of Interiors* and *Marie Claire Maison*. They were 10 or 12 dollars a pop and we would all share them. I remember the English *Elle Decoration*, you *had* to get the latest copy of that when Ilse was there—we thought that she was the goddess of everything. I actually ended up staying in that apartment for about seven years, but only because my career was so busy that I didn't really have *time* to move. It was a great place, only 10 minutes' walk from Bondi Beach.

Now, with our new house, my target was to have a haven to come home to after work, a very quiet, calm place with lots of breeze. I love moving air, especially in

Sydney when it can be warm. I looked at lots and lots of architects and chose one whose work was clever, but simple. I didn't want curved walls or crazy stuff. I wanted it to be the opposite to my day at work, which can be crazy. It's part of a row of terraced workers' cottages, so we only had five meters in width to play with, but we've redone the whole back of the house. My husband William is building it with his friends, which is like a big *boyathon*. Previously, he's done a couple of renovations, but otherwise he's only built fences at his farm. He's one of those handy Australian types and he's really tall with really wide shoulders, so he's good at talking to tradesmen because they get a little scared of him. It's great! All the structural stuff he does really well, but anything to do with a hinge or a door handle he says, "You'll have to ask Donna." He has his bit and then I have mine. He even got on his hands and knees and started digging out a cellar, which is my laundry and his wine cellar. I love doing the washing and cleaning and I love change, the whole process of throwing things away, giving things to charity stores. Even my son's toys I go though and cull. People have given him too many toys, stuff that he's never going to play with again. How many soft toys can one child have? I'm both a bath and a shower person, so we've designed a big bathroom with a big Japanese-style bath you sit in rather than lie in. William likes those stupid showerheads that fall from the ceiling straight onto your head, like standing under rain. But if you're a girl with long hair it's not so good. So we have two showers. Our bathroom is fantastic; when I'm having a bath, my husband always comes and sits on the floor or on a stool and talks to me. It's kind of our quiet meeting place. We discuss a lot of things in the bathroom. I hate the hotel feeling of two basins, so we just have one big one, big enough to wash a baby in.

The block is sloping, so we have really wide stairs leading to the kitchen. If they want, guests can sit there or on the stools and watch me cook. Everyone tends to come into the kitchen, so I've made it a very important part of the house, designed to be one big space with lots of room for people to perch and have a glass of wine and watch while I'm chopping. I do hate sitting and eating on top of the kitchen, so there's a dining table off the kitchen, to one side, and then it opens onto a deck with the mandatory barbecue, which is getting larger and larger every year. Mine has a wok burner on the side like a small kitchen. I'm not a state-of-the-art person, I don't have gadgets. I cook with a knife and a chopping block and a frying pan. It reflects my food, simple and modern and stylish. When we go away on vacation, the first person we will have to stay in the house will be the architect. He deserves it and it's important for him to see if anything annoys him.

OVERLEAF

From this view, the kitchen looks like one of those old operating theaters, which in a way, it is. During the day, light floods in from almost every direction, and at night it's lit by lights that wash down the textured wall and others that are concealed in the side windowsills to wash the ceiling. To create a calm and relaxed feel to the space I've used ranges of warm buttery whites and crisp linen whites, and replaced traditional cupboard doors with sliding panels. The shallow prep sink is set into the limestone surface of the island unit, which wraps over at each end and continues to the floor. The old table on the right, with its zinc top, was found by one of the stylists at the magazine. It is great as a side or drinks table when we are having parties and I love the mix of the soft zinc with all the wood. The wide stairs overlooking the kitchen are designed for those people who like to sit with a glass of wine and watch me cook their dinner. (There are many!)

I was very young when I first became interested in buildings, probably about eight years old. We lived in Indianapolis, Indiana. As I progressed through school and college, that interest increased. I don't know how I knew to start with the ancients, but somehow I did. One of my first drawings at school was of the Parthenon. I entered it into the school drawing competition but the judges disallowed it because they thought I had traced it. I was devastated but my mother was encouraging, telling me that it was probably the best compliment I could get. If you were to see that drawing today, you'd say it was pretty awful.

The college I attended, the University of Cincinnati, was different from most in that it had what was called a "co-operative" program. We went to school for two months, then took jobs in our fields of study for two months, and kept up that rhythm all through college. That was unusual at the time—the mid-1950s—and it remains unusual. I found a job with a small architectural firm in Cincinnati that had the two ingredients I wanted. One was teaching me how to put a building together, in other words the pragmatic part of practicing architecture, and the other was satisfying a more cultural interest. The firm's owner regularly got tickets to concerts and the opera and would give them to me when he couldn't go. It was primarily a residential practice, so I thought that most of the buildings that I would work on as a young intern architect would be small enough that I could see them through during the time that I was there. As it turned out, the houses we did were enormous and took a long time to complete. However, I worked there for six years, so I got my share of experience.

When I graduated from Cincinnati I went to the Graduate School of Design at Harvard and then studied at the American Academy in Rome for two years. Being in Rome was like heaven. I had my own studio and worked on imaginary projects, but mostly I went out into the city and traveled about, always drawing the examples of important architecture that I would see. I had a wonderful arrangement with my then wife: she would do the homework on the places we visited and rank the important sights, so I was confident that we weren't missing anything that we'd later regret. All of the Fellows at the Academy, scholars in various disciplines—art history, architecture, music, painting, and so on—regularly had dinner together in a wonderful hall designed at the turn of the century by McKim, Mead & White. This made for a very lively table and the arguments were sometimes fierce! At other times, I walked through the city with some of these scholars, all people I trusted, and they

gave me positive and negative critiques of my drawings. It was a life-changing trip; it completely influenced who I am today. It was while I was in Rome that I realized that character in architecture didn't just happen; it came from storytelling, from precedent, from various other influences. The columns of the Baldocchino in St. Peter's are the shape they are for a reason. If you allow your mind to comprehend that about everything you see (though you obviously discard some things), you end up holding on to certain ideas for life. In Roman buildings of many periods, and certainly in most Renaissance buildings, the stories were right out there ready to grab. That made the architecture of the past richer, and it taught me lessons that influenced my own architecture once I returned to the States. You can distinguish my architecture from that of my colleagues because I have insisted on doing something that has meaning to my clients as well as to myself. People often don't understand me when I say that Rome is an artifact; it's all of a piece despite its layers of history. When I came back I desperately wanted to find out if modern architecture could absorb the same kind of rhetoric that Rome had shown me, but it was a long time before I received commissions for whole buildings rather than just additions, so I couldn't try that out right away.

The first house I designed was for my college thesis. It was a house for myself, a building that could grow in time. Obviously I couldn't afford a big house, so I designed a one-room building, and devised a way of adding a second, third, and fourth unit; finally, all of the units made up a kind of public square. I never got to realize that project, but when I started to get commissions, they were similar inasmuch as they were additions to existing houses. At the beginning of my practice, I never got to do anything "in the front yard" as they say; it was always "in the backyard." The critic Charles Jencks called me "The Cubist kitchen king." I can tell you, I made the most of those little commissions. Whether the additions were small dining rooms or kitchens or whatever, they were intimate spaces where families could gather. We Americans always spend more time in the kitchen, leaving many of our dining rooms unused, so I wanted to create social spaces in the house, even when the program was thought to be utilitarian.

During those early years, the Museum of Modern Art recommended me to one of their donors, someone from the Rockefeller family, who wanted a house, a very big house. The potential clients wanted me to come and show them "all" of my houses. So I gathered everything I owned at the time and composed photographs of various combinations—

a chair and some fabric, a framed drawing, and another piece of furniture—so they looked like lots of different rooms. I was basically a set designer for a day. I got the job and was enormously relieved that the clients didn't want to come and see my "houses."

Some time later, as my practice developed, I started to get commissions from various industries to design products for the home. The first was a manufacturer of limited-edition art rugs and then a kettle for Alessi, which has become quite famous. That was a relatively unusual thing for an architect to do and it got coverage in lots of magazines, which led to calls to design other things. We now have a practice that includes architecture, interior design, and product design. I often talk about a condition that I call "domesticity," where architecture and product design came together in the interiors of a building, where you see a combination of all of the elements that contribute to the character of how you live in a space. That idea informs much of our design work.

Among my design heroes are the Viennese architect Josef Hoffmann and the English architect Sir Edwin Lutyens. If Hoffmann made a breakfast room, you knew that, like many English manor houses, it would be on the east to get the morning light, and you knew he wasn't going to paint the walls white. Instead, he would find wallpaper that was uplifting, perhaps a floral pattern that linked the interior to the garden. I love the idea that Lutyens worked with the landscape architect Gertrude Jekyll and allowed the house and the garden to be one, without looking like each other. We have a saying, "Bring the outside in," that to most Americans means placing a big Ficus plant in your living room and calling it a day. That's hardly what Lutyens or Hoffmann or I would have in mind. As an architect, I would love to have both the budget and the space to do gardens and to find ways to allow people (as they may have in 18th- and 19th-century England or France I suppose) to stroll the gravel paths through the landscape after dinner and end up at a folly or pavilion and have coffee, but grounded in what our society is today, not in European aristocracy. I would love to have support from a sympathetic landscape architect, but I've never found my Gertrude Jekyll.

The first house that I built for myself is where I still live. It was a shell of a warehouse when I found it one Sunday morning in 1969, with no plumbing, heating, or air conditioning and only half a roof, and completely overgrown with vines. From my days at the American Academy in Rome, I'm an Italophile and I could see that it was built like an Italian barn rather than an American warehouse. In fact, it

turned out that the builders were Italians who had come to Princeton in the 1920s to construct various buildings on the University campus. The building had a language that appealed to me and also, since it was a ruin, the price appealed to me. I had no idea what a house like that would ultimately cost; and thirty-some years later, I'm still paying for it. I started modestly changing it by covering certain things up and opening other things. It started at a time when I had very little money, so I did it one bit at a time. Of all the homes I've built, this one is the most gratifying, the most photographed, the most visited, the most everything. We get visitors from all over the world. When they step into the house, they are completely surprised by the intimate scale and by how I've used natural light, not to flood the house but in a very controlled way to create an ambiance and a subliminal connection between the interior and the garden. The house is filled with things that give me inspiration: books, artifacts, paintings, drawings, objects I've designed. The whole house is a big story. I've had a lot of practice with surfaces and finishes and their relationships; in other words, how to paint and color a building to enhance the reading of the architecture. In the way that two adjoining walls come together, there is always a little crisis about where one color should stop and the next one start. My house is painted in about five different shades of white. They're just colors that blend with the next one and make it seem darker or lighter. I'm quite pleased with that, but I tell people that one day I will polychrome the entire house. I haven't done it yet. A house is like a life: it evolves from year to year. There's always more to do.

OVERLEAF

My favorite room in the warehouse is my breakfast room, or solarium, which is adjacent to the kitchen and leads outside to a small garden. The fireplace is clad in faceted white tiles laid in a running bond pattern, like the tiles in the Paris Metro. This pattern is repeated at a larger scale in the painted wood paneling. With the quality of light and use of materials, the room seems to be inside and outside at the same time.

The translucent and gridded surfaces of the kitchen cabinet doors are reminiscent of windows and extend the connection between inside and outside established in the solarium. I have furnished the kitchen with an antique table that I rescued from the trash and refurbished, as well as with objects that we have designed for Alessi, Dansk, and Target, among others.

Food and eating and restaurants have always been very important parts of my life. I've had my own restaurant (St. John) in Clerkenwell, an area of east London just beside Smithfield Meat Market, for 11 years now, and we opened a second one in Spitalfields, which took nine years to develop. So I don't rush into things too quickly. I have no plans to open any more restaurants, though we've had a little flirtation with New York, which could be interesting. I've got a slightly "ropey" left side with Parkinson's, so I've had to step back from the kitchen now; my life is quite civilized, not cooking all hours of the day anymore, though I enjoyed that part of it too. I learned to cook from my mom and by osmosis, eating other people's food. When I met her, my wife Margot was a very good chef.

Probably one of my most telling childhood memories is of coming downstairs in the morning and finding the paisley tablecloth still there from dinner the night before, and a delicious smell of old cigar smoke and undrunk wine and coffee and so forth. I remember, as a young kid, sensing that something good had been going on and that I was missing out. My father was the architect Brian Henderson. His projects were not domestic; he did things like airport terminals. His work was of a scale that was quite hard to comprehend. Also airport architecture gets ruined instantly by Sock Shop and Duty Free and all those things. Architects have this image and then it's gone, so I think he found it quite hard. But he seemed to thrive on large schemes. We had a little cottage that we shared with a family in Wiltshire, and he built an extension to it, which I thought was very nice, very modern in an Aalto-meets-Mies kind of way. That was as domestic as he got. In the late 1960s, we lived in a house in Regent's Park, London, that was all fairly white and open and full of modern furniture—Vico Magistretti and Joe Colombo—stuff that is now having a revival. Strange when something you witnessed as a child gets a comeback. It's also quite interesting to realize that even that kind of designer furniture, at some point, begins to have a look of a time gone by. But my parents loved it. Home was always quite ordered. About the only thing they did was to treat the dry rot. There had been a lively evening, with dancing on the second floor, when suddenly the floor dropped by an inch. Immediately they realized that something was structurally wrong. So for a long time we had "acroprops" on the ground floor that were virtually holding the building up.

Naturally, growing up surrounded by modern things, it rubs off on you. It's very hard to shake it off. But I was determined not to be an architect; I thought that there was enough architecture in the family. So I went to art school and I worked in a kitchen, but those things didn't hit the spot, so I thought maybe architecture was what I should be doing. My parents never said, "Come on, son, you're going to be an architect." If anything, I was only encouraged in good eating. My mom cooked very well and my dad was a big eater and we traveled and ate very well in restaurants. They were a big feature in our lives. The theory is that our family was held together so well and for so long by a white tablecloth. It acted as a sort of bonding unit and it's always brought us back together again. The places we went were a mixture of nice interior and fine food.

Anyway, I studied architecture in London for seven years and during that time most of the buildings that I designed ended in a feast, to mark the completion of the building process in some way. It was sort of essential to the design that this feast took place. I also had this theory that you could do recipes for buildings, because I felt that there was a danger that when you have a two-dimensional drawing and it turns into three dimensions, it seems to lack some magic. So I had this idea that somehow the magic that happens in a kitchen could be applied to a building. It worked in theory. I was a student and it was fun. Strangely, my father and I rarely discussed architecture. When we did, it was certainly not the most relaxed conversation. But I owe a lot of what I know to him. In a way, I got more encouragement sitting around the table of an evening so, strangely enough, maybe that's what made me become a chef. While I was studying, I took over a restaurant in Covent Garden on Sundays and two chums and I cooked cassoulet or pot-au-feu for two hundred people one day a month. I felt at the time that I was in a kind of pinball machine, with the fickle finger of fate sort of knocking me about. I thought it was unwise to make too many plans or hopes, I would let fate decide. If I'd thought I'd be married or have kids or live here, I'd have said no, that doesn't sound like me. But things happen.

While I was still thinking that I'd be an architect, I was offered a job in the kitchen of an architects' office,

strangely enough. Later on, my wife and I opened the French House Dining Room in Soho. And that was it.

When I see a new restaurant, I see it partly as an architect, and partly as a chef. Over the past ten years there's been an explosion in restaurant design. I think it's good. I see a lot of over-design, or design for the wrong reasons, and that doesn't make me comfortable. I think quite a lot is working itself out now. I go to them now and then, a little foray into someone else's world. It's exciting too. I'm not sure that the *theater* element is necessarily a healthy element. I think that the decoration should be people having a good time, eating and drinking wine. I like to be able to see what I'm eating, too. The other issue that people are always talking about is noise. Noise is tricky. Noise is a lovely thing. In a restaurant, you don't want too many soft surfaces. They don't wear too well and they absorb grease. I think that you just want a clean space when you eat, so inevitably you're going to have a noise problem, one that we're constantly wondering how to deal with. I would suggest that a person who is deliberately creating a noisy restaurant must be feeling vulnerable themselves and they feel they must create some buzz. Those places that are overdesigned are OK I guess. No, it's not entirely OK. It's slightly disrespectful to their customers—assuming that they're not bright enough to have an enjoyable time without a "wham bam" interior. Maybe there are some people who are reassured by that. One of my favorite restaurants is in Paris and it's called Rubis. You go in and there's a row of tables and a busy bar, with all these old boys standing eating. I find eating standing up at the bar very hard, but they make it look comfortable and delicious. Then there are people sitting—a whole mixture of life. They generally serve one thing, like tête de veau or tripe or something each day. You generally have to wait for a table, so you stand there and you have your first icy cold glass of Puilly, and a few of the old boys turn around and look at you. They know how good that first glass is. It's a tiny space, with just the right elements in it. Not trying to impress you. The perfect lunch ensues.

The London apartment I am living in now used to be my parents' apartment when they moved to Wiltshire. What was once a very calm, svelte flat now looks like a bomb has hit it, with the children and everything. It's amazing how much stuff one gathers without meaning to. Pots and pans, cookbooks, they just sort of "gather." There's always room for one more pot, though my wife may screech. She's trying to bring order to it, tackling it head on. Hopefully she knows the parameters. There hasn't been too much consulting, but so far, so good. I hope she'll be finished soon—it's not a very big apartment. I get to see the odd beautiful interior. Other people's homes are always fascinating. The kitchen is quite telling, obviously. Particularly the kitchen table. If there is one or not; what size it is; and if it's covered with stuff and never used. Strange, somehow, that people will get a sofa before they buy a kitchen table. I find that bizarre, because the table also suggests merriment. It's also quite telling if the knives are sharp—particularly if I'm going to cook in someone else's kitchen. There's nothing worse than trying to cook with blunt instruments. Eventually I might like to own a country place. I could build something. But at the moment, that seems to be a thing that is quite grown up and far away.

PREVIOUS PAGE AND RIGHT
In a kitchen one wants to be comfortable, too, but I find that chairs can be quite elusive. Our kids seem to devour them in some way. They put their feet through them, or they use them as a battering ram or something. They don't seem to survive terribly well, so we sit on Alvar Aalto stools now. They seem to be indestructible.

The inspiration for the hotels I have designed—we have seven now—often comes from the areas of London that they are in. For the Charlotte Street Hotel I used art from the Bloomsbury group, and for our first hotel—in Dorset Square, which my husband and I did in the 1980s—I used cricket as one of my inspirations since it had been the site of the first Lord's cricket ground. Prior to that, Timmy, my husband, had done other buildings but they were for back-packers and for kids in college. With the new one we decided to go up-market, so we suddenly had to think about bathrooms and plumbing and everything. But Tim is a perfectionist—more than I am—so when he decides to do something the quality is there. I didn't want it to feel like a hotel. I wanted it to be more like staying in a country house in London. Also I didn't want a cellophane-packed experience and I didn't want any kind of pastiche on the past. People don't need to stay in a bland hotel just because it's safe; they can have an adventure. I had stayed in quite a few hotels by this time but I never really liked them. When I went to India the first time, one of the hotels was full, so I had to sleep behind the bar; that was much more fun. I never liked big hotels; they were so predictable. I'd rather go somewhere that was slightly dirtier, if it had more flavor, more character to it. Young people now are so interested in all the different facets of design, so much more aware of everything. They can say, "I'm a fashion person and I'm interested in this" or "I'm a media person" or "I'm a film person" and they can find a hotel that really suits them and hopefully they'll find other like-minded people when they get there. Also, it tells other people something about you.

Creating a new hotel usually takes us about two years: it's a small company, we do things really quickly. I start with the smaller areas and do the public rooms last. A hotel is an organic project; I might decide to change my ideas halfway through. It's very difficult to do that if you're working for someone else. When a project is finished I can tell if it's turned out the way I intended. I will see a lot more than other people can about a finished scheme; in fact I have to stop myself from pointing out the things that I think are not right because it prevents the enjoyment of somebody else. I learn from it. The other thing is that I'm looking at my work in every season: does it work in January or September? You can't really plan for that—I keep learning. You can place a mirror opposite a window in a north-facing room, you can put lights inside window boxes, but every day you're always just learning. I get lots of letters from people asking where they can get a sofa or a lamp or a painting. In fact,

some even ask me to give them a breakdown of everything in the room and I think, hang on, this is getting a bit laborious. They are totally aware of everything. I won't go back and change rooms that I've done, but I also wouldn't do the same thing twice—even 24 hours later. It's the way it is. I guess I'm a restless soul.

I was born in the country—Hampshire, in the south of England. We were lucky because it was very quiet, hardly any traffic about. When my parents first came down from Manchester, before the last war, they stayed with a lady in a house on the top of a hill just outside a village. It was a small house with small rooms, but it was surrounded by beautiful rhododendrons and a small garden; but then that was surrounded by land that had never been built on, so my abiding memories are of just going through fields of long grass up to my knees. I had two older brothers and my mother had a whistle that she would use to call us back in for meals. Beautiful. Eventually the lady sold the house to my father and moved to Devon. We never moved. It was a house we stayed in "forever." Simply furnished. I remember the smell of polish and sliding on the wooden floors. There was a huge walnut table that had a circular wheel device at its base and I used to sit under there and play, moving this wheel about. I still have the table and I look at it now and it's so small! My father would change the colors of the house but my mother wasn't interested in decorating. It was the old English idea: if you could remember the last time it was decorated it didn't need doing. She was not particularly tidy either. I remember at a certain age I was a bit ashamed to bring my friends into the house because there would be a whole pile of laundry in the kitchen, things that needed ironing, and the dog under the kitchen table with all the boot polishes. But actually, it was a great house—a family house.

My mother liked dress fabrics; she had a sewing machine and she taught me to sew. I'd look in all her drawers and there would be layer upon layer of fabrics from markets and all over. This was the 1950s so there were wonderful colored patterns and textures, silks as well as toweling, and stuff like that. So my life was more about making clothes than drapes at the window. I would see something in a magazine and then make it. I was the only person going around wearing something weird like that. It was fun. For vacations we'd go camping in the back of an old Austin automobile with a trailer behind. Both my parents worked. My father had the first espresso coffee bar in Southampton; it was really cool and it had a jazz club upstairs. Even when he got home late at night he would play

loud music and keep us awake. My mother worked at the BBC in Southampton. They were real doers. So when I began to visit the houses of my friends, it wasn't the rooms I remember but the fact that they had tea at four o'clock in the afternoon. We never had that. I was one of the original latchkey children. When we walked home after dark there were no lights, just the silhouette of the trees at the top of the hill. But I loved the isolation, and the isolation of rooms— being quiet in them. In my bedroom I didn't want wallpaper; I just pasted the walls from floor to ceiling with magazine pages. Something I did myself was much more interesting; we never discussed it, we just did it. Though the room was small my bed was very high—it was level with the window —so I could lie in bed and see the tops of trees and the animal life, and all that. I've always preferred looking out of windows to the rooms themselves; the light is so important. Even at that young age I was more interested in building things—a den in the woods—than things indoors. I hated dolls. I hated going into shops unless they were junk or antique shops. I liked old things. I left school at 16 and eventually got a job with an auctioneer. He was so nice, he would give me one small thing from each auction, some- thing like a mother-of-pearl glasses case or a book. I was learning things all the time, though I didn't know it. We were often auctioning the contents of entire houses and I began to understand about the scale of things. I saw how things looked when they were in a room and when they were out of it and I realized that everything actually is about scale. If it's a huge room you can have one really huge ugly piece and it will look great. In the same room when everything is a piddling size, it looks like nothing even if the things them- selves are beautiful. Being near Southampton, what I also loved was seeing the things from the life of somebody who'd been to sea and had brought back objects from abroad, like intricate wooden carvings from India. I liked the exotic things that at that time were not saleable. I hated the things that sold well, like fine porcelain and silverware.

Eventually I got my own place. That's when I began to think, how do you fill up a room, what do you do? In a weekend it's amazing what you can do. If there was a fire- place, I'd paint it. I was never put off by anything. If I sud- denly wanted circular cushions, I'd make them. The fabric would be the wrong weight and the pattern wrong, but if I liked the colors... I was a whizz. I'm not saying it was beau- tifully done. I used to change things every few months. By this time I was working for a shipping company, writing their brochures and newsletters, and they asked me to decorate

their offices. Then in the 1970s somebody asked me to do a room in their house. More than anything else, I had energy. I was tireless. I didn't have any preconceived ideas because I wasn't that sophisticated. I had always liked art and I would find someone who was able to paint or construct something. When it comes to decorating, you can tell someone where to get everything and show them all the ingredients, but the actual room when it's finished is such an individual thing. Like a perfume is different on different people, so is a room. People's rooms say so much about them. Interiors die when you leave the room; they need people, and life, and love. Eventually my parents got old, my father died and my mother moved into a home. But we kept the house; none of us could be the one to break it up. We would stay there from time to time and one night I got a telephone call to say that the house had caught fire and was burning down. The insur- ance had run out. I went to see it and, actually, I've never seen such a shocking thing, to see only rubble. There was nothing left of our family home. My parents had loved that home and now nobody else was ever going to live there. It was like Manderley. I had never really thought of having my own family home until that happened; the continuity suddenly seemed important. So my husband and I bought a house just a few miles away and that's where my three daughters live and go to school and we have dogs and horses, and my brothers can come and visit. For me it feels like going back to my roots. It's home.

PREVIOUS PAGE AND RIGHT
The best room I've ever done? There isn't one. I'm still looking for that perfect room and I think I always will be. Our family home is our house on the south coast. This is where my daughters grew up. We built on this big dining area next to the kitchen, with doors leading onto the garden, and it's where we spend most of our time. The kitchen table is French sycamore and above it is a chandelier from INGL Brown that I've hung with old brass and copper kitchen utensils. I designed the chairs, which are covered in a zebra-print fabric from Andrew Martin, and on the end wall, beside the Asafo flags from Ghana, is an old plate rack with a collection of huge English serving dishes.
OVERLEAF
The kitchen leads directly into the sitting room, where the French fireplace came from Apt and the two big sofas are my own design. Beside the fireplace are two pictures by Suzannah Linhart, and the needlepoint design on the two chairs was adapted from an old sewing bag.

I love seeing how other people live. I think I'm like a big sponge. I take ideas and I think: How would that work in my life? Is that a good idea, or is it just pretentious? I'm a sucker for the mags as well. I love to get the interiors magazines and look into some Hollywood home or other. It's usually deeply disappointing because they've had somebody else do it for them, so it doesn't reflect their personality at all. When I go into a place I do look at the books, but I also look at their pictures, and I'm likely to look at chairs. I love chairs; they don't have to be practical, they can just be objects of beauty. I once went to a party in an amazing house on Long Island. It was after a movie screening, and there were flunkies serving white wine or champagne, neither of which I wanted. So I went into the enormous kitchen, which was doubling as a bar. On the counter there was vodka and gin and every type of cocktail you could wish for. So I said, could I have a glass of red wine, please? "Oh I'm sorry, Ma'am," they said, "we're not serving red wine, because of the house." It's the only time I've been somewhere where that has happened. I was appalled.

Because of the transient life of a young actor, I was quite old before I got my own house. When I was born, my parents lived in a large semi-detached house with a gable, in a seaside town in Lancashire. I remember quite a few things about that house. It had what we called a lounge-hall, a semiformal waiting-cum-sitting room where the Christmas tree went up, and there were bookcases and the phone and the phonebooks. Then there was a larger sitting room, which had old gold-colored curtains with bobbles on the tiebacks that you could pull across, so I had a ready-made theater. There were also armchairs and a sofa covered in midnight-blue mohair, a Chinese lamp, and a radiogramophone. That is where my father sat to read the papers. He was a big trad jazz fan and my mom used to like Frank Sinatra and Nat King Cole. Then my sister, who was eight years older than me, brought home the Beatles' *Rubber Soul*, and that went on. I don't remember a great deal of classical music. The dining room was really only broken out for special occasions—you could go in there but it wasn't used very often. It had a very high ceiling that my mom had papered in a sort of holly-and-ivy pattern as I recall—in red and gold and green. It looked very striking and my mom had a lot of flair. As for my room, it had midnight-blue wallpaper with big silver roses on it, which I loved. I was one of those children who wouldn't go to sleep if there was something like a dinner party going on downstairs. Eventually they realized that I wanted to be part of things, so they stuck my crib right out on the landing with bright lights on—and only then did I go off to sleep. We didn't have many dinner parties, and my mom hated to be surprised when she was entertaining. If it was a party, it was a planned party. Her attention to detail was extraordinary. She always had her clothes made for her too.

When I was 10 or 11 we moved—still in the same town—but to an apartment in a tree-lined main street, but I didn't like that at all. I would get up very early in the morning and go for long walks. There are some great things about a seaside place, it's very atmospheric, particularly out of season, so I have some nice memories: the end of the pier which used to have its own repertory company, though I never went to any shows there; the floral hall; the Victorian swimming baths, which lured but terrified me at the same time. We never went abroad. For vacations we went to Cornwall, but I don't remember where we stayed. When I was 14 I remember we came to London to see the first night of *Gone with the Wind* at the Theatre Royal, Drury Lane. That was a very big event. I think we stayed in the Liberal Club. That was rather marvellous too.

At 15 or 16 I was a typical moody adolescent, keen to leave home. I don't think I had a plan but I was hoping to go to drama school in Bristol. This city has always felt like a sort of home, I have to say. When I arrived on the train that first time, I remember that the air felt great. I felt that I was somehow connected to the place. It's a university town with a lot going on and it was very stimulating. While I was waiting to get into drama school I affiliated myself with the local arts center, which had a theater group, and I was in *The Threepenny Opera*. To earn some money I did a series of jobs, including office cleaner. I also found lodgings in an assortment of rooms. I remember waking up in my first tiny room; there was a perfectly nice landlady, it was reassuringly close to the police station, and it had one of those gas fires where you had to put money into the meter. Somebody told me that you could keep warm by juggling so I learned to juggle; it worked, it kept your mind off the cold. I'd heard about a hay-box oven, so I went down to the local healthfoody-type store, which was quite new then—very exciting—people with cropped hair and earrings loading sacks of bulgur wheat and raisins and stuff. They gave me a spare crate. Then I got hay at the pet shop and used the oven to make porridge and stew; I know it sounds like salmonella hell, but it was fun. Later I lived in a succession of rooms with either ghastly or extremely nice roommates. But it was usually a basement with varying degrees of dampness. In one place I woke up in the morning with condensation all over me. You could rarely change the drapes or repaint, but I surrounded myself with objects I'd bought at markets or junk shops. It all felt like I was passing through in order to get to something else.

After Bristol there was a spell in London and five years in the rep—staying in lodgings in Manchester, Derby, Lancaster, Leicester, and Bristol twice. I remember one theatrical landlady kept complaining that I woke her up at night. My room was the garret right at the top of the house, so when I came in I would spend five whole minutes going very carefully one tread at a time so they didn't creak. Her son slept on a little mattress in the cupboard under the stairs. Obviously that's where he felt secure. The first house that I bought was after I made my first movie, *Dance with a Stranger*, in 1984, and while I was doing the *Blackadder* series. A very nice member of the cast said, "I'm living in south London, you should have a look around Lambeth." So I started looking at places south of the Thames and the real estate agent said one day, "I don't know if this will suit you or not—it's just come back onto the market." I walked in and I thought, I can breathe here. I think it was the proportions, there was the bones of something. It combined two things: it had an upstairs that felt like a house and a downstairs that felt like a cottage, and I was rather excited by that. It was my toehold onto the property market and stood me very well for ten years. At first I had to be there and experience it and let it evolve. So when I moved in I slept on a make-do mattress on the floor surrounded by dust for one summer. A lot of people would probably have thought I was bonkers—why didn't I want "more" or "other" or something—but a lot of things were happening at that time. I was away for large chunks of the time, but wherever I was I would be poking around in flea markets or junk shops, finding some little thing to bring back. I do it less now. You start to get things that you want to shed and I find it very difficult to do that. I have to hang on to things until it's all right to let them go; I can't be ruthless. Same with clothes; sometimes I get very excited when I discover some piece of clothing that has come back into fashion, and I still have the original. I didn't do anything structural to that place, but I did paint and decorate and put in a little kitchen. It took a friend on a visit from Canada to say, "It's a great place, but you're living so within your means." I kinda knew that, so I realized that I was going to have to bite the bullet and move. I thought if I spent any more money on that house I wouldn't get it back when I sold it.

Moving to Notting Hill Gate was absolutely terrifying. Looking back it doesn't seem so bad, but at the time it was the largest outlay I had ever made, apart from an automobile, and I'd always bought them second-hand. When I moved in here, I said to friends, I can't go out—you come to me and I'll cook. Everyone took me very seriously and came round. But within a month I was saying, Ah sod it—let's go round the corner. You rationalize everything. I've always liked that phrase "spend, spend and god will send." My priorities when looking for property would be light, and an indefinable atmosphere. Sometimes you walk into a place and you're hit by a kind of dead air: it feels like the life is being sucked out of you. Preferably the street has to "speak" to me too—some streets have bad feng shui. I thought I was looking for a loft, which this absolutely isn't, but the owners had opened up the first floor so that it felt like it could be a loft. Then it went up to three normal floors. It had the right degree of finish so that I could have left it as it was, but of course I never can do that.

I've been here now for eight years and I feel I have changed quite a bit in that time. I can't tell you exactly what I mean by that. A couple of weeks after I'd left the previous house it was still vacant, and I had to go back to get something and I noticed how quickly the place had changed. Doors were already creaking and everything seemed smaller. It made me think that it's your individual energy that holds a place together.

For a long time I had thought about getting a place in the country—without knowing what I meant by that; another craving to be somewhere else perhaps; another aspect of one's personality or another creative opportunity to do up a house and for it to be radically different. I found one in the West Country, near where my parents came from. It's not a cottage, it's a two-story house and while it's not overpowering it's lovely because there's room to maneuver. It's built of "glowy" stone, the ceilings are not so high, and it feels quite cottagey. Sometimes I arrive there quite late at night and all I have to do is to decamp the stuff from the car, have a glass of wine, and go to bed. It's lovely to be able to wake up there. I always worry that it's going to disappoint me—that I've been away too long—but it's never done that yet. I don't know if it's forever, but it's jolly nice.

It's an impossible thing to ask of a bit of rock wool and plaster, for it to be a repository for all the things you want of a home. I view finding a new home as a way of moving on, you know? There's something defined and rather sexy about it: you're saying, I'm allowed this, I can do this, I can spread myself here, and I'm grown up. I can have my books and my music around me, and they are in an ordered fashion—they're not on a couple of bricks and a plank. I can move between rooms; I can cook dinner for my friends. It feels like a civilized life, and anything might happen.

OVERLEAF LEFT

The little stuffed tiger is one of my favorite things. It belonged to my sister before me and I love the way it looks and feels. Standing on the Singhalese plaster shrine is a figurine of the original Siamese twins, Eng and Chang Bunker, who famously toured Europe in the 1860s.

OVERLEAF RIGHT

The thing that is most reflective of me, and what I'm about, is my bedroom. I installed the wooden shutters, the old floorboards came from Norfolk, and I stripped the fireplace. Above the Beidermeir chest in the corner is a favorite poster I've had for years.

FOLLOWING PAGES LEFT

The downstairs living room is divided from the kitchen/dining room by a sliding glass door so that it doesn't block the light. The open-tread staircase was there when I moved in, but I had the idea to wrap the stair rail with leather and painted it in these colors. The furniture is all pieces that I have collected, including the metal chest of drawers by Norman Bel Geddes.

FOLLOWING PAGES RIGHT

The lower part of the fireplace wall in the living room is clad in fossil limestone and the top is limewash painted by Kate Dineen, who also made the egg sculpture on the left, beside the Jacques Henri Lartigue photograph. The tall object is perhaps a grain scoop from Africa, which is also where the two neck rests come from, though I bought them in London.

The most remarkable and inspirational house I've seen belongs to the mother of a friend. We were invited to lunch and we didn't realize that we were going to see the most spectacular place ever created in the history of time. It was built in the 1950s or '60s for the Rockefellers by one of the architects of the United Nations building, on the most picturesque piece of land on earth, the Caribbean island of St. Bart's. It was an organic sort of modernist house built out of giant flagstones and it had all the original Danish modern furnishings with unbelievable patina. We had a lunch that I'll never forget, and then a couple of years later, it was destroyed in a hurricane.

My own family house was sort of a great modernist place. It wasn't incredible, but it was pretty good. It had good, high-modern furniture, good paintings. We lived in a farm town in southern New Jersey but me mum was a New York transplant. We moved into the house around 1971 when it was new, and they bought most of the furniture from a store called Design Research. It stayed pretty much the same, even when a lot of people started to "80s-up" their homes. However the panache—evident in the public spaces—all came crashing to a halt in the bedrooms; they were completely disheveled, done without any plan, and like the rest of the house, never changed. Me dad, though he was a lawyer, was also an artist in his spare time. He was a sort of modern minimalist and me mum was a bit more decorative and pattern-orientated. I have an older brother and sister. Even though it was this very small town, there was a small clique of progressive Jewish intellectuals, so I think the decorating style was really consistent with their intellectual position. Looking back, I realize that it was kind of groovy having a lot of friends who had modern, groovy houses, especially given the location, and I realize that it completely informed my own sensibility. The only thing I'd say is that my parents' best friends and next-door neighbors when I was growing up—the Goldsteins—had the single grooviest house on earth. At the time I took it for granted, but now, in retrospect, I still look upon Mrs. Goldstein as my muse. She wasn't trained or anything, she was an innately aesthetic person and went on to become a florist. Often, when I'm mired in the business side of my work, I think of Mrs. Goldstein and me dad and of their approach to art and design. They were both inspirational to me.

As a child I wasn't that interested in design or art, until, when I was 12, I went to summer camp and tried pottery, and then I became obsessed. After that, I convinced my parents to buy me a wheel and a kiln at home. At the end of college, I tried to figure out what I wanted to do with my life, and I decided I really wanted to be a potter. It was kinda my dream. I remember going to my pottery teacher (I was 21 by then) and she said, "No, you are terrible at it; you should give it up and become a lawyer or something." It was horrible, but actually very valuable. At that time a lot of my pottery reflected my interest in rap music and fashion. In her defense, I never really resolved things, my work was always half finished, so maybe she saw that, and not the potential. So I stopped potting. I moved to New York and got a job in the movie business. Luckily I was a terrible employee with terrible bosses, so I failed miserably. After that, more for therapy than anything else, I got a space in a pottery studio and I started to make only the stuff that I was interested in, without any regard to other people's opinions. Eventually I had so many pots that I filled up a closet in my apartment. They weren't quite what I wanted them to be, but I didn't know what to do with them. I had to be careful when I opened the door or they'd all fall out. I never wanted to be a gallery potter. I wanted to figure out how to make a living, and commerce seemed to be the answer. Eventually I got some orders from Barneys, the fashion store on 17th Street.

I thought it was the most exciting thing on earth, but now I realize that getting your first order is not that difficult, especially when you're underpricing yourself insanely as I was. The first four years were real slavery. I was making all these things for no money and working like a lunatic. I can't remember that I ever took a single day off, working 12 or 15 hours a day; I was like this weird automaton. I had this whole range of stuff. It was kinda horrible and kinda great, in the sense that I really honed my skills. I was living in Chelsea in a tiny, tiny one-bedroom fourth-floor walk-up and it really informed my pottery a lot, because I started to make things that I wanted to have at home. There is a directness and honesty about what I do that I really enjoy. Now I have my own stores, I can just make something and put it on the shelf and people can buy it. I love making stuff that people can afford to have in their homes. My innocent Pollyanna-ish side started to

evaporate fairly quickly, and a raging merchant started to emerge. I was lucky enough to find a great workshop in Peru to make all my stuff when it became apparent to me that I'd have to have a fairly diverse offering. I started to approach things almost as a fashion designer approaches a collection. Each season is about something different, almost as if the work could have been the output of several people, rather than just me. I've always been very influenced by fashion, and I can see that a consistent newness is necessary to keep the business vital.

From there I expanded to textiles, rugs, and lighting. Now I've become an interior designer as well. I never in a million years thought that this is what I'd end up doing, and it's really been the result of a lot of serendipity and I think meeting and working with the most talented posse on earth. It hasn't all been me.

In 1995 I moved in with me husband Simon Doonan, who is the creative director at Barneys. It was a total meeting of minds about interior design. He lived in a really great apartment with double-height ceilings, incredible moldings, beautiful fireplaces, great pre-war architecture. The furnishings were a weird fusion of Bohemian and mod. The perfect expression of Simon's style, and mine too actually. We now have three places: our place in Manhattan, then a house on Shelter Island, which is this rustic modern kinda thing, and a place in Palm Beach. Those three houses have really clarified for me what my design sensibility is, because I've always had a rather schizophrenic design taste, and I've been lucky enough to be fairly prolific and not have the enforced constipation that a gallery artist might have. My design philosophy is called "happy chic." Someone once asked Hardy Amies, the dressmaker to HM the Queen, "Why do you make her look so frumpy? Why don't you put her in very chic clothes?" And he said, "Because there's an unkindness to chic," and I thought that was very profound. Being chic is very exclusionary, and yet I'm a person living in the world and I want to be chic, but I also want to be inclusive and fun and be playful, so my whole design mission is to marry chic with happiness. Now that I'm an adult and I decorate and I see how hard it is and how many things can go wrong, I look back at my parents' choices with a new-found respect, and if I ever face a difficult decision or a difficult design problem, I just have to ask myself, what would Mrs. Goldstein do?

PREVIOUS PAGE

My house on Shelter Island, about a two-hour drive from New York City, is painted almost entirely white, to give it a beach-house feel. The floor in the guests' upstairs sleeping loft, which overhangs the ground floor, is painted magenta; the chairs are by the designer Geoffrey Harcourt, and I found the lamp in a thrift shop.

LEFT

Our bedroom, on the main floor, has high-level windows that look out onto the bay. On the right there is a modular metal screen from 2000 by a company called BiProduct, and on the bed, a throw of my own design. The date on the pillows refers to my favorite year.

OVERLEAF LEFT

The things in our Manhattan apartment den illustrate what I would call a tremendous tolerance for extreme visual stimuli. Some of the pieces, like the brown leather-covered Chesterfield sofa and the Tommi Parzinger chandelier, are classics, but others, like the horological collage of a vintage car or the life-size bust of Prince, are just fun. The cushions, the rug, and most of the ceramics, as well as the lacquered coffee table, are my own designs

OVERLEAF RIGHT

In the foyer, my hand-thrown pottery Aorta vase stands on a reproduction Renaissance oak bureau in front of a white-painted wall collage made from layered scraps of fabric and industrial carpet by the artist John-Paul Philippe. I'm constantly changing things around, and me mum is very bewildered by this. When I was growing up, it was like, that's where the sofa goes, and things lasted longer too. I personally strive now to make things that are not disposable, and I think that a lot of my influence came from that heritage.

I don't think that there was ever a time when it didn't matter to me what my surroundings looked like. They matter and have always mattered, in the same way that my appearance and what I wear has always mattered. It would drive me mad to live for any length of time in a place that I couldn't personalize. Even as a child growing up, we learned that you could customize everything, even if it was just a matter of deciding what colors you wanted to be surrounded by. I had quite a strange upbringing, in that, from the time I was born right through to when I left home, we lived in about 12 houses. My father was an officer in the army, constantly moving around, so I'm a bit of a nomad. In terms of my memory, there's a lot of confusion when I try to remember individual houses. They were generally quite big and with a lot of staff: a nanny (I had two younger sisters), a cook, a cleaner, and my father's batman, it went on. I remember we were never alone. The first house in Libya, I just recall the palm trees outside. We always lived out in "civvies," never on the military base, so it meant we experienced whatever culture we were living in. Strangely enough, my father was the visual one, not my mother. He came from an Indian army background and was part Indian, part Scottish. He was very creative; he took photographs and had his own darkroom, painted, drew, and decorated. He even made some of our furniture, which my daughter has now inherited.

Our house in Germany had a huge cellar and he did it out like a cowboy saloon, with swing doors and a bar and so on. It was wild. He loved country-and-western music and even wore a cowboy hat when he was off duty. My mother, meanwhile, was a dressmaker and taught us from a very early age to use a sewing machine and make our own clothes. But I really hated it when we all had to wear identical outfits and I guess that's what made me rebel. I think we were puppets to her very traditional Scottish yearnings. It's so easy to see these things looking back, isn't it? You realize why things have happened, and why you now do certain things yourself. My parents always talked about Scotland, they yearned to be there, and in 1965, when I was 16, we moved back. Almost simultaneously I left home. I just wanted to be independent. I hated school and I was no good at most of the academic classes, but I came top of the year in drawing. Even when I was very young I discovered that I could make money by drawing celebrities such as Elvis and selling them to my friends at school. Before I knew it, I had a little industry going. It was quite a shock when I got to Britain. The 1960s was just bursting out and it was a wonderful time to come: mods, fashion, music, everything had more variety than I'd ever imagined. I went to Carlisle College of Art and then to Newcastle, where I worked for a while as the assistant to a fashion photographer. I lived in a top-floor apartment, which I shared with three other girls; we slept in this big attic room and had a ball. We all swapped coats, so that our boyfriends thought we had more clothes than we did. I was nearly 17, and from that day on I started to wear black; it became my uniform. In those days black was different. I saw it as a way of individualizing myself. That was when I became a vegetarian too. After a few years, I did my degree in fine art at Manchester, but I never thought that I wanted to be a painter. I wanted to be a maker, and eventually print became a more important aspect of my work, and that developed into printing on softer materials. The other thing that I'd set my heart on was to go to the Royal College of Art in London. Rightly or wrongly, it epitomized all the things I felt passionately about. When I arrived, I found that it was full of a bunch of kids who were no different from kids in other art schools and I felt deeply disappointed. By then I was a single mom with a daughter, so I had no chance at all to indulge myself. I had a goal, I had grounding, and I had to make it work. At the same time, I managed to find an amazing place to live. The college let rooms in an old embassy they owned at the top of Queensgate, and I found that the best room was part of a ballroom on the first floor. But it was a furniture dump for the rest of the college apartments. Straight away I knew I wanted that room; it had great proportions, a fantastic 12-foot-high ceiling, parquet floor, and a massive bay window. But basically no-one had looked after it. So I said to the registrar, if I find somewhere for all of the furniture, could I have that room? He said, "I don't see why not." I redid that room all in a 1950s black-and-white style, and every weekend I went to jumble sales and I managed to collect some amazing black-and-white pieces: vases, tables, everything. The work that I was making went up on the walls. I suppose it was because of the way I dressed, but there were a lot of other influences too—Japanese culture and so on. They all came together in that room and it really pushed me forward. Work and home began to move closer together. I hadn't realized that until just now. Biba became a very important thing for me at this time, too. Even from Newcastle I had been sending away for stuff. Then when I started to come down to London it was *the* place.

Eventually I began to accept that I was a designer and not a fine artist, which is a massive thing. There was a feeling of betrayal among my fellow students—that I'd gone over to the other side, and maybe the weaker side. They felt that designers are not pure and honest in what they're saying, and that their criteria isn't strong enough to hold up on its own, and that's all rubbish actually. On the other hand, you reach more people, you stretch yourself more as a designer.

As soon as I finished college, two nice things happened. One was that I got a traveling scholarship from the RCA, and the other was that I became homeless. During the last term, my friend Graham Fowler told me that some of my designs would look good on fabric for garments, which hadn't occurred to me before. So we printed them on some fabric, and together we went to Paris. The first shop we showed them to bought the lot. I had no idea what it was leading to, but with my scholarship and his bank loan, we went to Japan. I had an amazing list of about ten names to contact and the first person on the list became our agent—within two days. He contacted Yohji Yamamoto and Issey Miyake and so forth. In a week, we'd done wonderful business over there and could see a way forward to sell my concepts on paper and fabric to the Japanese fashion market. That was the beginning of Timney Fowler and, after that, we did frequent trips to Japan for the next 10 or 15 years. This was in the early 1980s, and for a long time Graham and I were basically homeless; we lived in a lot of different places, council apartments, and all of that. It was to do with having very little money and we were trying to build up the business. By that time, I'd had my second child, and we were working from home—very kitchen sink—like Laura Ashley had done. After about five years in rented accommodation, I saw a sign for retail and work spaces in Notting Hill Gate, and on the spur of the moment, I decided to rent one of them. We had no business plan and no funding, I just thought that maybe we could do a shop somehow and use it to show people what we were doing. Up until then, all of our work was in Japan and nobody knew our names. So that it wouldn't conflict with our fashion business, we decided to do things for the home and keep the two businesses separate. At that time, there seemed to be so little on offer, nothing that was experimental or driven by a fashion element for the home, and I knew there must be people like us in the Notting Hill area. Soon after that, Joseph approached us and said that he was planning to open Pour La Maison, a lifestyle concept store on Sloane Street. "Can you work with me and help put this look together?" So I did. I worked with him on setting up the stores, and provided fabrics, cushions, quilts, ceramics, etc. The look was graphic, simple, stark and, of course, black and white. From then on, we developed licenses for Timney Fowler in America and Japan—for bedding, drapes, and other home products—and we opened a new store in the King's Road in London. All of the stores have been a showroom for our style and a place for us to explore different ways of thinking. They were like a 3D sketchbook of our thoughts. At the same time, we were needing bigger and bigger homes. Soon we had three children, and all the things that go with children. Gradually, through all these places, I discovered that I wanted to do that sort of thing for other people. I'm not disappointed when a place of mine is finished, but I'm never happy either. I am always looking

for the next way to do it, and one good way to appease that feeling is to work on other people's homes. It was very gradual; at first I was invited to look at the soft furnishings, and then they'd say, "Now can you sort our furniture out, and then what about the colors on the walls?" Before I knew it, I was working on the whole concept. If you do this sort of thing, people are always asking you for advice at dinner parties. It's like being a doctor—people want to know if they're dying or not. Sometimes, though, you can't give advice because you don't know any more than they do at that stage. I don't always know the answers, just because it happens to be my subject. I have to study what's going on and contemplate. A quick fix isn't always possible.

In 2000, we licensed the Timney Fowler brand, and from then on I decided to set myself the challenge of creating a new company and a new stores, which would have the same focus— i.e., fabrics and interiors—but with a different look, more toward woven, brightly colored fabrics. In a way, I've moved back to my roots in Africa, to see where that takes me. Travel is an important influence on all of us, the way we use our spaces is influenced by what's going on in the outside world. Politics very much informs the way we look at our homes, too; we have a left-wing government with right-wing policies, and we have a Tory party that is pretending to be left wing, so we're at a time in our homes when we're mixing things as well—styles and cultures, traditional and modern. Young kids, what they're wearing, their music, and how they express that through color and culture, is all part of it. Fashion and home is totally linked. Every day we live in spaces and wear clothes, so how could they not be? *How* they're linked, and which discipline informs the other, is what's interesting.

OVERLEAF LEFT
In this house, I moved the kitchen to the second floor next to the sitting room, so they link right through from front to back in one big space with the same feeling.

OVERLEAF RIGHT
You can see for yourself that I collect objects. I would say that their common denominator is mark-making, things decorated in the old-fashioned way.

FOLLOWING PAGES
This house is a bit smaller than the last one I had, but my family had grown up and I didn't need a huge house. There is still a garden, which I had to have, and it still had rooms to redo. It was another challenge. I don't have a checklist of what I'm looking for, the outside of the house doesn't matter. It might be in a street that other people don't consider suitable, but that can lead to a greater surprise once you're inside. I like that edginess.

The education of my eye began when I was 17. My father was in the Navy and we were living in South Africa when I met my first boyfriend, who was ten years older than me. He was a photographer, and he taught me all about films and photography; the history, but also who was currently hot in Paris, Milan, New York. I used to read fashion magazines and look and see who the photographer was. I started to become very educated visually. I thought I wanted to be an actress. I loved the idea of the theatrical environment. I liked people. I never imagined myself in an artist's studio by myself being "tortured." I was very untortured as a young person. In the late 1970s, my parents moved to New York and my boyfriend and I moved to Paris, so that was the end of that. I never lived with them again. I started to do some modeling and I used to do the makeup for my boyfriend's shoots. I was photographed by Steve Hiet, and Guy Bourdain lived up the road—I knew all these people. I'm only 5 feet 2 inches, but I was taken on by an agency who had very unusual girls. I began to learn by osmosis. I didn't go to such-and-such college, I was in pictures. When my boyfriend went to do photography in Milan, I used to go and visit him—that's where I saw some great apartments. From then on for three years I just absorbed. We had no television; we went to a different season of movies every week, so I saw every Italian, German, Swedish film ever made. François Truffaut's mistress lived along the corridor—if I looked out of my kitchen window I could see into her bedroom—so there's nothing I don't know about Truffaut. We used to bump into him on the stairs quite a lot. I'd forgotten about that, but I probably lurked on the landing hoping to be in one of his films.

Paris at that time was the place where everyone creative was, you know. We talked only about design, visual things. I learned how to cook there; I always liked arranging food more than making sure that the sauce was reduced enough. I love the look of food. I also began to have an interest in my apartment. We lived for a while in Les Halles. Flowers have always been incredibly important to me. Even if I had only ten francs for the week, it would be a bag of potatoes—so I could make lots of potato pie and things—and I bought flowers. You always saw people in the street with their baguette and a bunch of flowers.

One of the first purses I made was a Paris street scene, with a drawing of horse chestnut trees and a corner café. I was terribly influenced by living in Paris. My apartment had a mattress and a vase of tulips on the floor. I think that what I learned to do there was to edit. There was the underlying spirit of Portobello Road and all of that, but I learned to take away. It was slightly to do with having no money, too. I always bought things that were retro for my home (that's a very good point); no one else was particularly into that at the time, so I used to have a very good time at the flea markets. I've still got a lemon squeezer (I wonder where it is?) that I bought then. I would love to have bought much more. But it's good training I suppose. If you can only have one thing, what's it going to be? I went through all of that without knowing it.

I came back to London to do a play, "The Reluctant Débutante," and I shared a house in Fulham with a girl. After that I lived in all different place for years. When I finally got my own apartment, I had dreams of what it would be like. I knew that when I got something, it had to be different. I always wanted everything to be different from everyone else. On every level, every level. A very, very tiring thing to be. I bought a second-floor ballroom; it was a complete wreck. I built a bed in the center of it. You came in through these enormous double doors and there was a vast fireplace, which I made a lot of, and I had two sofas, one on each side, and an art deco trolley. I made a kitchen—white with light gray marble tops. No color —all white and a bit of chintz. Actually, I guess I did have color, I had a very, very strong-colored Chinese shawl bedspread. At the back, it went down three steps and there was a funny little bit that I made into a bathroom. My friends thought it was amazing, but they couldn't live in it. "How could you have a bed in a sitting room?" It was a long time ago, studio living hadn't really happened yet.

When I got married, my husband and I bought this house where I am now—Notting Hill Gate—and lived in the basement until we could afford to do the next floor and the next, and then we had a baby. This house has evolved in its own way. He had a say and I had a say, and that was how our home was going to be. But, meanwhile, I had to express my own creativity, and so I started my business, initially in the basement of the house, and later, my own office and shop in Ledbury Road. That's when the vision of what I liked started to come out. That was in 1996. But unlike in my business, where I'm often constrained by costs or production limitations, where I'm designing into a price point—shoes, gloves, purses, umbrellas, so many things—at home, it doesn't matter if this bit of glass that sparkles and lights up or something costs more than the rest of the kitchen, because it's up to me. Now that I'm on my own again, and I've got a bit more money, I can work with craftsmen, not just the odd-job bloke. I adore people who make things. I think that Manolo Blahnik was right when he said something like, "Trust your guts and find the best technician you can," to a group of designers. I have a contract to design china for Spode, and what I'm looking forward to is getting up to that factory.

What I want to do in my kitchen and dining room is totally in my head. Magazines about kitchens and bedrooms and bathrooms are my porn at the moment. But I don't do anything about it, I just haven't had the time or whatever, which is good, because what I would have done two years ago would not be true to me now. I've got much more confident. I'm much more interested in lighting than I was, I now understand the mood thing. What motivates me now is quality of life, and time to do what I want to do. I have two children who I put first. When I was young, I was very creative. I would do the posters for the summer fêtes and the raffles in our village. I used that bubble writing with each letter colored in for hours. My children do that now, too. I remember cutting up millions of magazine adverts. Biba was something that has never left me,

and Fiorucci too; I've always loved graphics, I guess. My aunt would ask me if I would draw Monet water-lilies so that she could sew them as a patchwork. I was quite bad at still lifes with apples and things; in those days art school was so limited. I do remember making things out of squeezy liquid bottles, and things they showed on the TV program "Blue Peter." I had quite a strong personality, so I thought that doing stage design might be a way of getting into the theater world. In the 1960s I was all set to go to St. Martin's College of Art in London, when my parents left for South Africa, but my being so young, they didn't feel comfortable leaving me here by myself.

My dream now is to be asked to do a hotel and to do a ballet. These are my long-term goals. The best creative moment for me came when I got my "florist basket" purse into the V&A. I remember thinking, right, if I'm run over by a bus tomorrow, I've made my mark; I will be remembered.

PREVIOUS PAGE
In the dining room, these decoupage plates by the New York artist John Derian hang above my favorite butterfly lacquer cabinet.
RIGHT
This picture of my daughter Madeleine in the sitting room was taken some time ago. She is wearing shoes from one of the yearly collections I design.

For me the only thing that's important is people. I always say that if I go to a house and it's very ugly and the people are very happy, I think, well this is a good house. If I go into a house that is completely designed, and nobody's happy, I really dislike the house. A house is well decorated if it combines with the owner rather than the decorator. There are lots of people who are very happy in ugly environments, but this can also be beautiful. If you see a photograph of an old lady sitting in her chair with her table beside her, it's beautiful, even if it doesn't fit into any design philosophy.

When Holland was rich, Edam—where I live—was an important place because the boats were arriving with spices from Indonesia and India and so on. So there were a lot of 17th-century houses and everybody had the same interior: planks (wooden boards) on the floor, white walls, antique cupboards, antique couches; everybody was following each other. It was a very Dutch look, quite different to English interiors, which were more completely antique decorated. In Holland there's not much ornament and the furniture isn't rich with details, it's much simpler. By the 1970s people were already starting to mix styles, using new Italian furniture. I always heard that England was quite late in changing from the classic period to the modern; I hear that it's only just happening now.

When I was young, 14 or 15, I had a very clear idea of what I liked and what I didn't like. I think it was in the family—everyone needed to have an opinion, always quarreling about everything you know? If you look at art, for instance, I liked Mondrian and Rietveld and things that were mathematical and clear and straight. I didn't like Gaudi and those people and I thought they were bad. During my studies it turned around of course, because I found out that this was just stylistic. You can be very good in organic forms and you can be very good in mathematical things, and you can be very bad in both directions too. I was completely wrong and I'd been a pain in the arse to everyone around me. Neither of my parents cared much about houses; they still don't. My father was an English

teacher; his environment isn't very important to him, he just reads books. It should be silent; that's what he needs, he doesn't need nice decoration. My mother only changes things when they don't function any more; it's the normal, old-fashioned way. There are still a lot of people who are buying things for their whole life. Most of the furniture I make will last forever, and people buy it for that, I'm quite sure.

I was always building and making things when I was very little. I made tiny furniture from matches, little chairs, and cupboards with two drawers, only 12 millimeters high. I just made them out of my memory. I always do that; even if I cook, I cook from memory. That's exactly how I design too. My inspiration doesn't come from special visits to museums and things. I just walk past a farmer's house or an old bus stop that is constructed in a very specific way, and I see some detail and I put it into my head. Then maybe three years later the details come out in a completely different context. I don't draw things to remember them; I just trust that the nice things will bubble up when they're needed. I always thought that the process would end, and now I know it's not ending, it gets easier and easier. The idea of making furniture from old wood came when I was doing my exams at the Industrial Design Academy in Eindhoven. Everyone in the course was making perfect pieces; at least they had to look like they were perfect even if they were only a prototype, because it's design. So naturally I thought I would do the opposite; I thought isn't it possible to make something with rough materials, with history. It's not that I don't like perfect things; it's just that it's not the only direction you can choose. I really liked old wood, and one day I was walking through a place that sold old building materials and I thought it was more beautiful than the materials we normally work with. It had a life, a history; it was cheap too. So I thought I'm going to make something with old wood, which is desirable; that first scrapwood cupboard is still selling now —better than ever. At first people said it was fashionable, but recycling is not the issue; it was not

the reason for doing it. Now they tell me that they still like it so it can't be just fashion. If you look at the whole collection, you understand that the cupboard is just one part of a bigger story. We now make lots of products that are all with the same mentality, but the materials are completely different.

In Holland we've changed the way people think about materials, and even about the way they should live. We make a big table, so lots of people can eat and be together; it's the central place. That's the most important thing in your life, being together. If I ask people for their five highlights, they don't mention being alone in the forest, they say when I was with my best friends, or when I met my wife or something, so I try to accommodate that. It's also something against always hurrying, taking time for the people around you. In Holland now, I've become a brand; on television, people say, "Ah, we're going to do it in a Piet Hein Eek style." I like that, it makes me laugh. When I was a student, a friend and I used our vacations to rebuild people's houses. When they were on vacation, they'd give us their keys and we would work 14 or 18 hours a day repainting and repairing and doing all kinds of things, and when they came back a week later the whole house was done. If you look at the commissions we get now, we almost never get home interiors, we get parts. If we are asked to do a home, I always end up not doing it. I say that people should do it themselves. I like to help but I often end up saying, just take out that wall and your problem is solved. They think that they should refurnish or something but the house is wrong. Everybody has a story about how they would like to live and the space should fit into that story.

My own house, where I live with my wife Janine and three daughters, is a 1950s brick-built house that has been painted white, so it feels like a vacation home. We've made the house twice as big by adding onto it and under it and next to it, but nobody sees it, as we just did it in the same style. It's a functional family house. Every corner is well thought out and slowly it's filled up with special things that I've designed. I like the things that have a story: the things we found, the things we bought

for very little money when we were young. I like it not being perfect and I don't think we'll ever get to the end. I've always been inspired by things that nobody else gets inspired by; it's the normal things, rather than the special things; the bus stop is more important than the art gallery. That's why the cupboard I'm making now, in 50 years it will still be a good cupboard, I'm quite sure.

PREVIOUS PAGE AND RIGHT
Geertje (one half of my twins) and all of my women are painting a box with an incredibly beautiful vase in it from a very talented artist designer in Holland. We don't dare to take the vase out of the box because the girls are so wild. Instead of enjoying the vase we decided to decorate the packaging. The space where all the mess happens is my study, which was for me the prime reason to rebuild our home, but instead of having my own space, it became a family hobby and working area. The floor is an old parquet from a military barracks.

A client who is building a house is building it to last for a long time, during which other people are going to use it. They're kind of privileged because they're building a part of the city, a little part of the overall townscape. What these little buildings make up as a whole group is almost more interesting than what they are as individuals. The idea that architects are going to work on small private houses for middle-class people is incredibly new—only about 70 years old. Most housing before that was part of the warp and weft of the city. Think of most suburban streets in London or Boston or Sydney.

In the end, the things that I think are most memorable and enduring do turn out to be streetscapes, rather than individual buildings. Now that all cities are becoming more stressed, you come to realize that in order to have a life, what part of town you're in—how easy it is to see other people, what kind of amenities there are around you— becomes more important than people's personal concerns with their own space, because humans are so adaptable. But if you live an hour or more away from your work place, if there are no parks nearby, nowhere to go out to eat, you can have the most beautiful house but a horrible life. Where I grew up, in a suburb of Brisbane, the idea that there was any kind of public life only emerged after the World Expo in 1988. Suddenly people realized that they could go out to be with other people. Previous to that, everyone just went to everyone else's houses for a barbecue. That's what going out meant. You would have three or four families, which didn't fit inside the house, so you always spilled out into this partial zone that was between the garden and the house. All of the memorable events—birthdays, Christmas—they all happened in this "pit" of the building that was the most ephemeral and fragile and underworked (usually with a concrete floor, steel ceilings, bits of plastic) because it was so hot, but invariably it rained. So people would have their living rooms and so forth—with all their Edwardian furniture and Axminster carpets and wallpaper and their ornaments—that nobody ever went into. I was always inter-ested in buildings. At kindergarten I was reorganizing the sandbox according to town planning principles (!); working out how I could hand in assignments for art that were really to do with buildings. I remember in grade 9, I designed a building and made a model of it. It was very big. There was a lot of difficulty getting it into the automobile to get to school. I don't remember what they said, but the whole thing was not about the reactions. This is the great thing about living in a culture where you don't do anything to be appreciated. It's very good for the imagination, because it's really all you can rely on. You become immensely robust. By the time I got into architecture school, I was already going to the library and reading a lot of books and periodicals about architecture, and I came to realize that there were a whole lot of ideas that I could see different buildings shared. It was almost like a secret knowledge and I had to try endlessly and patiently to find out what that was.

Living in Brisbane—and not having traveled overseas— I hadn't actually seen anything by way of buildings, or been in a society that took them very seriously. But I could see that in other countries and other societies and other times, they really did take them seriously, whether it was public buildings or private homes. I didn't divide them. Still don't. The only thing is that the circumstances of the commission of the home in our society are fairly different from those of public buildings. People who commission houses usually care quite a lot about them, whereas we've never done a big building for anyone who cared a damn. The only thing interesting going on in architecture all through the 1970s and '80s here, were houses. The terrific thing that's very hard for Europeans to understand about our kind of place, is that it's a frontier. There is absolutely building going on everywhere. By the time I'd finished studying and doing part-time jobs, I'd done three or four houses and a couple of little public buildings—completely done them. I had no targets at that stage—just to build. I began to realize that what made buildings substantial was the way that you experienced them, and that was usually related to very strategic planning. I was convinced that the plan of a big scheme and the plan of a small scheme were very much the same. I thought that what went on in a house was just a tiny version of what went on in a town; that there were public and private areas, and it was a sort of frisson between these two interreacting that made one of the key architectural experiences. The initial idea, I realized, was how the site was organized; how one house could exist beside another, and that trick of not making the house the object, like the modernists had, but treating the building as the negative feature of the design, with a perfect space in the middle and the rooms all around it. I was very big on that as a student.

The houses that we're doing now have that same principle. They are• almost like little towns in miniature. There is usually a town square and a number of addresses off the square, so that, rather than having a front door into the hall, they usually have a gate; that tends to make them more autonomous. Just like a town, there are big and small spaces. The private rooms, which I guess are the bedrooms or office, tend to be one sort of space, and then there's another space that's usually more beautiful, and that's the square. The thing that gives the rooms their quality is often their relationship to the town's square. This is where we put all the architectural effort. It's the exact reverse to the houses I grew up in. All the richness and brocading we now put into this outside space, and then the other rooms rely for their beauty on their attachment to it. It changes the proportions, it gives you a sense of the context of the building, and it lets you have an impression of the time of day and the time of the year—from the inside. In terms of materials, I would say that we tend to make homes out of authentic elements.

The beautiful thing about Australia, wherever you are, is the landscape. However small the project, it can usually involve thinking about or reminding you of the landscape. Making a building is a lot like making a movie. If it's a vision only about the end results—and doesn't take into account how you are going to get it to occur, and who can be persuaded at what time, and how much you reveal when, and who you involve to help—it's a pointless vision. Because all of these things are usually against you. People never support visions, they have to be coerced into them.

Even in domestic work, the client is often not well defined. We've done several houses for clients who were absent, or we've barely met, or who wanted a speculative outcome. We've done houses for clients who weren't in any way a family, and we've done a lot of work for clients who aren't interested in home, but who want some kind of project to keep themselves occupied. The best project is first of all a client who can agree within themselves—where there is a leader or a spokesperson. Ideally I want someone who is open to being fascinated, not someone who wants to toy with their own willpower—or ours. The shared responsibility between the architect and the client is to agree what it is that's interesting about the project, outside of the brief. If you make a project and all it does is satisfy your own whim, it's terribly limited. A whole lot of the buildings we now admire in history were in some way an experiment with a wonderful idea that was beyond just the client. So many of those houses from the Renaissance, for example, had a whole lot of wonder about them that went on and on. They didn't want just a house.

Building something for myself was never an ambition— still isn't. I don't have a home. I rent part of a house that I designed for someone else. In a way, that is because so much of my energy is taken up in projection that the last thing I want when I'm dealing with people's houses such a lot is to have one myself. If I ever did build one for myself, I'd be so busy trying to make it self-effacing; something tailored just for me doesn't make me feel good. I'd probably end up living in an apse or a swimming pavilion. So many of the great spots to live were never designed as houses. What I'd really like to do is a house in a generous landscape. Very few gardens in Australia are thought about as design, yet so many of people's memories of places are about landscape. If you think of all those famous Australian houses, they're usually about a house that's detached from the landscape, so that it gazes out—as if nothing's happened. I think that, as an idea, is immensely lonely and alienating. It would be really wonderful to make a garden where the ideas have such substance and conviction that the house part can be incredibly deferential to them. I'd like to do that.

OVERLEAF
Australians have always associated "homes" with "houses" and "apartments" with "boxes." This apartment, which clambers on top of itself to yield the living areas under its roof, has the sort of places, platforms, and pluck that might encourage a form of "real life" domesticity. It is not the "life" depicted in the selling brochures … but "life at home" can be pretty open-ended.

FOLLOWING PAGES
Life in this house is lived mostly outside, with this ambiguous space being the most memorable part of the site. It enjoys openings but not windows, sun but not heat, breeze but not wind. It acts as a room at the lower level and as screen to the world from the upper, private, evening level. In our culture, where there's no money and no history, no-one's interested in furniture at all. I don't think that we've ever done a house that anyone has ever fully furnished— ever. People just aren't interested in it. So knowing that, we often try to design the interiors so that you don't have to have much furniture, rooms with a lot of built edges like you see in North African architecture. I call it the democracy of the sofa. If we build a spot, even though it's fixed, it's potentially more liberal than a sofa. People can sit, lie down there, or sleep, or can take the cushions away and use them as low tables, make them into bookcases. You can't do that with a sofa. Sometimes we've done rooms where all that people have done is to add cushions.

If you saw me as a child growing up you wouldn't know whether I was Indian or Greek or Italian or something else, but the fact is that I knew that I was Indian. My father looked very Indian—he had very dark skin and black hair—so there was a very strong personal identity and we grew up as Indians, my brother and I. The Cheyenne, which is the tribe that we belonged to, are located there in Oklahoma and that's where my father was born, even though he would be quick to point out that it was not their historical territory. My mother, on the other hand, was Scottish American, even though she was actually born in China—the daughter of missionaries—where she lived until she was 14. But the way in which we were raised was very much aligned with our native background on my father's side. If you're talking about ways of life, or how we define our cosmos, much of that is intangible, but there are cultural dimensions to it that were rather tangible. For example, my brother and I learned to dance various Cheyenne dances, and there was an aspect of ceremonial life that was distinctly Cheyenne that my brother and I still carry on. I would dress just like other children but I also had Indian regalia that I donned on some occasions.

I was born in San Francisco, where we lived during the Second World War while my father was stationed at the naval base. Then in 1947 after the war, we moved to eastern Oklahoma, three or four miles outside a small town called Muskogee, and we lived on the campus of Bacone college, a former mission school and a type of transition home for young American Indians, many of whom had never lived in a house before. That was my home from the age of four until I was about 17. I can say with an absolutely straight face that I was raised in a four-room log cabin. I remember the inside of it very distinctly: it was paneled entirely in knotty pine boarding; there were two bedrooms, a living room, a kitchen, and a bathroom. My father tended the outside, he was a very serious gardener, and imagine my mom looked after the inside, although there was probably a collaboration. Both of my parents were very good cooks. The entire house couldn't have been more than eight hundred to one thousand square feet in total, and most of the furniture was simple local purchases. The distinctive thing about the house was probably the artwork, which was all my father's. He was an artist, a painter, and a sculptor and he taught art at the college. In fact both my parents were teachers; my mother (a trained musician) taught piano. Our living room, for the entire time that I was growing up, was also a studio, with my father's easel and his drawing table right there. He also had a studio in the art department on the campus, where 95 percent of the students between 18 and 20 years old were American Indian.

Somehow I expected to be there the entire time—it felt very stable. I remember a couple of times when my father was offered positions elsewhere—I was horrified that we might leave. I was shocked when I went back much later to see how very small it was, but for me then, it was quite commodious—a lovely place to grow up. Both my parents had family in California, so every summer we would hop in the automobile and drive out to visit them. That was the only traveling we did. Finally, when I was 17 I went to a small private residential university there in California, which is where my mother had gone. But frankly, I might as well have gone to the moon it was so different, so foreign to me. From there I went to graduate school at Harvard and then back across the country to law school at Stanford. First out of the box, I became a lawyer and my brother became a banker, so neither of those were close to being a pianist or an artist, but that was OK with them. My mother passed away when I was only in my 20s, but my father remarried and lived on into his 80s, so he got to see me in my present position as the director of the National Museum of the American Indian, and I think he took great pleasure in that.

I was in college for a total of eight years and, looking back, I see it as a rather transitory time. The nesting didn't occur until I moved to Washington DC, where I've lived for most of my professional life in the same house. I remember seeing it for the first time, it was very exciting. For one thing, it was a much bigger home than I had been used to. It backs onto part of the park, which was very important to me too—I wanted to look over the natural environment even though I was in the city. Where we live in Washington is very much a neighborhood; we all know each other and most of our kids were raised together, so that one of the ways of socializing is going to each others' houses for dinner, and in the early days at my law firm, my wife Mary Beth and I entertained a lot. Most of the houses were the same as ours really—we call them center-hall colonial; it's a simple family dwelling on four levels and was built in the 1920s, when this part of the city was developed.

At one point we did have a wonderful country house that we had built in the Blue Ridge Mountains and used for a number of years. Then for a while we lived in New Mexico in a terrific adobe house that we thought we might retire to. As a matter of fact, now the kids have grown up and left home we don't need all of this space. I am approaching retirement, and we're trying to make the decision as to whether we're

going to keep this house—which we probably won't—for the long haul. But the reason it is so difficult is because I was raised not just in houses, but in homes, and the distinction in my mind is that I have great identification with these places. Place for me has great importance. The home we have lived in for almost 30 years is a part of my being, if you will. It's not something I can just leave behind on a whim. I think that historically there was no difference between what native Americans felt about home, and what westerners felt. In our roots we are all profoundly attached to place. One of the reasons that native people feel so strongly about it is because we are tribal in culture, even to this day, and there is an importance attached to community, to family, and to home. Western society now has become so highly transient. People move all the time. The profound attachment that Indian communities have to particular territory is not only physical, it is spiritual in nature and I think that is a profound dimension of native world view that cuts across all of the Americas, from Cheyenne to Comanche, Cherokee to Choctaw, and the rest. My wife and I are in the process of buying property in Bali, and one of the reasons I'm doing that is because Indonesians look at things the way I look at them. For example, the seller explained to me, "When we're doing this kind of transaction we have to consult the community leader and the village leader. There are blessings that attach to the purchase of property and so forth." And I said, look you're talking to the choir here, I understand it exactly. To much of native America there was a permanence, a settled nature to their occupation. Not so the Cheyenne, but though our homes had to be portable, there was still a profound respect for that place because it went with us. I remember when I got married my father pulled me aside and said, "Now remember, amongst our people it is the wife who actually owns the tipi and all of its contents, so if you run amok, you may find your belongings on the stoop of your tipi—so just mind your manners." Cheyennes were matrilineal, so property descended through the female line. My point is that there was much that was in that tipi: tipi painting, tipi furniture, tipi art, beadwork, quill work; all of that stayed with us. We created homes that attached to us in very important ways; that were decorated in very specific ways by the people who lived in those places.

Even when I was a practicing attorney, I represented Indian tribes and communities and I was always involved in native cultural arts affairs, primarily because my father was an artist. So in 1989, when this really quite astounding opportunity came up—the establishment of the first National Museum of the American Indian—I just went for it with a vengeance. There has really been a renaissance of interest in Indian culture, beginning in the 1960s with the flowering of counter-culturalism, and Indians were the beneficiaries of that. It was partly a self-recognition in the United States of its own deep roots, and there was of course a tremendous amount of romance surrounding American Indians. They were known but not known. When it came to the building of the museum, we consulted broadly with the native communities before we began and it was designed in part by native architects. The principal designer is a highly regarded Canadian architect who happens to be of native descent too. Much of the building is evocative of native aesthetics: the color; the fact that it is very organic in design form; the use of natural light; the thinness and transparency of the visual membrane between the built and the nonbuilt environment; the connectiveness of the building to the land on which it sits; the fact that it is surrounded by an eco-environment that is similar to what was on that site when native people owned the land. I promise you, native people see these things. They were the first—well ahead of Europeans—to be able to think abstractly in artistic terms. They can look at our building and say, "I know that, I can see myself in this place."

This isn't something you can be taught, but it's the way you grow up; it's experiential. It's something that ends up setting in you a world view that is Cheyenne.

When the museum opened, I made a short speech to the 80 thousand people who gathered in front of the building on the National Mall in Washington DC: To those of you who descend from those who came—welcome to Native America. To those of you who descend from those who were here to greet those who came, I say—welcome home.

PREVIOUS PAGE

Ours is a "historic" neighborhood, so there are restrictions as to what you can do, and any additions have to be approved by the architectural review committee. But that didn't apply 20 years ago when we built an extension downstairs to expand the kitchen and eating areas. We had young kids and we wanted a place where we could congregate very easily. That's what I look at when I visit other people's homes, the places where the family actually live, rather than grand unlived-in places.

RIGHT

This is a view of the Potomac space in the National Museum of the American Indian in Washington DC.

Whether it's a residential building we're designing or a hotel or a restaurant, I think that the most important thing is to come up with a unique DNA, so that it has an authenticity to it and is not just a composite of various things we've seen and liked. I do think that people are very sensitive to authenticity. Talking to a client, understanding someone and what they're interested in and what their approach is, is critical; a bit like archaeology. If you're designing for the theater, which we do once a year, it's clear what the script is. In the case of a restaurant or a hotel, the script is really something you have to pull out of the chef or the operator and find out what is going to make it unique. One of the questions I like to ask people comes from my theater experience. When I'm talking to a director or a playwright, I want to know how the audience is going to feel at the end of the show that differs from how they felt coming in. Sometimes not knowing the answer is the most creatively freeing aspect, and it's one of the reasons why we move from one type of project to another so intently. I really think that the key to me staying creatively vital is to always take risks.

If you look at the role of hotels in the United States, and think about the grand hotels, in some way they were an extension of the public space. The Plaza in its heyday was a kind of living room for Central Park. There was a real shift back to that with boutique hotels, with their teeny rooms and all the emphasis on the bar and the restaurant and the nightlife. Now it's moving back, and we're getting a balance where the room really matters. Since we're nomadic, moving around all over the place, the room becomes our office away from home, our home away from home. When we are designing a hotel room we can have a lot of things that people don't have at home. Since guests are only staying for a day or two there's a chance to infuse a level of fantasy, so that when you're picking a hotel, you pick what fantasy you're in the mood for. If you look at what's going on in restaurants right now, there's an emphasis on sharing—food that you share, open kitchens, community tables— and I do think I see that filtering into how people live at home. We're doing a residential building in Battery Park right now, where we are creating kitchens that are like a teak enclosure on a ship. When you walk into the apartment it can be folded up quite small, but when you're cooking in there, walls pivot and open out, counters flip up, and you have this wonderful eat-in kitchen. In a way, it accommodates all the various moods that moving from hotel to hotel can. What we add as designers or as architects is more innovative ways to live.

Though I was born in Chicago, we moved when I was three and a half to a town in New Jersey, so I don't remember that house, but I must have been programmed as a city kid, because I feel at home in cities, although I guess I've always kept one foot in having a country outlet. I love contrasts and when I was young there were so many sudden transitions that weren't my choice. I'm the youngest of five boys and when I was two my dad died, and later my mom remarried and we moved to an amazing stone house in the middle of the forest. I remember

it as a place where I could experiment and play and perform magic tricks, build things, and my favorite place was this fantastical old garage that was whatever I wanted it to be. After a year or two, we moved to a huge house just two blocks from the sea at Deal and that was the first time I ever thought about fixing up a home. My mom had performed in vaudeville when she was younger and was a dancer. In this house, she redid the sunroom all in a Chinese style, with bamboo and rattan and bright oranges. I think she looked at this room as a kind of theatrical installation. The most active form of creative encouragement that my mom provided for me was music and dance. When she was working on choreography numbers, she'd rehearse them with me. The piano was always central in the living room, so music was very much a part of my life growing up. Then when I was 11 we moved to Guadalajara in Mexico. My stepdad had read some books about retiring to Mexico, so he sold his company and off we went. That was a big shock, on every level, starting with the fact that at that age, you really don't understand what it means to get into a station wagon and drive to a country where they don't speak English. You're going from sea level to several thousand feet above sea level. The quality of light is one of the things that I remember most: the light and shadow, the brightness, the vibrancy of color; also the public spaces. In a suburb by the Jersey shore, there's no marketplace, no bullring, no mariachi, so I guess my love of trans- formative communities, my love of public spaces and public theater, comes from there.

We lived in a detached house, the Mexican equivalent of a brown- stone I guess, which had a pool and a bamboo garden in the back. A total trip. The houses were substantially more modest than in New Jersey, furniture was much simpler and there was probably less differentiation: simpler materials; tiled floors; TV wasn't a central element in the house. Most of the living was done on terraces and on the back porch, not the front. There was a respect for privacy and people did their outdoor living at the back. I got to know all the neighbors immediately and was fluent in Spanish in six months. It was total acceptance on my part and we were all very happy down there. At 12 I began to get very interested in the architect Luis Barragán and my focus moved from theater and magic to buildings and spaces. My mom died when I was 15 and after that I just wanted to get back to New York, where my brothers were. At archi- tecture school in Syracuse I had a room in the attic of the fraternity building and I remember, because the walls were very funky, I got a staple gun and rolls and rolls of red burlap and wrapped the walls and floor and ceiling in this red fabric. I had a large drafting table, a bed and one of those "butterfly" chairs, which was my relaxing place, and there was a stereo on the floor. It had everything I needed and was my own little home. I didn't think about it at the time but now I realize that it was the red of the bullring. After college, my first apartment in New York was on 14th Street between 7th and 8th, above a restaurant that seemed to be burned down every two years for the insurance. Living down the hall was a primal scream therapist called Parks White, so for free, I gave him some ideas about insulation. In the center of my room I put that same baby grand piano that reminded me of my parents and connected me to my previous homes, and the rest of it I built with hammer and nails and a few friends. We even painted murals on the walls of the stair leading up. The other floors were all vacant. Three or four years later I moved to a teeny studio—only about 500 square feet—on 30th Street and Madison Avenue. You know when you do your apartment for the first time, every inch matters; this was like doing the interior of a ship, like a little nest. I loved *The Grass Harp* by Truman Capote, and the way he talked about that tree house being a kind of retreat from the world. By this time (1981–2) I was working as an architect. I designed a nightclub, some recording studios, and this apartment for a couple, one of whom worked from home. The whole apartment was configured as a series of gentle steps, like an Italian hillside village. Imperceptibly as you moved through the apartment, you ended up upstairs. I'd always used levels and steps on both my apartments and I felt like the act of stepping up could create zones within a given space. You could take a small studio space, and by stepping up into the bed area and then up again into the bed, not only was there more of a cocooning, but it could create separations between different areas that allowed you to move from place to place, not just from corner to corner. In 1985 I started the practice with two projects, one was a woefully underbudgeted Japanese restaurant on 46th Street called Sushi Zen, with a really insane sushi chef who would chase everyone around with a meat cleaver. The space was 25 feet wide, no daylight, no view, but in the way that designers often do with their first job, I put in every good idea I'd ever had. At the same time, we did a ground-up house in Pound Ridge for a very rich, very interesting family that wanted to have a lot of party and celebration space. I realized that my primary interest in the house *was* the public space. There was a huge amount of feedback and awards, particularly for the restaurant. It's not like I *chose* restaurants, but this one became the armature for all these ideas that I was interested in, and launched a 20-year career in hospitality and restaurant design.

Around that time, I decided to build a house for myself on the roof of a building on 68th Street and Columbus overlooking the Upper West Side. Again it was a teeny weeny one-bedroom house, but this time, every inch of it was built in. I had multiple levels, so you stepped down into the living room, up to the bedroom. I became focused on how you choreographed space and how you moved through space. I became fascinated with the way light moves and changes during the day and affects paint. I was constantly repainting the apartment, seeing how different colors resonated with natural light. I'm also sure that there was more lighting per square foot in that apartment than any other apartment; I had multiple dimmers and circuits, uplighting, down-lighting, and so forth. I lived there from 1987 to 1993 when I met my current wife and moved to a loft in Tribeca. It was a hard thing to move

because the space was tailor-built for me. It certainly wasn't built to accommodate two people. When I walk into a space, whether it's a restaurant space or a domestic space, I think what I try to find is the unique characteristics. In this new loft, it seemed to me like a kind of spaceship. Being on the roof of the building was like being in your own little time machine. I was intrigued essentially by the view and the light. I find it much easier to choose furniture and to be definitive about fabrics when it's someone else's home, because it's different when you're living with it yourself. When I go to visit somebody's home, I think I look at the relationship of things. The arrangement of spaces and objects tells you a lot about what people do in there. If there are two very fixed sofas with a coffee table that's just too far away to reach—with art books on it—you know that it's a place to look at and not to be in. I think about theater and restaurants as a two-hour mini vacation, but a home is a very different thing. In contrast to the 68th Street apartment where everything was done when I moved in, I've now started to enjoy the imperfect process of adding and changing things, certainly now that we have two kids. The house has evolved over the years, to be about us as a family. The kitchen was never the center of activity until we had kids, and now it is. I guess when it comes to my home and picking furniture and things, it was a really freeing process when I started to think of it not as a permanent fixed-in-stone thing, but something that would evolve and change based on where I was at, and where my wife Marsha was at, and most importantly, where our kids were at.

OVERLEAF LEFT

Mood, atmosphere, and creating dramatic effect is often what my work is about. Our concept at the Washington Square Restaurant in Philadelphia is opposites attract; A study in dramatic contrasts; modern meets baroque, the restaurant is actually in an art deco building circa 1929 that was built for an advertising agency, but the garden lounge area pictured here takes a turn for the modern. It is neutral in color with simple furnishings. Walking through the garden, the teak flooring and white canvas furniture create a symmetrical organization, culminating with a glowing white bar. We maintained the inside-outside relationship by creating a semi-enclosed space with overhead floating fabric panels. Along with the semitransparent lampshades and random patterned cushions, they help give the scheme a softer, more domestic appearance.

OVERLEAF RIGHT

By contrast, this room has no windows at all, a different approach for creating drama. Adjacent to the kitchen, the Hibachi room is one of the private dining rooms at Nobu Fifty Seven, which we completed in 2005. Enclosed within walls and ceilings lined with a unique black terrazzo inlaid with rings of bamboo, this area was created to be a visually dramatic backdrop for the theatrics of the food preparation; its effect being both shocking and strangely soothing.

New York became my home in 1985. For almost a decade, I lived in a very eccentric loft-style apartment in Chelsea that had giant eight-foot-high windows that all looked out onto an airshaft. It had virtually no daylight and hand-me-down furniture, and there came a point when I simply didn't invite visitors in. I slept on a miserably thin futon on the floor, and I almost negated a sense of home and comfort. Then slowly I started to get writing work for film and television and my career began to accelerate, and as that occurred I became more and more invested in my surroundings. I developed a real hotel fetish. As I traveled more for work, I found that sometimes I would be put in relatively posh lodgings. My surroundings were always so much more comfortable than they were at home, and I never knew what it meant to pine for home. In hotels, the mattresses were better and the thread count was higher and the environment was more rich and lush. Finally I began to think, I can't go back home; I could live in hotels for the rest of my life. Eventually I moved out to Brooklyn and got a very lovely apartment on the top floor of an elegant old brownstone, and for the first time, gave myself the requisite budget and time to forge a home. Then almost immediately it became kind of an obsession. Looking for my first apartment was a huge part of my education and so was unrestrained voyeurism, because I saw how other people lived and what was possible. When I go to other people's houses I look for vestiges of their own history, the astonishing revelation of character that comes from the display of prized objects, not because they're beautiful, but because they're meaningful. I look for the objects that promise a story— they are the things I want to learn about.

When I was growing up in Texas, culturally it was relatively impoverished. My parents were educated people, so they were very vigilant about exposing my siblings and me to culture when they could. My father wasn't one to take us out into the backyard and toss a ball around, and he wasn't one to go on hiking or bicycling trips, but he loved antique furniture.

He would take me to rural antique auctions as a small child and I'd sit and sketch the people in the audience while he bid on different pieces. I think those people traveled a great distance to those events, they were usually the more moneyed, the more artistic, flamboyant characters who would gather in places like Forney, Texas, to buy credenzas. Before the auction began, we'd wander through the warehouse and look at all the lots. My father had a very broad taste and so he would first be attracted by a piece and then go to great lengths to learn its history. The house didn't look haphazard or chaotic, but I think the pieces were eccentric. There was a kind of mad elegance to it, but it was definitely singular. Eventually it became almost like a cluttered showroom, and was the bane of my mother's existence. In the way that

families keep secrets, he'd often pull me aside and say, "Don't tell your mother, but I've just bought eight of the most beautiful Turkish rugs," and then he'd hide them at his office or in the garage so mother wouldn't know he'd splurged again. It's almost impossible for me to separate the object from the memories of my dad. I remember that he'd come home from an auction pumped up like a boxer from a fight, and proceed to describe procuring a piece in glorious detail. It was like listening to a hunter home from the hunt, so that no matter how much he'd paid—no matter how much the item was worth—he always got it at a remarkable steal. His idea of contentment was a quiet afternoon alone in his study sitting at his Chippendale desk with a really good book, surrounded by his gorgeous items.

As children we were relegated to the upstairs. Dad was fairly precious about the antiques and kept the living-room door closed, so my friends, when they came, didn't have a lot of access. But any child unfortunate enough to evince even a moment's interest usually got a two-hour lecture. Instead of a paper round in the morning, or taking out the garbage, my task every week was to take this old earthenware pitcher and fill each of the little pie tins underneath his favorite pieces of furniture with a modicum of water. I was the humidifier to make sure the wood didn't crack in the parched Texas air. My sister slept every night in a giant Jacobean bed with gargoyles carved along the posts— not the most hospitable environment for an eight-year-old girl. Initially she resented it, but I think she grew to love it. It wasn't until later, when my brother and I had left home and gone to university, that dad finally overflowed into our room.

Both my parents had a passion for art, so for the longest time I thought I was going to be a painter, but when I got older I gravitated toward the theater and thought for a while I might be a set designer, and then I found my path in writing. In the same way that my father plucked furniture from previous centuries, I guess I—in my writing—had a habit of plucking historical figures from times that preceded me. My first full-length play was about the artist Marcel Duchamp, and next I wrote a play that was later a movie called *Quills*, about the Marquis de Sade.

I was on a tour of Berlin in 1992 with a childhood friend, who was at the time a news reporter, when I first met Charlotte and became obsessed with her story. The wall had recently fallen, and there was a real thirst for stories of survivors from East Berlin. Suddenly a lot of interesting history was coming to light. So Charlotte Von Mahlsdorf had been written about in the local press, and she'd published an autobiography, which was on the bestseller list. So I can't claim to have discovered her. Anyway, we contacted her and she invited us to come out on a Tuesday night at 10.00 pm and view her collection of 19th-century German antiquities. She was a night owl. I was not remotely prepared for what I found. We met her on the porch of the house and she proceeded to give us a tour and explain the provenance of each piece. It wasn't unlike those home tours that my father used to give to the neighbors. It's strange to say that this elderly, pixyish 65-year-old East German transvestite reminded me of my father, but she emphatically did. They shared the same passion. At the same time, she seemed one step ahead of my dad, because not only could she tutor me in antiques, but she could tutor me in the very art of living an alternative life in an oppressive world. I remember that the first room we went into was filled with oversized music machines. At one stage in her life, she earned her living repairing antique music machines, so she had lovingly restored all the mechanisms.

The whole house had been returned to the state that it would have been in 1895, had it belonged to a bourgeois Berlin family. The books, the matchboxes, were all true to the period. It was as if Charlotte inhabited a kind of living diorama of the time. She had a particular fondness for Neo-Renaissance Gründerzeit and Neo-Gothic pieces. A lot of the furniture came from her Tante Luise, who had an estate farm in East Prussia, but she had been hoarding furniture since prior to the Second World War, when as a child of 10 or 11 she worked for a junk collector. With a wheelbarrow she would collect furniture from the houses of Jewish families who had been deported, or after Kristallnacht when furniture was shoved out of the windows and such. She said she wasn't looting, but rescuing objects that would otherwise be destroyed or burned for heat during the war.

The house itself she first saw when it was a grand manor house, then it became, for a while, an orphanage and then a school. Then after the war it was in very poor repair, so in the 1950s she set about procuring it. Approaching the government, she offered to restore it if they would let her live in it and have some kind of squatter's rights—and they said yes. It took her almost 33 years to make it habitable. It's hard to describe Charlotte. I think of her as a charming granny, but if you see photographs of her, she had a thick neck and big strong hands that *could* move furniture or restore a breakfront. I said upon leaving on that first night, I'd love to study your life and write a play about you. Can I come back? So for the next two years I scraped and saved enough money to fly back and forth to Berlin and spend more time with her. Charlotte at that point had got enough local attention. She had become used to receiving visitors who came with almost intimidating hunger, and she was an innate performer. She knew she'd found in me a devoted audience, and she was ready to perform.

I guess that what elevates a craftsman to an artist is his subject, and I don't know if I'll ever find a subject as compelling or as rich or as special for me as she was. My recourse was to work next on something demonstrably different and I think, having completed *I Am My Own Wife*, both of my next theatrical projects will be musicals—so in form, they are a radical departure. When we moved to the current apartment it was both daunting and thrilling. Looking for real estate in New York is both depressing and expensive. I also felt the need for guidance, so I retained an extraordinary designer called Miles Redd to help me. He is young and flamboyant and has a real sense of humor in his design. I never knew how passionately I cared about door fixtures and toilets until I knew that I was choosing them for all time. I bought design magazines, I went to showrooms, I became a little bit obsessed by it.

I recall one thing that Charlotte truly taught me about design. In 2002, after she went to live in Sweden, she returned to visit the museum that was once her home, and she had a heart attack and was rushed to hospital in East Berlin. According to a newspaper report, she was lying on a stretcher in the emergency room when she cast her eyes to the heavens, and her last words were, "Mien Gott, what a beautiful chandelier." So when I next went back to Berlin, I knew I had to go to that hospital to confirm my suspicion, that the lighting in the emergency room was, in fact, fluorescent.

I want to continue living my life with my partner, David, and sharing adventures that yield objects that find a home in ours. So that the apartment becomes a reflection of a shared history and a body of experience that represents who we are. Someone who passes through the apartment, even if I'm not home, can emerge with a sense that they've spent an afternoon in our company.

PREVIOUS PAGE

This beautiful old wooden desk was used by the U.S. post office on the American railway. The piece would fold up into a large mailbox with slots on the outside, and when they stopped at the local station, the postmaster would board the train, unlock it, and it became an entire portable post office. Afterward, he would close it again for the rest of the journey.

RIGHT

When I first bought this apartment my father very kindly shipped me a number of the pieces from his collection, so these rooms have an added resonance for me, because not only are they beautiful objects, but also they have rich childhood associations. I would hazard that it has a slightly more unified look because a lot of the pieces are oriental.

Every generation thinks that basically they are better at two things—one is acting and the other is parenting. They're quite happy to admit that society worked better 50 years ago, or government was better a hundred years ago, or whatever. They don't care about any of that, but they all think that actors are better actors, and that they themselves are better parents. But of course every generation has its own flaws, and our flaw as a generation of parents is that we are too involved with our children. We don't give them any space. We want to be part of them all the time. People say, "She's not my daughter, she's my best friend," and all that crap. I think that a degree of space around a child is both healthy and necessary. I was born in Cairo, my father was in the embassy there (with Burgess and Maclean in fact) but they came back when I was one, so the first home that I remember was in Wetherby Place in London's South Kensington. I remember the house very well and I still have bits of furniture, pictures, and things that I inherited. There was something about that house. It was a tall London house in the way that they are, the old kitchen in the basement had been converted into a separate flat. On the ground floor there was the drawing room at the front, and then you went up and there was the house's one bathroom, and a separate john on the mezzanine. You can't imagine that now, of course. Then up again and there was a spare bedroom and my parents' bedroom at the front, and up another staircase and there were two night nurseries—one for my eldest brothers Nicholas and David, and then I shared the other one with my brother Rory. Then there was a day nursery and another room, which was called the train room for a long time. That eventually became my bedroom for about the last year we were there. So it was a kind of separate place. If you were sent to bed, which was the great punishment then, it was missing out. Of course, now I can't imagine anything I'd love *more* than being sent to bed, but then you really were totally isolated.

We used to have this game in the nursery called "the death of Sydney." In those days our groceries were delivered from Oakeshotts in Gloucester Road, and they would come on a bicycle —the orders would be placed in a sort of box on the front. Of course in those pre-credit-card days, you just rang up and ordered, and the bill was sent at the end of the month. They were always brought by this very old man called Sydney, with whom we were all quite friendly, but one day a strange boy brought the groceries. This happened a few times, so we begged our mother to ring and find out what had happened to Sydney. Anyway, she did and was very shocked, and told my eldest brother the story, who of course immediately told the rest of us. Apparently, Sydney had run himself a bath, but had forgotten to run any cold. So when he put his foot into it, the scalding water made him start,

and as he did, he slipped into the boiling water and *died*. So of course, the image of this absolutely seared into our childhood imaginations and we evolved this game called "the death of Sydney," in which the sofa in the day nursery became the bath and we all took turns to play Sydney, the landlady who found him, the health authorities who came to the death scene; I can't tell you how complicated it was. The best role obviously was Sydney, because you got to jump around in the boiling water. My parents didn't know anything about our nursery life—it was all going on two floors above their heads and we had a sense of being ourselves, separate from them. I suppose we were privileged as opposed to unprivileged, but we were not particularly rich or anything.

They lived in that house for 20 years, and in 1959 they bought a house in Sussex, keeping the basement apartment as a London base and letting the rest. I remember the very first day we went to the new house. I couldn't believe it, we went in and all our furniture was already there. It seemed to me a kind of magic. My mother had done it all with the removal people and although they couldn't move in until completion day, the woman who lived there had allowed her to put all our furniture in beforehand, which was rather nice of her. My father grew up in the tradition that you move in and if that's where things were, that's where they stay. My mother wasn't like that. She said, "No, we'll knock this wall down" and so on. So we grew up in the tradition that your home, as you buy it, is only the canvas, and it's then up to you to turn it into the picture you want.

That house became my home for my growing-up years because we moved there when I was nine, and then when my mother died in 1980 or '81, I bought it from my father and stayed on there until 1988. When I finally sold it my father was very generous. He said, "Just because something is wrong for you now, doesn't mean it was wrong for you then." That first summer was wonderful, one of those kind of Edwardian summers that we get here occasionally. The house was much larger than the one in London, and we became part of a county gang that exists in the country. I attempted writing and we put on plays in the attic. We were always encouraged to paint, and to cook too. The people we knew in London lived—on the whole—in rather similar houses, but there was more variety in the country, and we would go and stay with friends or relations who had huge, falling-down country houses, and that was very exciting and thrilling. But in those days —the 1950s and early '60s —there was an element of defeatism going on, a sense that it was all over, that the money had run out. You would be taken around and they'd say, "This is where the groom used to live, and this is where the nurseries were." There was a time in the late '50s when you could buy these *huge* places for tuppence, because everyone thought, it's over, the servants have gone, this way of life is dead, nobody wants these places. Did you want your whole life to be enslaved by a house? Those were the terrible demolition years. Then in 1974 there was an exhibition at the V&A called "The Destruction of the Country House," and suddenly the country woke up to the terrible destruction of a huge part of their heritage that had been going on, really, since the First World War. After that, things changed. People started to think that there was a new kind of life that could be lived in them, converting the stables to offices, or pulling down this wing but keeping the main block, or whatever.

There had been this whole thing about it being well bred to put up with discomfort, which is odd when you think that their parents' generation, the Edwardians, had been the most luxurious ever seen on earth. When I was young, the two rooms that had to still be uncomfortable were the kitchen and the bathroom. It was terribly common to have carpet in the bathroom. I remember my mother arriving in Sussex and saying out loud, "I don't care if it's common—I'm sick of lino." The kitchen always had to be decorated as if the servants were just on a day off, when of course they were gone. The whole business of admitting that you live in the kitchen, having a proper table in there with proper places to sit and all the rest of it—that was much later. Toward the end of my school years I was taken up by a couple called Sir Ralph and Lady (Pommy) Lawson, friends of my parents, who had a home called Brough Hall in Yorkshire, not far from my school. I would go to see them pretty often and they were incredibly kind to me. It was a very beautiful, very interesting house that had been added onto in different periods. For the first time in my life, I became aware of the beauty of a house and its history. I asked them millions of questions; it became a house I loved and it became my bridge to an understanding of houses. From then on houses became a great interest of mine. There were a lot of houses that I already knew, but when I was younger it was just a free lunch. I have a predilection for soap opera, so the stories of the families are pretty important to me, even to this day. It's the same for my wife, Emma, it's one of our joint interests; we love houses, and now we *have* an interesting house, which of course is the greatest treat of all.

We met soon after I moved back to London and began doing up the house I had in Chelsea, so she was thrilled that she could have an input from the very early stages. It was quite a traditional house but I had a little bit of money at this point, so I was able to shape the rooms, and for the first time in my life I had a little library, which was exactly the way I wanted it. I loved that room. At the time, I was starting to get much more work as an actor. It was a very optimistic time in my life and that house was

a very happy home for me. Gradually our life became bigger than the house, the work took up more space, and also we'd both grown up in the country and we wanted our son to have that same experience, because rather like learning French or riding a horse, if you haven't done it as a child you don't ever quite get it. By then I had written this film *Gosford Park* and won an Oscar and everything kind of changed for me, and I realized that this was our opportunity. If we were ever going to do this adventure —I was already 52—then this was the time. We both had a desire to buy a "project" house, one that needed to be brought back to life, to be revived. A real house. We both felt we wanted to do it and die there, and hopefully have our grandchildren living there, but even if that didn't happen, we were never going to do it more than once. Emma found this house first, and out of our list of ten imaginary things we wanted, it had nine of them. As soon as I saw it, I knew I wanted it. It is an Elizabethan manor house that had been refaced Carolean in 1633, and in the 1840s its access had been changed and a new Victorian arrangement had been built in the same style but on the other side, and so the dining room and the staircase hall and the library were all added. I've always wanted a big dining room because one of the rooms that got small and more or less disappeared was the dining room. We can have a log fire and it doesn't bake us all to death. Having lived here now for three years, we've changed our minds about several things we were going to do, because we now understand the rhythm of the rooms much better, and when we've entertained, which we've done a lot, we've seen how people move from room to room; the role that a room needs to have and so on. Also, you need rooms that work for different seasons and that kind of thing. It wouldn't work for me to move into a house that was already done, because I think it has to grow out of the people who live there. At the same time, it won't spoil it for me when it's finished, I can assure you.

OVERLEAF

Once when I was staying at the Lawsons' at Brough Hall, I took a wrong turning and found myself at the top of a staircase, and I could hear this row going on—it was coming from the kitchens —and I suddenly had this incredible sense that there wasn't one group of people in that house, there were two, and each group was equally valid and equally alive with equally complicated lives going on. When it came to filming *Gosford Park*, I basically knew how the system worked, but for the detail we found three elderly servants in their 80s, who had all been in service in that year, 1932. They were on set when we shot all of the scenes of the servants' duties. It creates a patina of authenticity, and you get a sense that this was a life.

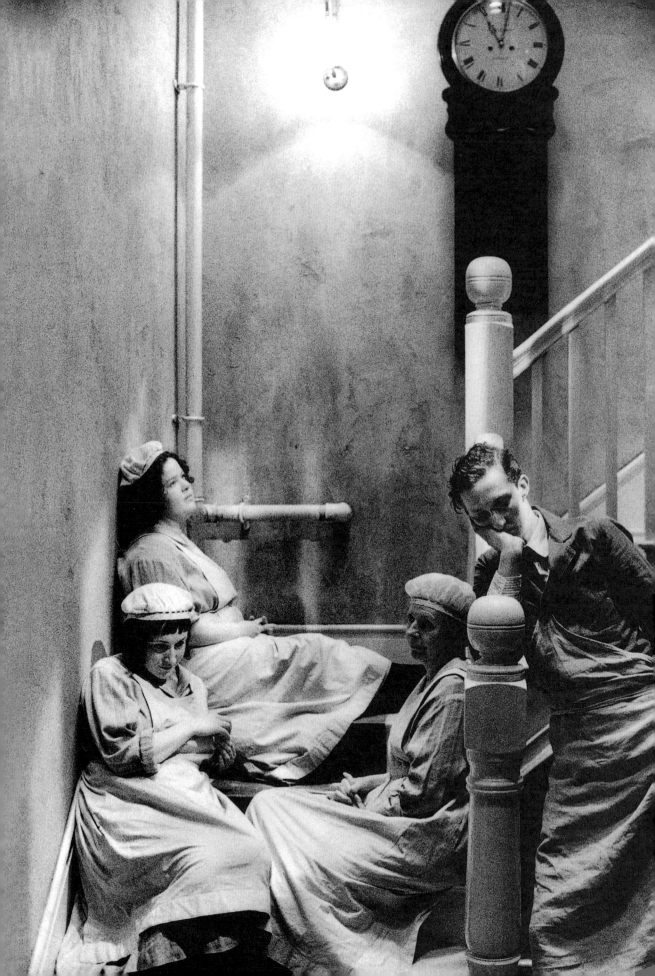

I remember the first night that we moved into Alnwick Castle so well, sitting in the dining room with my husband eating dinner. It was a chop that was really tough and it stuck in my throat. I remember thinking, God, I don't think I can bear this. Nobody had rung us up to ask what we'd like for dinner. I'd always done my own cooking for 16 years and suddenly there we were, butlers coming out of our ears. I thought, I can't complain, it's my first night; I mustn't let my husband down. But I knew that if I'd been at home, in our beautiful Georgian farmhouse only about half an hour away, I would be eating a plate of garlic prawns in front of the fire. My husband saw what was happening and he said, "Look, don't worry; it isn't going to be like this forever. I promise you we can change things." My husband had been looking after the estate for his elder brother when he wasn't well enough to do it. But when he died, Ralph said, "I think we should go to Alnwick for the winter, see what's what, how it's running, see what the staff are like. We can then make a decision about how and where we want to live."

The castle had been run as a museum. There was linoleum on all the floors and it was gray and it was depressing. We lived on the top floor, which was the nursery corridor. Six of us were sharing a tiny, tiny bathroom. The children were distraught at leaving their lovely house just down the road. At first I didn't know where to start and I didn't have a huge amount of confidence at that stage, so we went very slowly and we really started again from scratch. Soon I realized that my husband meant what he said; that we really could change things and that he was prepared to do so.

It's taken ten years. One of the first things I did was to make a room where we could live as a family, because I like to know that the four children are all around and I wanted them to know that they could find us in the same way that they could in the last house. So I made this enormous kitchen, which is directly below the enormous library—one of the most beautiful rooms in England. But underneath is the opposite, it's this modern kitchen which is all open, with a huge billiard table at one end and a sitting room at the other, and an Aga cooker. It used to be the servants' quarters—a lot of little rooms. When we opened up some places and removed doors and whatever, I could see the wonderful honey-colored stonework behind it all—huge great blocks. The castle dates from 1309; how can they have plastered that over? So I asked the builders to get rid of all the plaster, which they did. Then I got very, very modern lighting and lit the stonework—and it works. The whole

room is very, very contemporary. At that point I realized that you can actually do anything if you know what you like, what you feel is right. It also taught me that experts are not always right, and don't worry about what people think of you. That's been the greatest learning curve in the last ten years. I also realized that life wasn't going to be easy. In the other rooms of the castle I wasn't too concerned and I realized that there were a lot of things that I needed advice about what could be done, not about what was correct; I will always fight about what is correct. In the state rooms I've moved a little more carefully, but even there, just because something has been yellow for the past two hundred years doesn't necessarily mean it has to be yellow nowadays, as long as you're using the best people to do the job and you're not just trying to make a statement (flashy or gaudy). I don't feel any desperate need to duplicate; at the same time I've never done anything on a whim simply because I didn't like the color. If you do something at Alnwick, it's a year's work.

I'm a great homemaker and I love moving things around. Even as a young child growing up in a really wonderful big town house in Edinburgh, I was constantly changing my room around. My parents used to say that they never knew where to find me when they'd come and say goodnight, because they didn't know where the bed was going to be next. To me Edinburgh was a most beautiful city. There was always a lot going on and it was a buzzy house. I had two sisters and a brother (this was in the 1960s) and I remember my parents having very wild parties and I would come downstairs early next morning to find people lying all over the floor. That was the way it was and I loved it. Then when I was 12 or 13 we moved out full time to a place my father had on the Scottish Borders. To be honest I wasn't a country girl; I was a towny at heart and I missed Edinburgh, and I missed the house there. My grandfather had a beautiful big country house, but in the 1960s, he knocked it down, thinking that nobody would be able to live in that way again, with so many bedrooms. So my parents, for some reason, decided to move into the gardener's cottage and build onto it. This was a terrible time because there wasn't room for all of us, so they put us children into a cottage nearby, with two nannies. I remember hating it, and I hated the nannies too. I hated the lack of privacy; the place was so small that you couldn't get away from anybody. In fact, I was very impatient and very bored by country life. I think I was creative, though I didn't realize it. I didn't particularly like being a child; I was dying to be grown up and get on with life. Looking back I see that as a teenager, I should have had a job. I'd have been much happier and it would have given me a sense of purpose. I never thought of getting my own place, because I met my husband when I was 17 and Ralph and I got married when we were 20 and 21 and went to live with his parents in Surrey for a year. After that, we got our own place in Petworth. That was quite scary, moving into your own house at 22, but I loved it. It was a cottage—not at all pretty—in a dark, wooded area, but Ralph never liked it, and couldn't wait to get away. Normally I don't like dark places. After seven years, we moved to Northumberland and now that I'm getting older I realize what I like and what makes me happy. I love the sun—that's the only thing that could ever take me away from living in Britain. Sunshine, and having breakfast outside, is the ultimate luxury.

I'm very aware of people and how they feel and their attitudes. People say that what they love about Alnwick is that it feels like a family home. I always leave the children's things in the library—drawings, silly Christmas presents—so that it looks like we've just left the room, but we'll be back. My husband is not remotely interested in furnishings or clothes, or even himself; he's an outdoor man, interested in the countryside. So it was very clear from the beginning that Alnwick was my job. But after the castle was finished, he realized that I would need another project. So he suggested to the agent that I was offered the garden. At first I had no idea of what I could do, what the boundaries were. Now I realize that he and I set the boundaries, but at that time I was in everyone else's hands. I knew the garden and I could see that it had incredible bones but it was derelict. Once I started to clear it out I got this vision of what I wanted to do. I've never, ever felt that you should be recreating history for history's sake, I don't think like that. English Heritage said, "You are destroying one of the most important gardens in England." That's when the big battle began. What I wanted was to create something that was as good as, if not better than, anything that was built two hundred years ago, and I had one of the greatest teams in the world to do it. I suppose they didn't know then that I was as committed as I was. They just thought that I was arrogant. We've now built two-thirds of it and we're expecting up to six hundred thousand visitors next year. Everyone's been calling it the Duchess's garden but it was never my garden; it's a big public garden, we have 150 full-time staff at the moment and 17 managers who all have to follow my vision. For instance, I don't want children in school groups to come here and walk around looking at fact sheets. We've put the classroom up in the trees with a huge plasma screen. Why build an apothecary garden when there are a million of them around the world. No child wants to know how people are cured; they want to know how they're killed—hence the poison garden. Those plants don't kill without man's intervention, so we have two drug-education programs working and the children will go up into the tree house and learn all about it. This place was built unashamedly to be busy and noisy. I want to hear children screaming with laughter. I also want the garden to be just as busy in the winter. You do that with lighting; I'm doing an incredible lighting program. So in the winter, instead of turning the water off as they do in every garden around the world, we would actually light every single step of the cascade with electric blue lighting, so you see water and ice moving down the hill together. It's just looking at different ways of doing things. The people who still don't understand what I'm doing will have to come and see it when it is built.

We only live in the castle now in the winter. It has a very wintry feel to it. It's cosy, not cold or drafty; it's very warm and incredibly comfortable and it feels like a family home.

I love seeing people comfortable and happy. I would love to be a minimalist, but I can't be. My eldest son (he's 21 now) is like me, he would be contemporary if he could. He has the same love of light and air and open spaces as I do. Through Alnwick, I think I've shown him that if he chooses one day to live here, he can do things too; he's not stuck in a time warp

OVERLEAF

Apart from Windsor Castle, Alnwick, the setting for the first two Harry Potter films, is the largest inhabited castle in England. The designer, Robert Kime, helped me refresh some of the state rooms, adding some of the newly restored pieces of furniture we saved from auction, and designing some of the fabrics, etc. The library houses approximately 13,500 books, with the earliest published in 1475. The Ninth Earl of Northumberland (1564–1632) had assembled one of the finest personal Renaissance libraries in England. I love things that take your breath away; an experience where you stop and you think—Wow!

FOLLOWING PAGES

Directly below the library in Prudhoe Tower, the enormous family room includes a billiard table, a modern kitchen with an Aga cooker and, at the other end, a cosy sitting room. The tables and chairs were made by a local craftsman. This room was the first thing I did at the castle, and the moment when I first trusted my instinct.

My earliest memory is of masses of honeysuckle on the walls of our house. We lived in something called The Gardens; my grandfather had this beautiful house and we lived in the park. I used to wake up every morning and know that we were never going to be there, so I was brought up with this incredible beauty that you knew you couldn't get your hands on. I've always wanted it; I still want it. I think that beauty is very sexy. It wasn't the size, it was the elegance. Once a year, as a child, we used to look out over these incredible gardens and look at the world we'd lost, and it was a red carpet with people going up all dressed for the hunt ball, and the house would be spotlit. It was the only house in England to have plates on it—to have Wedgwood zodiac signs. It made me, I suppose, obsessed with tarot cards and the zodiac, and with very strict beauty, which I still like in fashion. People think I like really funky stuff. I like classic with a twist. I like things that are cut beautifully and I think it comes from that house; it was really severe. It was called Doddington Park and it was designed by Samuel Wyatt, who was the younger brother of James Wyatt, who did a lot of houses. Plum Sykes recently got married in a Samuel Wyatt house, which was her cousin's, Sir Tatton Sykes. She was wearing a giant emerald bracelet that was perfect with the house and it looked great. You see, I think people have to plan their house so they look good in it. Wallis Simpson's clothes were amazing, she was my heroine; but not her house, it was too busy for the clothes.

I had two sisters. My brother died—he drowned in the swimming pool of that house, in the garden. Our house was so ugly: it was a pink house with horrible pink grout. My room was blue, and I've always had blue wherever I go. My apartment in New York was light blue. Neither of my parents had any interest in furnishings; they were socialites. They poured crème de menthe over each other every night. Then my grandfather had this murder trial—*White Mischief* thing—and everything was sold from the big house. My father didn't *want* any reminders of those things. But I have inherited two pieces that are going into my new place. One is a pope's table that my grandfather got on the Grand Tour, and it's got snakes and peonies, which are my favorite flowers, and the snake is winding its way around the

flowers, which I love. Hard and soft. I like very severe beautiful tables with very soft cushions. That's what makes something very erotic, like a penis going into a vagina—same thing. I was brought up in a house in Cadogan Square in London. That was amazing. It had these beasts on the floor—black beasts with hair flying and funny noses—and amazing doors. I'm obsessed by doors. (The Hermitage; for me it's the most beautiful building in the world because of the doors. The tsar had every single door made differently, and it gives it such an individual feel. Making an entrance. I never thought about that before.) We had these malachite tables that remind me of Russia, and this great round table in the drawing room, with a vase of flowers in the middle— that must have come from Doddington. My parents entertained *a lot*. You could extend the dining-room table by adding extra leaves, from four people to six to sixteen. My mother got a friend, Andrew Rolla, to do the interior. Do you remember when trompe l'œil was very popular? We had this absolutely hideous fake trompe l'œil hall that was orange and cream. I knew it was wrong because I'd seen my grandfather's house. I knew what you should have and what we *didn't* have, and maybe that's been my problem all my life.

When I was 16 I was chucked out. My father had met this woman and my parents got divorced. My mother moved from Cadogan Square to Lennox Gardens, where she had a gray suede hall, ugh! My mother went very suede. She had suede sofas. I hate that. After that, I literally lived like a vagabond. I just loved living in other people's houses. That's my thing. You can't afford what they've got, so why not enjoy it while it's going? As a fantasy. I was very influenced by someone I stayed with called Maria St. Just, who was the muse of Tennessee Williams and she played Maggie in *Cat on a Hot Tin Roof*. She got a group of Russians in to paint her house and they make little pelmets, like a theater set. It had pistachio green, like the inside of the nut, on the walls and the sofas were … I don't remember, but she had one little sofa opposite another little sofa. I love it when you can talk to people opposite. When you just have one lame duck it's hopeless.

I went to New York and bought a fantastic apartment. It was a classic—the second floor of a brownstone. It had a beautiful square drawing room, lovely light. I knocked through the two bedrooms and had a huge four-poster bed and big cupboards for my clothes. That was the first time I really had somewhere. I was 24 and my grandmother had died and she'd left me some money, so I spent it on that. I worked for Anna Wintour at American *Vogue*, so I wanted it to look good; I wanted some self-respect. I used to go out with Andy Warhol and Jean-Michel Basquiat. We used to really live it up. It was slightly "rock 'n' roll," the whole thing. The apartment was on the wild side, but very classic. I had a Mary Fox Linton black-and-white sofa. I cooked—I love cooking—and I had a very modern galley kitchen with a black rubber floor. Then I got married to somebody and then divorced two years later. I finished my job with *Vogue* and left New York.

For the past eight years I've been living in this little two-up two-down hatbox in Lambeth, London, but it's a horrible area; I can no longer live in terror. I can't walk under the bridge at night for fear of being murdered. Location is the most important thing. I've now decided to buy this flat in Eaton Square—classic, first floor, very good proportions. I was only looking for three weeks. I'm very impetuous. It's a bed-sitter basically, but I won't make it a bed-sitter because of proportions and scale. I'm not really a good home person; my husband is the same. I'm not very cosy by nature because I've never had a real home. I've lived in 29 houses. I've got a friend called Camilla Guinness who's going to do it up, otherwise it just won't get done. I just don't want to have fights with Detmar—my husband—over sofas and chairs. She can arbitrate. I think when your husband has a strong point of view, you have to show him photographs and drawings so he feels in control. We're going to do a portfolio, so I can say, do you like this sofa, this chair; do you like the chandelier hanging here? What he wants is organization. He doesn't want chaos. I've got a great chandelier that came from my father's house; it's been in storage for nearly three years. It's absolutely huge—really beautiful; Waterford 1760. People don't hang them properly—much too high. A chandelier is meant to act as a light on top of the food or something. It has to be down, so the eye goes, wow! It's something people have got to learn. I hate shopping. I like buying

art. I love auctions. The nerve-racking bit of it. You see it, you fall in love with it, and you feel like you're buying it for the correct price. I like to support artists; it's good for them and it's fun for me. You must support the culture you live in. Stability is very important. I've been so ill from not knowing where I belong. Since I was 15, I've never put my key in the door and thought I was at home, never. My mother never gave me a key. Having got Eaton Square I'm not going to be going anywhere else.

OVERLEAF
Looking directly onto the square, this room is used by Detmar as a gallery space for conceptual art, as well as our dining room. The table dates from 1670 and originated in the Cigi Palace in Rome, via Doddington Hall, whereas the chairs came from junk shops. The candlelit chandelier is by Samuel Wyatt and above the non-functioning fireplace, where Detmar plans to install a video fire, is an inlaid framed mirror from Turkey.
FOLLOWING PAGES
Some of my Philip Treacy hats, including one fragile creation with feathers shaped into dollar signs, are displayed around the room and the walls are all lined with a silver-gray glitter wallpaper that reflects the way I make up my eyes.

When I was going to the Slade School in London in the 1950s we didn't go to people's houses. My friends didn't have houses. We were all in lodgings. I lived in various lodgings, in Gower Street, in Portobello Road, behind Grosvenor Square, and in the Slade hostel near Euston for two years. You couldn't paint them or do them up, but I did have my own place in Edinburgh that I kept going back to. In the mews behind my parents' house there was a garage, and above it there was a place that I turned into a studio. I remember it being very exciting because it had a separate address, although it was just through the garden. I didn't sleep there. Nevertheless, I didn't like Edinburgh. I really didn't know anybody there, and I connected London with glamour and having a good time. As children my brother and I were taken to London quite a bit. I remember the pigeons in Trafalgar Square.

In 1948, when I was 22, I decided that I wanted to be a barrister, so I came to London to join the Middle Temple and do the bar exams. But I was always failing the exams because, while the other students were studying about conveyancing and contracts and divorce, I was sitting in the courts. I thought that was more exciting. I suddenly realized that law was not for me, so instead of passing the exams, I started going to the Tate gallery to copy pictures. Painting was something I thought I could never do, but I had private lessons with a tutor in Chelsea and he said that I should go to art school. My mom was really pleased because she always said that law is sordid. She knew that I would never be as good as my father.

I grew up in a four-story house in Edinburgh. My brother and I were kept on the top floor, completely separate from our parents. We had a nanny and we had all our meals up there. We saw my mother all the time, she was always coming up, but … I mean … we could have gone downstairs, but somehow we didn't. We would be taken out by the nanny and sometimes when we passed his library, my father would want to see us so we would be taken in, but normally we weren't to disturb him. He was a barrister, and later became a member of parliament. In a funny way, I didn't really know him. I was nine or ten when I went off to boarding school. I didn't like it. It was horrid. I ran away twice.

My ideas about painting were completely changed by a scholarship I got from the Italian government to travel around Italy. A friend of mine, Myles Murphy, and I were there off and on for about a year, and then I kept going back after the scholarship ended. What impressed me most were the colors. Before that I thought, rather stupidly, that colors were best if they were bright. I was amazed when I got to Italy, to find that dark colors could be equally glamorous and I was surprised that I didn't *know* that. I remember an automobile journey between Siena and Rome, noticing the dark soil and the white pigeons on it. People say that it must have been because of the light, but I've never been hung up on light. People ask, "Do you have a light studio?" I don't know what they're talking about. Most of the colors I use are straight out of the tube and I could paint them in any light. I don't know what north light is.

I think it's all rubbish. So, I started to use raw umber, and I've used that color ever since.

After Italy, I went back to live in Scotland. I couldn't afford to live in London. I was lucky. Eventually, I started looking for places back in South London. I remember going around with a friend on a bike trying to find a property. When we found this place, it was divided into bed-sitters. There was a gas cooker and a sink in every room, an outside john and one inside, but no bathroom. It was in a very bad state and we only got it on condition that we did it up. It was a seven pounds a week rent for four floors—the whole house. That was in 1962 and I'm still here 40 years later. I didn't want it modernized. We got a grant to put in the bathroom and we got builders; it was quite easy to do. I'd been used to decorating. My mother was always altering and having things repainted at home. But they never changed the furniture; in fact I have some of it here, that cabinet and that bookcase and some of these chairs.

There's no connection between me as a painter and me as a decorator. I could be a banker. I just feel quite ignorant really. If you look at that screen and that chair and the wall, well, they just got like that. There are actually three different pinks, but it's not calculated. That would be impossible. I just thought, that suits. But if I put that blue chair here it wouldn't suit, but I couldn't possibly work that out. I just deal with what happens and what I've got. I don't really like all-white rooms and I don't really ever admire other people's houses. Sometimes I think, I don't know how they can live like that. Maybe they think that when they come here. Take London; I just happened to live near Waterloo when I found this place, so anywhere south of the Thames I feel is sort of OK. I just can't understand north of the river—I'd rather go and live in another *town*.

I wouldn't mind moving, but I'd really rather live in my place near Siena. I found it 25 years ago. It was a ruin and cost 10 thousand pounds including a chapel and six acres of land. It's a beautiful place to wake up in and to paint in, but I wouldn't feel quite as secure there as I do here. You don't know who's going to turn up.

In London, my place is cluttered with a lot of things that I've bought to paint. Still lifes. I've sort of always collected things. A lot of the stuff is completely rubbish. There are some valuable things but there are some that were tuppence. They're not treasures, but once I get something I don't want it to go away again. This room—all this junk—I just see it as security. If I get in a muddle in my head, I think, I can go back here and nobody can touch this stuff. It may all be rubbish, but here I can shut the door and lock it and nobody can get in. I turn the phone off and, you know, it's a great thing in life just to feel secure, isn't it?

RIGHT

This room has been painted these colors for about 12 years. I'd really like to put it back to wallpaper like it was before, but I'm getting used to it like this now, and it suits the furniture.

My first apartment after I came down from Cambridge in 1956 was a dampish but rather nice basement apartment just around the corner from here in Regent's Park Road in North London. I was a just-married medical student, and later I became a doctor. We didn't have enough money to buy pictures, but we had what was then called a radio-gramophone and we listened to records, and we had a big double bed in the back room. Then, in 1961, I made a little money out of *Beyond the Fringe* and I bought this house, and I've been here ever since. It was all rather bare to begin with, but without being aware of it we just bought things very slowly and cheaply. We did buy furniture, but at first it was all secondhand. I don't think we ever bought anything new. We never decorated anything; for a long time we didn't even paint the walls. Then we painted them white and they've been the same color for 30 years. I mean, it's acquired a sense of decor now; people coming here are rather startled by the way it looks. I don't know what they expect, but I suppose it isn't in any sense a designed house. It's very unlike what most people have in their layout. Eventually we had to buy some couches and some old carpets, but most of the purchasing has been to do with pictures or things. We did have a vacation house in Scotland, which I bought for seven hundred pounds —again that was 40 years ago. My children had all their vacations there, but then they grew up and went to America instead. Now they wish they had it back.

My mother was not domestic at all, she was a writer you see, and she could scarcely cook. From her descriptions in her novels, you can detect that she had a very, very acute visual sense, so she saw things but didn't have any interest in creating decor; absolutely none, she wasn't interested in wallpaper.

My father was a military psychiatrist during the Second World War, but he also painted and sculpted and sometimes he would draw his patients. During the war we moved out of London, and we had one house after another as he moved to different military hospitals, but I have no feeling of discomfort or rootlessness. All I knew then was that every now and then lots of things were loaded onto a trailer behind the car and we'd go somewhere else, with the six Rhode Island Red chickens that we had to give us a supply of eggs all clucking at the back. Home was simply somewhere that my sister and I went back to after school.

I was a very outdoor child; the things that I remember are watching the Flying Fortresses coming back from their bombing raids over Germany. In 1945, we came back to this rather musty home in Queens Grove, which had been requisitioned by Polish officers while we were away. It felt cold and damp, but we gradually warmed it up and refurnished it; that was our home. I can remember every detail of that house. My father was a great one for buying beautiful furniture fairly cheaply. I can't remember a dinner party at our house, ever. I don't think we had any social life; it may have been a thing of the time.

I don't think that I became visually aware until I began taking photographs in the 1960s. I also began collecting enormous amounts of what people would call junk in those days. I collected group photographs, and through the paintings of Morandi I got very interested in old bottles. Half the crockery in the kitchen here was all bought from a junk shop nearby. We still use it when we have people to dinner, which we do almost as rarely as my parents did. Now the house is absolutely crammed with objects. I'm very interested in what I call declassification; you pick something up and put it together with other things, and suddenly they become much more than the sum of their separate parts—they have some unity; there's a rapport between them. If I happen to find a painting that I like, and I can afford it, I'll buy it. If I see an extraordinary bottle, I'll buy a bottle. If I see a shoe last, I'll think, hang on—that's a very beautiful sculptural object. I don't make a distinction between works of art and works of beauty. If you saw a shoe last in a cobbler's shop, you wouldn't look at it twice, but when you see it isolated from its function, it starts to say, have a look at me, you may find me interesting, not withstanding the fact that I'm useless. I'm a passionate devotee of the negligible. The things that are either on the one hand incipient—in other words they're about to become something—or things that have dropped off the edge of being useful and no-one knows what they're for. I don't really like this notion of "the arts"; I think it's pretentious and stuck up, and actually almost invariably shows that people don't open their eyes. We are surrounded by a complicated world of things that have been made for all sorts of purposes, and if you put them into a different environment they suddenly start to attack you and draw your attention. It's scarcely a consequence of a skill; it's all the result of breaking down frames and categories that define what is proper to have in a sitting room and what is proper to have as a work of art. I've never thought about what is proper or improper. I'm talking about an absolutely ontological idea: that there is no such thing as the arts. It's a denomination created by rich people for rich people, who are absolutely incapable of opening their eyes to things that are not art.

If you have your eyes open, you are startled again and again and again by the commonplace. I actually think that the function of a great deal of art should be to redirect your attention to things you would otherwise overlook. It's the overlooked, the negligible, the disregarded, the abandoned, and the derelict that is actually where the payload is.

My approach is partly to do with the fact of not knowing anything about art when I started. I've been very fortunate, exactly the same thing happened to me in the theater—I drifted into it by accident. I didn't think about "the arts" then; now here I am absolutely embroiled in it, and very, very aware of it in the decor I get my designers to create for my productions. I know exactly what period and how I want it to look and how I want it to be lit, because I do look at paintings now, in very great detail. I know how people stand; I know that I have to get my actors to stand in a way that is consistent with 18th- or 17th-century stances. If you look at pictures, you see exactly the way people held their hands on their chest, or how they gestured. That has become, in the last 30 years, one of my principle pre-occupations with directing.

My source of inspiration is that I collect reproduction postcards from almost all of the art galleries that I've been in, so I have an instant reference for how I want something to look. For me it gives authenticity to a scene, not identifiability. I don't go to the theater at all; I haven't been for ten years. When people ask, "How do you do your research?," I say I've been doing it for 50 years; I've kept my eyes open, I have a vast library in my head, where I can pull files out and say, aaahh, yes....

OVERLEAF
Home is where you go back to. It's where everything is familiar. It's all to do with an accumulation of things that you have put together year after year. This drawing room on the second floor of our house in Camden Town is just such an accumulation of artworks and artifacts. Among the things on the mantelpiece is a large Hispano-Moresque plate, a Balinese shadow puppet, some medical models of the brain, and a cow bone. The object on the right was a prop in my television production of *Othello*. It's a sundial that I had copied from one on the table in the Holbein painting *The Ambassadors*. The two framed drawings of hands are 16th century and the little portrait is, of course, Rembrandt. On the small round table to the right are three plaster casts of my face and those of my two sons when they were boys.
FOLLOWING PAGES
Arranged on this old sideboard in the music room is a group of my favorite objects, including (far right) a Nigerian ritual mask, a 15th-century Florentine bust of a girl, which my father bought, several wooden hat stretchers, a shoe last, some wooden letters, and, on the left, a self portrait by Stephen Conroy. On the wall are two framed pieces of Kuba cloth, and, above them, a plaster-cast reproduction of an Ashurbanipal hunting scene, which I stained to make it look more mellow.

Originally, there wasn't any relationship between my work and my home but now there is. I live in an 18th-century early Georgian house in London's Spitalfields, and my work didn't fit into the style of my home. I realized I'd been dealing with some kind of schizophrenia for the last ten years. What's happened now—somehow—I've got more depth and integrity in my work; any of the work in my latest exhibition could go into my house. It's the same spirit. Something's come together. I've worked really hard at it. I'm trying to get my life better, and my home is one of the things that has really helped. I've always stitched—I've always made domestic work, nesty, homely—that's what I do. It's an organic process. If you look at my work, there's a hell of a lot of craft involved—not good craft—I'm not saying I'm good at it. Textiles is my thing. In my bathroom downstairs above the mirror I've got an appliquéd elephant that I made when I was six. That's the only piece of my work that I've got hanging up. My grandma encouraged me, and at school we had scripture, during which we had to sew. At playtime, we had to sew things that we liked, hence the elephant.

My earliest memories of my childhood are all sad. Every one of them. We lived in east London. The house was sad and my mom was sad; she was always waiting for my dad to arrive. It was nicely furnished, quite oriental-style, quite Turkish—influenced by my dad who was Turkish—so all these things came from Turkey. My twin brother and I were about three when we moved to a hotel in Margate. That was *really* strange, because it was a giant 80-bedroom hotel with lots of extended family in our life —lots of staff—and lots of strange people looking after us because my mom and dad were so busy all the time working. My mom ran the hotel. It was an adventure, but an adventure that I didn't like, and now I have quite vivid dreams about that hotel. I was always running around prying through the keyholes at people. I liked looking at the sea. In fact, I've just gone and bought a place by the sea. I like it, but it can be very sad and emotionally traumatic. It can conjure up strong emotions because of the nature of the sea, but I enjoy that. I'd rather have nature bring out my emotions than I bring the emotions out of myself. I could never live in a forest, the trees would frighten me. I like the sky and I like sunset and I like horizons. I like to be able to see the end of the world, if that makes sense.

When I was tiny we used to go by car to Turkey, where we stayed by the sea, near Istanbul, for two or three months of the year. My dad left us when I was seven. He didn't leave us, actually; he went bankrupt and the hotel got boarded up

and we were homeless and had to squat in the cottage which had been for the staff, but then became our cottage. We lived there for six and a half years, I think. There was no cocooning, no protection going on. That's why I am fiercely independent now. That cottage is where I discovered ghosts, and the next house we lived in, that was definitely haunted, horribly haunted, scarily haunted. It's what you sensed—you'd walk in and it would feel as though someone had gassed themselves in there. Very unhappy and very malevolent.

I came to London when I was 15, with a holdall and some David Bowie records. I'd outgrown Margate and knew there was a bigger world out there that I had to go and investigate. I was trying to create my own thing, which is very difficult when you're 15. Two years later, I went back to Margate. We didn't have a house by then, we were completely homeless, so I had to live in a DHSS (Department of Health and Social Security) bed-and-breakfast, and that was miserable. I was there for six months. If anyone has ever been homeless … it's a horrible feeling. That's why I now have a cottage in my garden so that any friends who are hard up and need somewhere to stay, can come and stay. You never forget being homeless. Having a bowl to wash in because I didn't want to go to the bathroom, and all my things in boxes around me. I didn't have much. It was very difficult to get my own apartment, with no money and 17, but then I noticed that the windows above the Kentucky Fried Chicken shop had no drapes so my mum went to see the real estate agent. She didn't want to tell them she had two children, obviously no one was going to give an apartment to a woman with two teenage kids whatever. It was a one-bedroom apartment, and when she went to sign the papers, they said, "We're really sorry, but we've actually already given this apartment away." We were so upset, but then they said, "There's another one upstairs but it might be too large for you." It had three bed-rooms, so we moved in to this apartment and we were so happy, it was brilliant. It was home, above the Kentucky Fried Chicken shop. Brilliant. Then a couple of years later, I left and got my own apartment. I went away to Turkey and when I came back, the landlord had boarded up the windows. It took me a week to get all my stuff out. That was pretty horrific.

Then eventually the council gave me a really brilliant apartment in Cooper Close in Southeast London. Now this was my first real home and I loved it. All my neighbors became my friends. It was a time in my life when I was quite lonely, and they became my family, my sanctuary. It was a tiny little apartment, all brightly colored: one room red; one room orange. Over Christmas, I painted it all white with the cheapest white paint I could find. I got my big studio in 1989, ten years later, but I kept the apartment on for a year because I thought, if it doesn't work out I need to have the security of knowing I have a roof over my head. By the time I left I was the only person who hadn't bought their apartment, and they all said just buy it, because I had the money, but I said no, I want someone else to have the same chance with this place as I had—in terms of stability and confidence. So I handed the keys back. Later, when I got an accountant, I realized that I had enough money to buy a house, which I had for a while, and then I bought my current home in Spitalfields, and that I will never, ever relinquish. It will be my home for the rest of my life. It's early Georgian, built in 1729, a five-floor townhouse with north- and south-facing light that goes all the way through. It's got a weaver's loft on top, which is my bedroom. It's got a really beautiful, almost Tuscan-looking walled garden and then the cottage. Before I bought it, I went there about five times at different times of the day and night to sense the atmosphere. It's got ghosts, but they're really nice ones, and I saw them on the second night I was there, going down the stairs: three men laughing, all laughing. This is the first house in my life where I haven't been afraid by what's inside the house.

I travel around the world a lot. I hate trendy hotels, I like old-fashioned comfort. Sometimes when I've stayed in hotels, I've taken the pictures down and hidden them because they were really horrible. In the late 1990s when I traveled a lot on my own to shows, I'd go back to the hotel and draw and then put the drawings up on the walls. I'd even move the furniture to make room, or play around with the drapes to make them more personalized. I've also moved the bed a few times. But now I can stay in hotel rooms that are large enough for me not to have to move anything. I'm always interested to see how people live, and if it matches their persona. When people come to my house it's always a shock. First of all, it's immaculately clean and tidy. I have a housekeeper who works five days a week. Dust just appears every day. I live in an antique, it has to be looked after constantly. There isn't one straight stair or one straight door or anything; it's all crooked, absolutely lethal. Another thing, my furniture is all antique as well. My kitchen is Arts and Crafts; above that, the next floor, I call my Freud museum. I've got a 17th-century Wake table, an early Victorian child's coffin cradle, a Georgian settle, not what

people expect. Then upstairs, the Victorians had come in and said, "Let's modernize it"—so they stripped out all the paneling and put in a big Victorian fireplace, so it looks different from the rest of the house. I've got a 19th-century French/Italian three-piece suite that's in an oriental style. It's really quite Victorian, that room. I love modern design, but not at my home, thanks.

I also plan to have a place down by the sea that is just like a luxurious hotel suite: widescreen TV, fantastic stereo system, giant comfortable sofa, very simple bed. Everything can be replaced very easily. I'll be a different person there; I'll be really quiet and have a different mental attitude. I can just imagine me in the winter, sitting with the TV remote-control watching BBC World.

I made my own drapes in the London house, not like my art, but just like *drapes*. A little bit madder than the normal stuff. I'm frightened of the dark—that's why I've put the kitchen in the basement instead of on the first floor. If I didn't, I'd never go down into the basement. So this way, I've extended the house, and made the kitchen the cozy hub of the house. The main thing is that I feel that my house looks after me. It keeps me safe.

PREVIOUS PAGE AND RIGHT
On the third floor, I've devoted one room for use as my dressing room. All my clothes are hung on an open rail along one wall, and opposite the windows I have a series of chests of drawers. From the windows there is a wonderful view onto a Hawksmoor church, and in front of the restored fireplace is a child's tiny wooden bed in which sleep two Egyptian dolls. Around the room, I have other Egyptian-style artifacts, including a bust of Nefertiti.

Activity is what gives atmosphere. I can't bear the idea of a place being so organized that it's like a prison, but in order to be reasonably spontaneous, you need a degree of order, and that order has got to be preplanned and underpinned. That's the beauty and the danger of building your own house: you have to be realistic about who you are, especially if you are sharing with someone else, you need to prioritize, and sometimes concede, but that in itself is quite an interesting process. You need to build something that would make you a tolerable being to live with, cupboards to hide your mess, etc. Books are my life. I live in a world of ideas—buying books and looking at books is vital; I go crazy if I can't find them so I need to have them where I can locate them. I can't bear crawling around the floor looking for a book I desperately want to refer to.

My home for the past three years is an apartment in London that feels as though it's been cut to fit. Just two rooms: a bathroom and a library in which there is a kitchen and a bed. I like living on one level. Open-plan is great in many ways because obviously it makes the best use of a limited space. At the same time, we do need intimacy, so I suspect we're all trying to find ways of creating a new segregation within open-plan, to provide areas of privacy without actually being in lots of different rooms. It's a primal need to have something behind you. We are not comfortable sitting in an open space; we want the visual beauty but we also want cosiness.

In my apartment, I designed the sofa so that it has high sides. It's quite hard to find something that has a high back. Modern seating is all very low and looks beautiful, but we are much happier with a high back; it's like a little room within a room, like old-fashioned country house sofas and wing chairs. We feel safe. When I write about a safe, happy home, this is what I mean, not locks and bars on the windows. There are a number of things that make us feel more protected. Very bright light doesn't make people feel secure or relaxed, and temperature is another important element. Feeling cold makes you feel slightly threatened and we all know how comfortable a roaring log fire makes us feel. These are deep psychological "buttons" that we must acknowledge if we are to be as free as we wish to be.

We are living in the era of the polycentric home where everything is moveable. You can work in bed, cook in the dining room, and eat in the living room. This changes the rules of the game entirely. We have to start rebuilding the rituals of home again, because the whole idea of having a living area, a sleeping area, really doesn't apply any more. But if it all goes, you need to create tiny focused areas: the male den, the female boudoir, the library, the games room. Even though the functions have changed, we are desperate again to have rooms that have ritual. My favorite is the bathroom; it's my most creative space. When the temptation is so great to multitask, the bathtub is the one place where you are forced to focus on just one thing. It's so physical. You can actually hear your heart beat. People break into two groups: showerers and bathers. Showerers like lots of stimulation; bathers are more internal. That's my theory anyway. Deep down we are all one or the other.

I grew up in an atmosphere of inspiration and freedom. The first house was tiny. My father was the economics editor at the *Sunday Times* but my mother had been to Chelsea Art School and was an early hippy. She was very arty, so gave us terrific freedom, whether it was the first tiny house in Notting Hill where we splashed paint about and made our own wallpaper, or the second, in Kent, which looked romantic but was huge and derelict. There was no furniture, but we were allowed to transform our spaces and do whatever we wanted. Presumably this saved quite a lot of money, but my brother and four sisters thought it absolutely grand, whether it was creating a garden and a waterfall from imagination or, in my case, the ultimate "Biba" bedroom in a very dark shade of purple. We had no limitations other than money, but as far as imagination is concerned, money isn't really something you are aware of at that age. My mother just left us to get on with it. Growing up with someone like that was an adventure. She could be quite eccentric, creative, and impulsive too. *The Thief of Baghdad* might be showing at the cinema, and she would suddenly decide we must go and see it. The fact that it was on in Manchester and we lived in Kensington 180 miles away, and the five of us would have to hitchhike there and back, was not a limitation. Even when we once had to sleep the night in a ditch. She simply said "Let's go!" Life was an adventure. It meant that I never had the feeling that there were boundaries. No limitations. No barriers.

I've lived in other houses and in other countries. I once lived in a very beautiful apartment with 18th-century paneling throughout. It's a question of appropriateness isn't it? It was the perfect place to be transient in, but it didn't feel like home. I wouldn't like to live in the past, in a museum-piece or a historical recreation. I love the houses in Spitalfields, East London, but I am more interested in how you recreate those values today.

I don't plan to move again, but if I did it would probably be to a hot country rather than a different style of house. My partner comes from Columbia, so maybe we'd move there. All you need is a pair of shorts and a tin shed. Of course, it would be an architect-designed tin shed. Something small and cut to fit. Your "footprint" can be much smaller if it fits your life pattern. People often have far more space than they need and they don't think enough about how to use space. I don't judge people by their homes. Some people don't care about their environment. It's just not a thing that's important to them. Other things are. It's not to do with good taste or bad taste, it simply doesn't exist.

If people have any kind of love of the visual world, it shows, even if they're 18 years old and simply paint one wall a bright color. I like it when I see people who are engaged by things around them. I love color, but it doesn't need to be there as a permanent fixture, it can be a more mobile thing, things that come and go. The same is true with seasonal changes. In winter my space evolves and I gather warmer things around me. The light outside is different. My own apartment is pretty archetypal. A big table, a big sofa, big bed, and a bath, that's it. So I can change it without changing much. Having said that, I find it much harder to make decisions in my own space than for my interiors projects, but that's partly because I'm aware of too much but also I never get a chance to redo it all in one go, as I would a client's space. At the moment I'm more interested in the insides of things, cupboards for instance; I'm constantly trying to find ways to resolve the "now you see it, now you don't" division so that you know it's there, but not there.

At the same time, I've never been a great collector (apart from books). Once you've moved countries a few times as I have, it's just too much trouble. I always lose a box here or there; in a sense that is quite liberating. Also, in my family I ended up being the one to melt down all of my family home. Dad died and all his stuff ended up on my doorstep. It sounds brutal, but without people things have very little meaning for me. Obviously there can be one or two exceptions—photographs, and if there's the most exquisite object. I don't need too much. In the scheme of things, it doesn't really matter.

OVERLEAF

My London apartment is a bit like sleeping and cooking in a library. It was built to accommodate my ever-growing piles of books, which were threatening to engulf me in my last place (plus I could never find the one I needed). Looking from the kitchen, the bookshelves on the right form deep alcoves around the windows, and on the left, tall doors conceal everything from my clothes to tools. The space was once a pornography printers (historically the trade of the area), and I've left the floor and the iron columns as a reminder. The high-sided sofa is one I designed for George Smith; the two chairs are by Hans Wegner; the chandelier is from the 1930s and is French. You don't need to change much to change the look completely. For the moment the rug is a Bauhaus design by Gunta Stölzl and the patchwork lampshade was made by Squint. But I feel a green moment coming on. Behind the bookshelf (which divides the room but keeps the sense of space) at the far end, is my bed.

I think that the whole nature of inheriting a family home is particularly important here in England, isn't it? Of course, it can also be a terrible burden. People should shape their homes, their homes should be a reflection of them, but people who live in important homes, like the Duke of Devonshire, it shapes their whole life. It is a big responsibility and it changes your personality. I do believe homes should be a reflection of your personality. They are a very important part of who you are, and to have a home in which you're comfortable—and I don't just mean physical comfort—is a very important part of life. You come home and you think, this is who I am.

My family home was a very nice traditional Tudor-beam, English, East Anglian-style building that had belonged to, and was furnished by, my grandparents. The thing about children is that they are very conservative, they hate change in their home. So this was perfect for me and my brother, because nothing *ever* changed. As far as I can remember, my mother never bought anything for the home in my lifetime. I think my grandparents bought the sofas and chairs that were in the drawing room when they bought the house, and although they were re-covered, they were still there when my brother sold it many years later. The fabric of the building was the fabric of our lives. At the time, I probably thought the house was more important and more beautiful, and the things in it better than they were. Truth be told, we didn't really have anything of extraordinary merit, no great paintings or anything. My dad was a great "chucker" and he loved chucking things out. My parents were divorced when I was only eight years old, but we stayed on there with my mother. Curiously, one of the central raison d'êtres of the family's existence was keeping the home together. When I used to go back there in my 30s, the same airplane wallpaper was still in my room that was there when I was a boy; the same toys were on the shelves.

My dad worked in the city as a bill broker. He was a much more restless soul than my mom, and one of the things he didn't like was being stuck in one place. He never liked to own his own home. He felt it was a *chain*; he liked the idea that he could go off and live somewhere else, even if he wasn't going to. The idea of my having a shop came when I was at school—two friends had fathers in retail, one was the boss of Marks & Spencer—but I had no idea what our merchandise might be, it might have been fashion. When I saw the huge Biba store in London's High Street Kensington in 1973 it was a seminal moment for me. I thought, this is what I want to do; the atmosphere was awesome. The romance, the theater of the whole place. A friend of mine, Andrew Gillespie (he knew only just a bit more than I did), and I opened a little shop in Richmond in 1974. We had no grand plan; we sold accessories for the home: rugs, lamps, and things. One day a customer came in who had a new office he wanted decorating and said, "Can you come up and see what's cooking?" I took the only two books of fabric swatches we had and just talked my way through it. After that job I realized that there was something in this fabric business. By the end, of course, we had fantastic fabric from every supplier in the land.

One of the first houses we did was for my old classical tutor and housemaster at Eton. He asked me to do his drawing room. I shudder now to think about it; we didn't show him anything, we just did it. He's retired now but he has since told me that for 15 years, "That room was the backdrop to my life." After that we did masses of work, hundreds of projects large and small. I just learned what to do. It was a long while before I did anything to my own apartment. For 18 months I lived with only a table, a bed, and a director's chair. I can live unbelievably simply at home. Even now, I wouldn't say that I am fantastically interested in interior design. I *am* interested in the separate elements: silk, ecat weaving, hand block printing; the whole essence of producing things. Silk is a good example—I mean, how can you make this incredibly luxurious and glamorous thing from something that's secreted from a worm? I'm interested in factories and the *people* who make things; eventually my friends said, "You must buy a sofa." When you do your own place, you think that you must do it perfectly. But I now know that nobody should ever try and do their home like that, because nothing is the perfect answer, you should always let it evolve.

The moment that my design point of view was really crystallized was visiting the Jim Thompson house in Bangkok 25 years ago. Until then, I was probably following whatever trend was current, a pragmatic decorator. His style of decorating, with oriental antiques and artifacts, using parts of old buildings he had rescued from all over the country, was amazing. Though he was American, he took on board the culture of the country and immersed himself in it. When I travel, which I do a lot, I'm really not aching to see people's houses. I'm less interested in design than I should be. When I go to see the latest apartment by an interior designer in New York I'm less moved than if I go to see a Syrian door in a museum. I'm not a junkie for interior design, though I now run a huge business in Central London selling furniture, fabrics, accessories, and artifacts from all over the world. If I see some amazing object in Timbuktu or Thailand—a canoe or whatever—I don't think, I want to keep it, I think, I want it for the business. Just to have all the fun of acquiring it, bringing it back, opening the crate, bringing it to the store is enough. Maybe my store is a substitute home?

My current apartment is very personal in the way it looks; it kind of tells a story of what my interests are. It says what I want it to be, as opposed to being just a decorated apartment. If you asked me, "Do you want to be the person who lives here?" Well, I would quite like to be that person. Some people might want white leather sofas and a very "clean" Italian look, they might like to be a James-Bond type with big TV screens and all that, or they might want the classic English country-house look, with a Labrador and so on. That's great. It's not a fantasy if you can make it happen. This comes back to the issue of how much you shape your home, or how much you let your home shape you. There are some designers who I admire enormously and I think how nice it would be to have them do a home for me. Stephen Falcke, the

South African designer, is great. When I saw the Saxon Hotel that he did in 1999 it was the first time I understood the potential of using African artifacts in decorating. It was not an African home, not a lodge; it didn't look tribal. It was a mixture of many different cultures in a very contemporary way. I would love to have the fun of working with him on a house for me, but I haven't got a spare home to do that with, and I haven't got another life to give over. Your home is a bit like your clothes. As you get older you discover the clothes in which you feel comfortable. It doesn't stop you looking in stores or magazines to admire other things. I might think, when I look at the houses done by designers, that's a clever color combination or I love that piece of art used like that, but I don't think, I want it.

Books are a very important part of decorating, more important than drapes. They tell more about you than you would like. They help define who you are because they reflect your influences. They are also very beautiful but desperately underrated objects. Cheap as chips (French fries). I don't keep books that I have read unless they are very special to me. I throw them away. In fact, I don't acquire a lot of things. I do have an amazing three thousand-year-old Egyptian mask. How I wish that I had been Howard Carter. I'm embarrassed to say that I got it from an auction house and not from a tomb. I'd *much* rather have pillaged it.

OVERLEAF

Before he mysteriously disappeared in 1967, James H. W. Thompson, the American credited as rebuilding the Thai silk industry, lived for 25 years in Thailand. His house was created from a combination of six traditional Thai-style teak houses that he found and purchased in various parts of the country and rebuilt on the banks of the Klong river, using carpenters that he brought from Ayutthaya province. The houses were taken down, neatly stacked on barges and transported by river to the site in Bangkok, where they were reassembled as one complex in seven months, with the work completed in 1959.

I was born in the same small city in Japan where Kurosawa made many of his movies. It's called Himeji, not far from Kobe, in the province of Hyogo. It's not too far from Kyoto either. My father ran a traditional Japanese-style small hotel with rooms for about 30 people to stay—about 10 rooms—so people were always coming and going. I was the fifth of seven children (four brothers and two sisters). My mother and father had their own room, but we all slept together in two other rooms—on the tatami mats of course—so there was no privacy. It was a traditional house, about one hundred years old I would say, which my father bought when he had some money. My mother had a few people to help her with the cooking and the housework, but if the guests wanted to eat in, she would get extra help, like caterers. They didn't eat in our part of the house, but were served in the hotel. I remember there was a beautiful garden, but I wasn't an outdoor child; I didn't like sport. I preferred to stay in the house.

I did drawings but my parents never encouraged me. One of my sisters went to a sort of craft school and learned to cook and sew things and from her I found out about fashion and flower arranging. Of course my mother was always arranging flowers for the house—ikebana—and quite often she would have a man come to the house selling kimono. I remember being very influenced by those. We also had geisha who would come to the hotel quite frequently. They were another big impression.

My father loved antiques, but in Japan antiques are not like they are here in Europe. They are small objects for the tea ceremony. There was not much furniture in our house: a table, some armoires. I don't think any of the things were inherited from their parents. Sometimes I'd go to the houses of my school friends, most of them were much smaller than ours. A normal house in Japan at that time had one main room and two or three smaller ones, plus a kitchen. They all looked very similar, and most towns were very traditional, but after the war they changed a lot. When I was young I was not at all interested in the Japanese house. I preferred the ones that had a European-style room. Some had just a salon or a library in that style and it was considered quite avant garde. I remember seeing one that had a ceiling that was painted red. For me, that was a *dream*. If I saw one now, I would think it was quite kitsch.

There were no foreign magazines; the first things I saw from the West were the movies. I remember seeing *Little Women*. For someone in Japan that was like a *dream*: the house; the bed. I remember the first time I saw a canopy bed (baldacan), I wanted one. I went off to university, but it wasn't a success and I left; I didn't like it at all. Then in 1958 I left home and moved to Tokyo, and was one of the first male students to be accepted at the Bunka college of Tokyo, a very prestigious fashion school.

Up until then, it was not normal to have boys learning fashion design. The courses were not traditional Japanese, they were European. Living in Tokyo then I had no money. My parents were not happy that I'd gone to a fashion school, they would have preferred me to have gone to university and then work in a bank or something more acceptable. Tokyo was very far away. After the Second World War, the city was still very poor, and most students lived in a very small room with no kitchen, no bathroom, and no rest room. In my building, the rest room was one floor below, and we all washed in the public bathhouse. Every area had one. After I left fashion school I began to work in a small fashion design studio for lots of different manufacturers. At last I was being paid quite good money, much more than young people would usually get. In Tokyo at that time, there were some apartments designed for westerners in a European style. That's what I wanted. I was very ambitious, it was very expensive and I thought that maybe I wouldn't be able to afford to keep it. But I was also very, very happy. It had a kitchen, a shower room, a bedroom, and a salon. I bought furniture too: a chair, a sofa and—for the first time—a television. There was no design concept, it was only European style. I bought some beautiful flower-print fabric and I covered the chairs. People thought that it was very unusual. This was in 1961 and I lived there for two years. At that time there were preparations going on for the Tokyo Olympics and they wanted to pull down our building and rebuild it so I got a lot of money to move, and for the next year I lived in an apartment. Then with the money I'd saved, I bought a boat ticket to France.

At school I'd seen my first fashion magazines—*Vogue* and our teacher showed us *Elle*—which we'd never seen before. I'd seen lots of movies too. On the screen, Paris looked very beautiful, but I arrived in the winter. It was cold, gray, and raining and again, I didn't have much money left. I had to be very economical and I felt very lonely and very sad. I missed Japan and I didn't speak French so I enrolled at the Alliance Française and slowly I started to make friends. Eventually spring came and Paris and its architecture looked much more beautiful.

Coming by boat was an incredible experience for me. Having never been out of Japan, suddenly I saw all these different cultures. The boat stopped at Hong Kong, Singapore, Saigon, Colombo, Bombay, Djibouti, Alexandria, Barcelona, and finally Marseille. I got a big shock. It left a very strong impression on me that I still remember so well. In the beginning I just wanted to go back to Japan. I felt very homesick, but I'd told all of my friends that I was going to Paris for six months, so I couldn't go back. After two or three months I started to get settled and I felt very free. In Japan, there had been lots of things that I had kept secret, a lot of things that I couldn't do or say. In Japan, they were very traditional. For the first four or five months I didn't work. I had no contacts, and I asked a few Japanese people who worked in the fashion houses, and they said for Japanese it's very difficult to get work. After six months my funds ran out, and I asked my mother to send me some more money, and she did. She sent me money twice, but after the third time she said no, I must come home. Then, just before I left, I got a job and began to have an income again. For nine months, I stayed in a small hotel and when I got a job, the owner rented me an apartment she owned. For the first time, I had my own Paris apartment. In fact it was not far from here, in Avenue Parmentier. I was on the sixth floor and of course there was no elevator. But for me, I was so happy. There was a salon, a kitchen, a bedroom, and a guest room. It was great. It was already furnished, but I went to the flea markets and found so many beautiful things, I gasped. I also began to go to museums and galleries of course. Then after two years, I went back to Tokyo and found it unchanged and disappointing. Paris was so much more beautiful. Then slowly I discovered Japanese traditional culture—my culture—for the first time. I saw it with a completely different eye. I noticed the textiles; the kimono; the theater; slowly, slowly—each time I went back—until I became completely Japanese again. I could never have seen that if I hadn't come to France.

At first, working in that Paris design office, we had to follow the trends, but when I opened my own shop Jungle Jap in 1970 I said to myself, I must find my own identity. I am Japanese, I can't be like a French designer, I must use my roots, but in a new way. So when I did some very square shapes—they were like the kimono shapes—I brought modernity and poetry to it. In the beginning, I lived in different places almost every year. I liked change, and I liked to live in different areas of the city too. Of course I traveled around the country, but I preferred Paris. Then at the end of the 1960s I thought, why didn't I go to London instead of Paris? That's where everything was happening: the King's Road and swinging London. From then on, I went often.

One of my *dreams* was to live in Paris in a house with a garden, and for a while I lived in one in the 16th arrondissement. But my desire was to one day build a house in the middle of Paris with a Japanese garden. So my friend and I looked at about ten places but none of them were big enough, or they were in the wrong style and a Japanese garden wouldn't have worked. When we found this place in 1991 it was just a big, square wooden warehouse that had been used to store garden things, set in the inner courtyard of a block of apartments near the Bastille. With the help of an architect, we pulled it down and rebuilt it, which took about two years, then I stopped. Half was not finished but I moved in and started to live here; 18 months later, I finished it.

That was in 1995, when these pictures were taken. Since then, I've changed the furniture twice and a few years ago I moved my bedroom, so that now it has a view of the garden. It's a difficult house to describe, because—unlike a traditional Japanese house—this one is on several levels. You come in at ground level through a bamboo garden courtyard, and then on the next floor, there is another garden, with a cherry tree that flowers twice a year and a carp pond full of rather fat fish. Most of the plants came from Japan, including the tree, and the gardener too. As you can see, the furniture indoors is all western and the layout—though it has a strong Japanese feeling—is European too, almost like an open-plan loft. People were quite shocked that I had a swimming pool in the salon, but I like the reflections on the water—and I used to swim once or twice a day, so it made sense. I also collect a lot of things. I love elephant statues and I have quite a few now, including one in the entrance hall that's nearly five feet high. I also love African carving and native American artifacts. When I go into other people's homes, the first thing I look at is the atmosphere.

Now that I live alone, this house is too big for me. I really love it, but now I think I'd like a change. My *dream* now is to live near the Seine with a view of the river. Maybe a small penthouse with a terrace? I miss the sky and the sunset.

In 1999, after 30 years in the fashion business, I celebrated with a huge fashion event which retraced my entire career, and then I announced my departure from Kenzo, leaving the company in the hands of my partners, LVMH. After that, I spent three years traveling the world—making new discoveries and painting portraits. During that time, I also bought a lot of things.

Now I'm back again, working on a project I call the workshop of the five senses, "Gokan Kobo," which includes fashion, times and decoration. My designs are a mixture of influences from my travels: a combination of both East and West; luxurious materials but at accessible prices. It's a sort of melting pot of design, inspiration, and craftsmanship. I think my decoration is a reflection of myself, and I would say that I am a "diverted classic."

Several views of my Paris house, some taken years apart, show how it has evolved. The pool in the main living space, OVERLEAF, for instance, was first shot in 1995, BOTTOM LEFT. The living room, FOLLOWING 3 PAGES, looks out onto the second-floor Japanese garden and has also evolved over the years, as my interests change and my collections grow. The large painting in my studio, OPPOSITE the low table, is by Jean-Michel Basquiat, and the still life in my bedroom, FINAL PAGES, is a collection of shells and tribal artifacts from Africa, Borneo, and Tahiti that I have built up over many years.

Though I've designed and built many homes for other people, I don't really want to build a spectacular home for myself. I've been struggling with the idea of building something in Africa, but that would be the most difficult thing, and I've realized that I'm not ready yet. As a child, I don't think I had a home in the sense of a physical place that I can always refer to. The first part of my childhood was so disparate: we lived in a different country almost every two years. My father was a diplomat, a civil servant for Ghana. He had a Pan-African agenda that took him to parts of East Africa, West Africa, North Africa, and the houses we lived in were given to him as part of his work. Once he had completed his education he got a job, and suddenly he was traveling around the world. He married my mother, and she decided to follow him. They had no home at that stage so they had nothing to miss. We were part of a transient diplomatic community; home was always like a hotel to me. So my house was not a material space, it was actually a psychological space. I was fortunate that my mother and father were a strong unit and they enveloped me and my two brothers, cocooned us in this intimate emotional space. But I always remember feeling really disconnected because I couldn't make the same references about home that other people could make. As a child, I remember that being quite a traumatic position; being torn by the inability to carry things with me, or to have any kind of tangible part of where I was or where I was going. I knew that in no time at all we would move to the next house. This went on until I was about 11, when moments of stability started to occur.

During our stays in North Africa, I remember being acutely aware of the difference between our compound and the houses outside. How North Africa and the Middle East had a completely different urbanism. The sense that the private life was not played out in the public realm; that the home was a very discreet world, not one of porosity of community, but a reinforcement of the family. It was an inward-looking system that articulated the cell unit of the family, and the nature of the streets carried that through. Totally walled architecture, small windows, hardly any perforations. Certain people were only allowed to go as far as a certain point, going through layers of status to reach intimacy. Children, of course, were quite lucky in being able to see the back, if not necessarily the front, areas. It was

the first time I'd seen buildings that defined how life was being organized, and that was very striking. I realize this in retrospect, but at the time I just thought there was something very different to my house. As an outsider I could see something that to them was ritual, custom, tradition; it would have been seamless. I just didn't know then that it was architecture.

By contrast, when I later visited Japan I saw in the traditional houses what to my mind was almost no privacy. But actually there was incredible privacy: it was the privacy of the mind, human beings respecting certain traditions. The Japanese had created psychological boundaries by which spaces were defined. These too were cultural ideas about how you live. That discovery was quite shocking to me. Eventually we came to England and after moving a few more times—less frequently by then—my parents settled into the house they still live in now.

After I'd graduated and traveled a bit, I realized that I needed to complete a kind of thesis that was building up in my mind. To investigate a sensibility that at that time I began to equate with artists. The architects I encountered had lists of making, and not lists of thinking; they always seemed to discuss technique and ways of articulating it. Whereas with artists it was ideas, and how they could be made manifest. I became gripped by that. So that's when I decided to go to the Royal College of Art instead of an architecture school. I wanted to be close to the kind of courses that artists would do. I started to see spaces in terms of a catalog of different possibilities. I remember in my early 20s suddenly starting to objectify space. I would go to places and be absolutely fascinated by them as phenomena; as constructs of cultural fiction. They became not homes, but compositions of things: air, light, proportion, material. With a group of friends I visited the villas of Le Corbusier and Mies van der Rohe. We'd just save up our money and fly off to Barcelona or New York. I was kind of obsessed with how people could make new space. I loved modernism, and what it meant. I was struck by the work of Adolf Loos, and his ability to make connections across time, as well as predicting the future. Most of all, I found that I was always interested in homes, rather than civic buildings, and psychologically, it must be this quest I have about the idea of home. I see function in many different ways. Early in my career, function was a very powerful element, but now it's not so important. The house is changing so much. The whole idea of the function of a house is totally fashionable; for me it's purely an emotive terrain of different possibilities. It's no accident that I gravitated toward artists and creative people to do my first houses, because I can have a conversation in a much more articulate way with them, and they are very questioning about the nature of what a home might be. It's not about the modules of kitchen cabinets, it's about how you make certain distances between different states of mind, by passing through air and space; about how you experience the world. Technology makes the home more elemental, it cuts down the "stuff" you need. Technological minimalism is the real servant. I deploy materials just to articulate certain differences, but it's not about that articulation, it's really about what these materials are to each other and what they mean to a human being. That is the drive in doing houses for other people—it always plays out differently—but for me, it's essentially the same. Whereas once I was working mostly in London, now I'm working much more internationally—in China, Colorado, Miami, and South Africa—all on domestic projects. Clients think that maybe I'll bring something different to their project, but I want what they have; I'm bringing them back to exactly where they are, drawing my inspiration from the locations. That's where I get new energy. The home projects are things I love and keep going back to. They're my "watercolors" now.

I only know if I've got it right when a job is completed. Within a collection of projects, what has become clear is that by making a concept physical I can now judge it. For me, the home is an ongoing investigation in the sense that I'm trying to find a resolution when I know there is none. Yet I've seen lots of resolutions, but somehow I'm looking for my own. It's about me completing what I think home is, by not ever achieving it, and that's what drives me.

OVERLEAF LEFT

I remember being acutely aware, during my stays in North Africa, of the idea of space in the private home, and how people articulated that and even organized their relationships around it. This is a contemporary picture of the Kasbah Alt Mouted in Morocco, though the elements are essentially timeless.

OVERLEAF RIGHT

The Müller Villa in Prague, built in 1929 for Dr. Frantisek Müller, is one of the most completely preserved examples of Adolf Loos's work. In designing the building, Loos acted not only as an architect, but also as psychologist, creating a house specific to the owner's individual needs. In the hall and cloakroom, the repeated square motifs Loos used in his other interiors are painted white, the floor tiles are terra-cotta, and the ceiling is painted deep blue, a color the architect likened to an early evening Venetian sky. Loos thought it was his most beautiful house and designed all of the interiors, including the light fittings.

FOLLOWING PAGES

In this four-story London terrace house, we excavated the garden to the same level as the basement and inserted a side-to-side glass wall, which pivots upward to extend the dining area. The kitchen worktop links the space to the front sitting area, all the floors and walls are clad in black basalt and a series of steps link the area to the main staircase of the house.

One of the most memorable rooms that I've ever been to in my life is in the Palazzo Borghese in Artegna, outside Rome. It's the country residence of the Borghese family and dates back to the 17th century. There is one room dedicated to Pope Paul V and there is an incredible kind of history and culture tied up in this piece of architecture. I remember that we had lunch in a beautiful corner room with big windows cut into thick stone walls; the quality of light and the painted fresco on the ceiling; the view across the valley to a distant town. It was very beautiful and I felt like I'd tapped into an amazing cultural moment.

I was always interested in houses and it's been a thread throughout my career, regardless of what I've done, whether it's studying architecture, selling fabrics or working in interiors. It was always the home and design in the home that was common to all of it. In a way, my current job as editor of Australian "Vogue Living" magazine ties it all together. I went to Bali on vacation recently and I walked into my private villa at the Four Seasons Jimbaran Bay and I thought, I could live here forever and I'd be perfectly happy. It was built in the traditional Balinese style, but with a certain simplicity in how the buildings were detailed and the privacy was dealt with, so that you feel like you're living like a prince; the architecture of luxury. Balinese architecture has had a big influence on homes in Australia, but often in a slightly clichéd way, I see it a lot in my job: "inspired by Bali." The downside is that I also see some really bad buildings and the scarring that goes on, and I see stuff which is so appalling and it's going to be there for hundreds of years and everyone's got to live with it. I'd rather have something that is controversial or difficult or confronting than something that's just banal. Contemporary architecture is a very identifiable and very creative genre here. Australia is quite unique in that it's the home of the home. Every architect expresses themselves through building houses, even very early in their careers. There's the space for it and the culture for it. If you're an architect in Europe, by the time you're 30 you will have done interior architecture or renovations or little insertions in a very dense architectural fabric. If you are an architect in Australia, by that time you could have built ten houses. I think that one of the areas where Australian architecture comes into its own is in the interstitial space—half inside and half outside—where it connects the two. We talk a lot about outdoor rooms, and I guess these are a variation on the traditional Australian verandah. I hear a lot about the close collaboration between landscape designers and architects, and many architects in Australia have very strong ideas about how their building melds with the landscape. It may be a characteristic of the best contemporary architecture here, that it considers equally the landscape and the built form. It all becomes part of the palette of the design.

I grew up in subtropical Brisbane, where the traditional Queenslander house is on stilts with a verandah at the front, often also at the back, and sometimes, if it was a grand house, all the way around. You will get wrought-iron railings that are quite ornate, or you'll get very simple crisscross wooden railings. It's a very particular, very idiosyncratic kind of building; very charming. The theory is that they came via colonial India; verandah is an Indian word. Our house had a corrugated-iron roof that was painted green and the woodwork was white with a green trim. The verandah is a kind of liberating space in a way because you're not enclosed. You have a vantage point looking out across the trees, and since Brisbane is hilly, very often a view across town. I feel like I spent a lot of my childhood on the verandah or under the verandah or climbing over the verandah. For me it was a magical space. One of my earliest memories as a child is of lying down on the floor in the heat and feeling the air coming up through the gaps in the floorboards from the cool space below. I slept out there sometimes, underneath a mosquito net; the sound of the crickets would be almost deafening. I remember once waking up in the middle of the night to flashing lights, to see a Queenslander house that had been just literally sawn in two and stacked on the back of a lorry with a police escort. It was being driven slowly down our street at three in the morning. It wasn't uncommon for these houses to be cut in half or extended. The roof was supported by internal posts, but people often cut through the walls or ripped them down and moved them.

I had a real passion for architecture and for homes, and I remember as a child I used to draw plans a lot. My great uncle was one of Sydney's early modern architects. His name was Arthur Baldwinson and he and his wife lived in a very modern house in Sydney. He was known as the "artists' architect," because he designed houses for many of the leading contemporary artists of the day. He had died by this stage, but when, at the age of six or seven, I'd come down to Sydney with my father, mother, and sisters, we'd stay at my aunt's house and I'd sit in Arthur's untouched study for hours, just looking at all his architectural pens and pencils and nibs and his drawers full of plans. I was just sitting there and absorbing the feeling in this very modern room, looking out across to the harbor. I realize, that was when my passion for architecture began. I knew when eventually I went to study architecture that I didn't really want to be an architect; it was just something I knew I wanted to know about. I found it thrilling; I really did. I remember history of architecture lectures and being absolutely enthralled. However, when I left and began to work in a small architectural practice in Brisbane, I could see what a hard slog it was being an architect. I could also see that the woman I worked for had a very successful business and people clamored after her as the architect of their house, but some weeks she couldn't pay herself. It was a really rough career.

I do have a dream about building a beautiful house and garden for myself one day, but it is only a fantasy. I see some amazing houses and when I am in them I really enjoy being in that place for that moment and I'm grateful for it, but I don't own my own property. I don't own anything really; it's only been in the last little while that I've started to gather possessions. I've seen some exquisite things and I feel that I have them all in my life already. I've never really wanted to own things, so I live a fairly transitory life. I'm in a rental apartment, with a lot of books and some framed works of art that I've gathered, and I keep gathering from friends. I don't have much else. A daybed by the window; I love the sensuality of a daybed. I can lie around and look at the view. I have all my things in clear plastic storage boxes under the bed. These are the boxes that for the past eight years or so I've used to transport myself around in. I'm just parked here at the moment. I don't care what my friends think; they're all into expressing themselves through their homes but I like the feeling that I'm not attached to a particular style or way of living. I feel freer when I'm not encumbered by things.

I still draw plans funnily enough; I have one on a drawing board sitting here beside me now. I love making a graphic representation of a space on a piece of paper. It's a very therapeutic thing to do.

OVERLEAF

This is the verandah of Beaufort Hill, a colonial house built around 1900 in Clayfield, a suburb of Brisbane, Queensland. I don't know who actually built or designed it but it has had two significant well-documented periods of ownership: a Mrs. Elworthy (1907–1915), the widow of a grazier with extensive pastoral holdings around Gympie, a gold-mining town to the north of Brisbane; and Mr. Edward Albert Hawkins (1915–1962), also a grazier, philanthropist, and antiquarian. It was his townhouse. These were both very social periods for the house according to photos, and the verandahs figured largely as the place of entertainment. Mrs. Elworthy gave afternoon tea there to neighbors and friends. Mr. Hawkins held parties. Furniture was stacked in a corner, the player piano was wheeled out on to the verandah and costumed couples danced "till the wee hours." This photo was taken in the Rotunda, which is a domed round-shaped projecting bay placed across the corner of the verandahs at 45 degrees, a design feature that helped capture all the prevailing breezes; very important in our sometimes sweltering subtropical climate. Verandahs are in fact the defining feature of the Queensland colonial house. By day, they were largely informal areas, accommodating both adults and children, often cluttered with daybeds, cane loungers, tables, chairs, and pot plants. French doors opened from most rooms onto the verandahs, and on occasion they also served as open-air bedrooms if the family grew too large to accommodate inside the house.

Wherever I go, I'm always looking at houses and the way people live. Sometimes, the more exotic, the more interesting it is. I'd much rather see those than tombs or ruins or temples. When I visit people's homes, I always look at the big picture. I never like anything drab or dull because it means that the owners are boring people. Light is important to me, and so is texture. I love great hardwood floors, great fireplaces, great art. A kitchen would be important to me, because if someone had a modern or a clean kitchen, I'd think that was interesting. I'm always looking at the details too. When I'm looking at new houses, it's totally instinctive, my eyes wander all over the house. Even in a restaurant or a shop, my eyes are wandering. I'm intrigued with symmetry. If something is balanced, I feel comfortable. If something is out of balance, I feel it's not right. If there are two windows in a room and a chair is between them—as opposed to under one window—I get the sense that these are balanced people. If you like the people and you feel comfortable with them, then their environment seems more pleasing and inviting.

When I was born, we lived in Elmira, New York, in a house that was totally American colonial, which was very much the norm in our community; they really didn't know about contemporary design or modern or Louis XIV. There were some pieces of furniture that I recall my aunt would refer to as items she grew up with: traditional classic mahogany pieces. One of my fondest memories is during Christmas, when it was snowing out, the house was decorated, we had music playing, and my eight brothers and sisters were excitely waiting for Christmas day. That house was pretty stable, things remained much the same, and it was probably due to the fact that we were living a very humble life. My sisters were aesthetically minded and they would be continually giving the house a bit of a "fluff" if you will—maybe changing the arrangement of the furniture. I would notice how much change could take place visually as a result of that. My mom was so busy being a mom that she allowed them to do whatever they wanted with the house. I was number two: first boy, second child. I shared my room with my younger brother, and I covered as much of the walls as I could with sports posters and pictures of my heroes—music stars and sports stars—and I had a bookshelf with all my sports trophies and favorite things. When I was 11 or 12, I became a newspaper boy in an area called Strathmont Park, a very wealthy area with impressive houses. I was fascinated by the outsides, but then once a week I would collect payment and people would sometimes invite me inside. I was in awe of the way some of those people lived, and it inspired my dreams of living a different type of lifestyle one day.

I was sporty when I was younger, but when I got into my late teens, I became very interested in music. I was always drawing and sketching. My dad was a jeweler and a watchmaker and I would go to his workshop and see him designing and making things. By the time I was 18 I was anxious to get my own apartment, and when a family has so many children it's almost a relief when one leaves. I went to college for a while, but I wasn't much of a student and after one semester I quit and concentrated on a small shop I'd opened called People's Place, selling jeans. You couldn't really find mod clothes, bell bottoms or rock-'n'-roll type clothing in Elmira in 1969, so I went to New York City and bought a lot of cool mod clothes from the streets of Greenwich Village and sold them to my friends, and created a dynamic business. That first apartment was a true hippy abode. I had a water bed; Indian prints all over the walls and ceilings; incense burning and black lights; posters of Jimmy Hendrix and Janis Joplin. It was very psychedelic; a lot of sitting on the floor and listening to music. At the time, all of the great music was coming out of London: The Stones, The Beatles, The Who, The Kinks, Led Zeppelin, and all of the great rock groups. I loved the way they dressed and the way they looked—so I went to London. I wanted to see how the whole fashion business operated in England; I got a job at Jean Machine on the King's Road and lived in a furnished apartment on Brompton Road. That was 1971, the time of Granny Takes a Trip and all of those fabulous shops. Biba was a big inspiration too; I realized that it had created a lifestyle that people wanted to be a part of, and saw that I could expand my business and roll it out as a Biba-type concept for the States.

In 1972 there was a flood in Elmira, the whole downtown area was under water. Some of the pictures of New Orleans reminded me of it. At that point, I opened a new store in a larger location followed by a number of shops on college campuses in upstate New York. I started to sell not just jeanswear but dresses, purses, accessories, shoes, fragrance, records, and my business really took off. At the same time, I wanted to start designing what I was selling. When I told my friends and family that I wanted to become a designer, they said, "You're crazy, you have to go to design school, you have to learn how to cut patterns and do all this technical stuff." But I said, no no no—I will just hire people to execute my ideas. And I did. I was taking ideas from everywhere, just like a sponge. I took my sketches to local factories, with fabric in hand. I went to Hong Kong, to India, wherever I could possibly go to get the things made. It might seem amazing looking back, but nothing stopped me because I didn't realize that I wasn't supposed to. I was doing what I loved, not concerned with spreadsheets or with risk. I just did it.

When I got back from London, my friend and business partner and I rented an unfurnished house in the country in upstate New York. It was a sort of modern upside-down house:

one side was all glass and we looked out over the hillside. This was just after the movie *A Clockwork Orange*, and we decorated it all white—white walls, white carpeting—with some very stark brightly colored modern furniture. We thought at the time that it was pretty cool. We didn't want it to look like *anything* I'd grown up with. Growing up in a traditional home with a traditional family poses certain issues, and one of them is called *clutter*. Everyone had a lot of stuff. I wanted to live more of a minimal lifestyle without a lot of stuff on the walls, on shelves, on tables. Op art was a huge inspiration to me. I don't think my parents quite understood it—the kind of music we were listening to; we had long hair; we were wearing weird clothes—and they were curious as to what that funny smell was in the house (the incense and a bunch of friends sitting around half dazed).

The pendulum swings back and forth in fashion and it's the same for me in home too. We stayed in that house for quite a long time for me, about five or six years, then I switched to a sort of American folk-art theme, a lot of red, white, and blue —that sort of thing. It was an old red schoolhouse that I bought. Very charming, small, and quite rustic and very authentic. It had been a one-room schoolhouse and someone had put in a sleeping loft. There were very large windows, high ceilings with beams, and a garden with a brook. Four years later I moved again; I got rid of all those rustic things—sold them or gave them away. It was exciting because I really wanted to move on. If I collect something, I become fanatical about it for a very short time and then I tire of it and go on to something else. I think change is fun, change is very interesting. I'm always looking forward to some sort of change by moving to a new place and, once in it, making changes. I always wanted to move to the next level in both social and financial terms. I wanted either a bigger place, or something more interesting or with two fireplaces or maybe this time with a terrace or a backyard—just different experiences. At this time I also decided to sell my six retail stores and move to New York to start a fashion design firm. I had been spending a lot of time there anyway (this was 1979) so it wasn't a matter of changing my persona or thinking too hard. I just needed to get settled and team up with the right people. I wanted to really focus on the work, so that meant that my home needed to be really simple, not cluttered or complicated. I found a loft apartment in Ithaca. I had modern pieces, no rugs on the hardwood floors, track lighting, high ceilings, not much on the walls. I'd also just gotten married at the time; my wife was also a designer and she agreed that the apartment should be simple and "clean." In the beginning, I was very much leading the way, but our roles have switched over the years and when we bought the next house in the country—in Connecticut this time—it was she who decorated the whole thing. I was so busy with my Tommy Hilfiger business. The interior was all done with Colefax and Fowler and, although I think they do nice work, it really was a bit too traditional for me. After the Duchess of Windsor died, their Paris house was sold and I bought a lot of the furnishings, so we do have a lot of rather interesting antiques in the house. It is actually a bit too big. We also have three other houses. We wanted to be near the seashore, so we have a house in Nantucket that is very traditional Americana; nautical. In Vermont we have a ski house that's done in an Austrian Bavarian theme. It's become a sort of hobby to do this, something I enjoy as much—if not more—than fashion design. I love imagining what it would look like and then making it happen. It's all about who you work with; if they're experienced and competent then it makes it *much* easier. Initially Colefax and Fowler were very English country style, but when we did the Vermont house we said we wanted it to be very Austrian, so they came back with a lot of Austrian fabrics, Austrian antiques, German and Austrian accessories. I do love to go to antique shops and flea markets wherever I am. We also built a house in Mustique in the Caribbean, which we did in a sort of British colonial style. There was a theatrical designer by the name of Oliver Messel who designed and built a lot of the early homes on the island, and when we bought the land there I wanted the house to be in the Oliver Messel style (he had passed away). So we bought some of his original plans and designs from the builder who had worked with him and used these to plan our house. In fact, just thinking about it makes me want to be there right *now*. I would love to have a house in London or in Paris or the South of France or wherever. I like the challenge of doing something new. But you really can only have so many; it doesn't make sense to have more homes than you can possibly digest. I've just given up the New York loft and I'm trying to think of the next step. People are all the time calling up and saying, "You must come and see this place or that place." I'm also looking at a house in the Hamptons at the moment.

I know I've said it already, but I like change and I think change makes the world go round, so probably if you asked me about these things in two years' time, I'd say I don't like modern, I don't like Austrian, or whatever. The thing is that I get bored very easily—and after a while, my instinct is to move on. Enjoy it for the moment, but then … next.

My house in Mustique consists of several buildings, including the main house, OVERLEAF LEFT TOP, seen from the back, and four guest cottages, OVERLEAF LEFT BOTTOM. Down by the beach is a seating area that is ideal for cocktails at sunset or for just relaxing and entertaining, OVERLEAF RIGHT.

Ever since I've lived here in Bulawayo, and probably for one hundred years before that, there has been a little street market along one side of the city hall. Each stallholder had his space marked out on the pavement where he or she could sit and sell flowers or handicrafts or curios. All of a sudden the police swooped on them, destroyed their goods, confiscated their produce, and now won't allow them to sell there any more, even though they had all paid their rent and bought a license. It's just been wiped off the face of the map. If the police see a hawker now, he's got to run for it. We have three or four fresh-produce markets and those fruit and vegetables used to go to the hawkers who then walked around the streets of the suburbs selling them. They were not making a vast fortune, and admittedly they probably didn't pay taxes, but they were providing some kind of service. Not any more, now they've all been closed down too. Go into some of the better shops in town, and you can still buy all kinds of luxury items—at a price—but you can't buy basic commodities. Sugar is totally unobtainable, but you can buy meat if you can afford it. I can't. It's getting scarce because the government has totally ruined the beef industry. There are a lot of cheap Chinese goods; light bulbs will last you perhaps a week. Shops are struggling on, but all over Zimbabwe factories are closing all the time. The country is bankrupt, so the services tend to break down. For instance, we don't have any garbage collection because there's no diesel for the trucks, and the sewage disposal system breaks down because there's no money for the chemicals. Here at the farm, we have a telephone, but it doesn't always work; the electricity doesn't always work either, usually every time it rains.

The staple diet is maize meal, and that is in very short supply too, but it's what most of the people live on, so they feel that if they haven't eaten maize today, then they're starving—and they are. Most people can't afford bread, and it's usually rationed to one loaf per customer. It makes me think of the rationing in Britain during the war. I was born in north London, but the only memory I have of that house is the bearskin rug on the floor and how nice it was to crawl on. In 1940, when I was four, I was evacuated to America, and for the next four years I lived with my mother's relatives in upstate New York. I do remember that house very well. It was a beautiful wooden house on two floors, three hundred years old when I was there, so now it must be four hundred years old, or nearly. My aunt and uncle were filthy rich, which was nice, and I remember they had a huge four-poster bed, an absolutely beautiful thing. The floors upstairs

had very wide wooden planks and there were gaps in between, through which you could see down into the rooms beneath. The house was built on the side of a hill and the gardens went down to a stream. Higher up the hill were the stables and a very large vegetable garden and a gardener's cottage. They had a couple of cows and a pig or two, and horses and things, but they weren't farmers; my uncle had a company that made surgical instruments, and their son was ten years my senior. He was off at West Point most of the time, so I played with the gardener's kids. The high point of the year was when the meadow was cut by hand scythe and the hay was brought in on an old horse-drawn wagon, and we were allowed to ride on top.

I was very happy there. Most of the food was produced on the place. They could afford to buy whatever they wanted, but my aunt was a very keen gardener and she did a lot of preserving. Apples were stored for the winter and we had maple trees, too, so we never went short of maple sugar or maple syrup. When I was six, my aunt bought me a pony; it was an idyllic childhood, but I wasn't spoilt. They had an African-American housekeeper called Julia Wiggin-Thompson who basically brought me up for those four years. I loved her dearly. She was about the size of a house, she couldn't get through normal doorways, she had to go sideways; she was immense. I remember she had very large hands, the size of Kentucky hams, which she applied to my bottom when I needed it. During this time my mother, who had been working in New Hampshire, came to see me from time to time, and then in 1942 she and my father, who had remained in England, had a big bust up and eventually divorced. I didn't know anything about it until years later, but she went back to England to try and sort it out and two years later sent for me to follow her. By that time I think people felt that the war was never going to end, and she wanted her "baby" back. It was still difficult to travel, but I was put on a boat along with seven other children, with a label around my neck like a parcel, and instructions not to take it off, under pain of death. We sailed from Philadelphia on a Portuguese boat bound for Lisbon, and from there by plane on to Bristol. I think that everyone thought it was a bit dodgy, but I don't remember being frightened. I didn't know anything about war or danger, but I was very airsick.

Back in England, we moved around a lot for the next few years, as my mother got jobs—usually fairly menial: housemaid and things like that. In six years I went to eight different boarding schools. I did see my dad for one weekend, but that was really the first and last time. Then in

1946, we came out to Africa. My mother's brother was teaching in Salisbury and said, "Come and join us here." At the time, king and country were urging you to go to the colonies, but they didn't tell you how you were going to get there. You couldn't get a passage to Africa for love, money, or anything else, but eventually we found what were called Liberty ships. There were two ships sailing: the one we were on was an ex-naval minesweeper, the other one was a wooden ship with a mast, so it could sail as well. There was no official crew; the passengers did all the dogsbody (grunt) work, and you paid through the nose for it. Both boats were totally unseaworthy, continually breaking down, and when we finally got to Freetown the crew of the other boat all mutinied. My mother, too, decided that she'd had enough, so instead of going on to Cape Town, we went overland by wood-burning train from Lobito, through Angola to Elizabethville in the Congo (staying in a very smart hotel in E'ville); then down through Northern Rhodesia to Lusaka, entering Southern Rhodesia over the Victoria Falls bridge and via Bulawayo to Salisbury, as it was called then. An amazing ten-day journey.

Eventually my mother bought a property in Rangemore, outside Bulawayo, where she spent the rest of her life running boarding kennels for cats and dogs. I guess that was my first real home, and I realized that once I'd put down roots, I wasn't going to leave. It wasn't much of a house; we added bits to it, improved it, built kennels. It didn't provide a luxurious lifestyle I can assure you, but it was home. Our house comprised two big rondawels with a little gap in between, which was covered with a tin roof to form a verandah or a porch. Round rooms—you find them all over Africa. Evidently the early settlers when they arrived had the local inhabitants put up something for them to live in, and because that's how they built, they were rondawels. They became quite the thing to have: one or two or three or even four clustered together. Even when they began building with bricks and mortar instead of poles and mud, they carried on building round homes. In our house, one room was for living and dining and the other was a bedroom. The kitchen and bathroom was on the back, and eventually, as I got older, my mother built on another room for me.

The farmhouse where I live now is the same: two very big rondawels built from local stone—there's no shortage of rocks around here—two-foot-thick walls, partly to keep out the heat and partly, without cement, they need to be nice and thick to help them stand up. But it's the same old Rhodesian farmhouse style. The roof was thatch when we moved in, but I don't like living under thatch. It's the fire hazard, not the bugs; the wildlife you get used to. I had a freer childhood than I think most children did, certainly today, even here in this country. My mother gave me almost complete freedom. She would say, "I'd like to know where you're going, and who you're going with." The only rule was that I had to be back before dark. As I grew up and became a teenager, I began to appreciate the different standards of living of my various friends. I can remember some lived in even poorer conditions than I did, and some who lived a great deal better: larger, better furnished, better kept houses; perhaps more than one servant; better silver, table linen, these sorts of things. I don't recall ever being jealous or envious.

I met my husband in Durban while I was at college there, and for a while we lived in very modest apartments. At first we made most of the furniture ourselves. Swedish designs were in vogue, so a lot of the pieces had angled legs. My husband, Terry, was quite good at do-it-yourself and I'm not bad at it. In 1960, we decided to move back to Bulawayo and opened a business doing printing and advertising and public relations and display work and exhibitions and anything else we could lay our hands on. Then after ten years, we bought this farm; Terry was always very keen on growing things, and I was keen on livestock of any sort. This area of Matabele Land is euphemistically called semi-arid tropics. You can cut out the "semi" as far as I'm concerned. When we bought the land it was quite small. I've added to it since. Most of the soil is not too bad, but it's not arable. Most of it is rocky hills—good for goats. The whole of the 1970s were very good: we had plenty of rain and Terry made a fairly decent market garden. There was plenty of water in the boreholes and vegetables grew very nicely. But since the drought in 1980–81 we haven't had a decent year since. In fact, we are on the fringes of the Kalahari Desert, so when it's dry, it's very, very, very dry. There were a lot of things that needed doing to the house, but we were building up the business in town, so any money we made went into that. Then after four years, my husband moved out; he took the business and I kept the farm. It was more or less amicable. I had two kids to bring up and I did not want to live in an apartment in town. I was prepared to give up quite a lot to stay here. Dominic was 19 and Alison was going on 17 when, in 1975, I married my second husband, Peter. He adored the children and they adored him. That's when we made quite a lot of alterations to the house, put on a new roof, and generally sorted it out.

At the present moment, I'm not prepared to spend any more on it when I might be thrown out at any minute; and believe me, I've fought long and hard to retain this farm. I guess I'm very lucky that I'm still here. They've tried very hard to chase me off—with death threats and flashing bits of paper in my face that I'm not allowed to read. The first time they came around I wasn't in the house, I was down by the main gate. There were five pickup trucks, about 15 or 16 men in their late 30s or early 40s, to terrorize an elderly white woman. For about an hour they were shouting and screaming, threatening to do this and that. Their language was pretty interesting too. Considering some of them didn't speak very good English, they certainly had a good command of swear words. I don't mind saying that I was shit scared. I was completely surrounded, but on that occasion, they didn't actually touch me. In fact, it was quite funny because the leader had obviously rehearsed a speech. I was accused of stealing land and exploiting the people and doing all sorts of things, and I made the mistake of responding, which made him stop and lose his thread—so he had to start again from the beginning, word for word. This time I let him finish. I've since discovered that you don't argue; it doesn't matter what you say, they will twist it against you. On other occasions I've been prodded and pushed around; they try to provoke you into reacting so they can respond. You don't stand with your hands on your hips and you don't cross your arms. They're bullies, and bullies are also cowards. If you react, you've had it. Not long before that, one of my neighbors further up the road from me had been set upon by three hundred of them. It took them three hours to kill him. Several farmers have been killed and several driven off their land—with or without violence. Plenty of them have ended up in hospital, had their homes burned down, their cars burned. Some other friends of mine were on their way home to their farm when they were attacked and their bodies put on the hood of the car and set alight. This is going on all the time. It's still happening. They kept coming back to my place every Saturday afternoon, and after a while it became a bore for me and for them too, and their visits became further and further apart. But they're so unpredictable; if they've been taking drugs, you never know which way it's going to go.

I've been trying to negotiate with the authorities to let me carry on farming and they just say, "Yes, Mrs. Manyathi" (that's my Sindebele name—it means mother buffalo). Even in a meeting I had today, they promised me the earth but nothing happens. I have three pedigree herds of cattle and a line of thoroughbred goats that I've built up over 20 years, but they've taken away all except 32 acres of my land; originally I had 2,377 acres. It drives me mad, but it also makes me tired. I get very frustrated and depressed about the whole thing. One bag of feed now costs as much as a ton used to cost. But I refuse to give in because that's what they want. I still have a few of my staff left, some of the older ones who've been with me the longest, but at least half of my labor force have absconded over the past two years. I'm sure that they are getting threats too. My husband died in 1980, so it's just me now. I guess I'm just stubborn. Damn it, I've done a bloody good job of farming here. It's in a much better condition than when I took it over, and I've put 30 years of my life into this farm. Everything I've earned went into it, my children grew up here, it's my home.

RIGHT

Outside the dining-room door, the verandah is furnished with some colonial-style teak chairs that belonged to my mother, a fridge we used for cold drinks and, by the door, a tall drum from the Batonka tribe of the Zambezi Valley.

OVERLEAF LEFT

Part of the sitting room is centered around the fireplace, where we have fires in the winter when it's freezing cold. The horns above the mantlepiece are from a wild Kudu bull that I shot when I found it injured years ago, when there used to be herds of them around here. All of the furniture is just pieces we've bought locally. Above the window is a long pole used for crooking sheep.

OVERLEAF RIGHT

This is the other end of the sitting room. The big coffee table is a plank on some oil drums, and in the far corner is a mirrored drinks cabinet. Above the window are some bucket hooks that we used at Rangemore to draw water from the wells, and one or two that I have collected. There's nothing special about this room, it's just where we live.

FOLLOWING PAGE

The dining room occupies one of the original rondawels, and is where we have all our meals. The English Windsor-style chairs were made here in Zimbabwe from local hardwoods, and above the fireplace is a poster that my son Dominic gave to my first husband—that tells you how long it's been there. The concrete floors throughout the house were once polished dark green.

When I was growing up, the greatest length of time I spent in any one house was in Sheffield. It was a lovely old granite stone villa near the university. It had the classic Victorian features: high ceilings, nice big door frames, three floors. The kitchen was huge. My mother was a very good cook, but she never taught me. I'm afraid that is a skill that has bypassed me. I don't recall whether she did anything to make those places more personal; I'm not really the person to ask. When I was young I was always a very outdoor child, and then later in Sheffield, I only ever remember the kitchen being full of friends of mine, fellow athletes who seemed— with unerring regularity—to turn up at mealtimes, so I very rarely remember eating a meal without at least three or four friends there. I was born in London but as a family we moved around a lot because of my father's various jobs as a production director. I didn't find it disruptive. Funnily enough, one of the great things it's given me is the capacity to be able to relate to the world outside London. Selling the concept of a London Olympic games, but as a UK-wide project; having spent a large chunk of my early life up in Yorkshire, having been educated in the East Midlands, actually gives me a much bigger picture of the UK than most.

In our houses, there was always a mixture of old and new things, which is a style that I've tended to adopt in my own houses. Some of it was inherited from my grandparents, but I remember as a family we were always very keen on walking. On Sundays, it wasn't uncommon at the end of the walk to stop off at places like Broadway or Chipping Camden in the Midlands, where my parents would explore a row of antique shops. That was basically how it was done. My parents came from very different backgrounds. My father came from very humble origins in the East End of London and got a scholarship to Westminster School, but although my mother's mother was from west London, her father was Indian—and my mother was brought up in Delhi as a young child. She went back to India quite a lot, and at home we had a lot of prints and paintings and odd things of an Indian origin. It wasn't unusual to see the female side of my family wearing saris. My uncle was the former Indian ambassador to London, and to Washington and Geneva, and he was in one of Indira Gandhi's cabinets. It's to my great shame that I only visited India five years ago, but I have now been back twice a year since then. I find it fascinating and I realize that there is a large part of my heritage there. At the age of 12, I had no idea what I was going to do for a career, and then I finished third in the 60 yards race at the Warwickshire primary schools' track and field. Then we moved to Sheffield and my father discovered somebody in his cutlery company who was a track coach at the local athletics club. That was how I got into training. I effectively left home at the age of 18 when I went to Loughborough University, and within six weeks of graduating I broke a world record. That was the year before the 1980 Olympics, and from then on my life changed quite quickly. Up till then, I had been applying for jobs and had got an interview with one of the big London banks. But I realized that I wouldn't have enough time to do a full-time job and prepare properly for the games. Fairly quickly, sponsorship began to follow. I don't mean that I was amassing a fortune, but the need to go out and do a nine-to-five job was not strictly necessary.

At the same time, I was fully expecting—after the games —to do that kind of job. Then of course I won the Olympics and a year later this sport had effectively started on its long road to becoming an open sport rather like tennis.

I bought my first apartment, in London, in 1982, but basically I only used it for the weekends. I was never in the country long enough. I remember various girlfriends coming through and being appalled at the wallpaper and things. The one in the kitchen had beer mats on it. Not, I hasten to add, anything that I had put up. So I changed things, probably under duress at the time, but I was fairly unconcerned. Most times, I was just throwing a kitbag onto the floor after coming back from a race or on the way to the airport for another. From there, I moved in the mid-1980s to a Queen Anne house on the Thames at Twickenham. I came across the building when it was a complete wreck, with six inches of water on the ground floor and a six-foot bow in the front wall, so it had to be painstakingly put back together. I had a lot of help from my younger sister, who was doing a degree in fine arts at the time. Now she's a very good interior designer. That was probably the first time I'd lived somewhere that I really did consider to be my permanent home—where my books and my music were. It was pretty much towards my late 20s before I had a place that I could close the door behind me and call my own home. I have to tell you, I'm not a wallpaper person. I don't think that I've ever lived in a house with wallpaper. I just prefer a wall to be fresh.

I lived in that house by the river till the late 1980s/early '90s, when we moved into a converted farmhouse in Surrey. This time, though, it was not a listed (historic) building, so once we got planning permission we basically just got on with it, with little hindrance. This time, too, the kitchen was designed much more for someone who's running that end of the business—if you like—more than me. I was never concerned with getting any publicity from any of my houses, because I've never, ever let anybody into my house other than close friends. I've never done photo shoots or at-homes. It's just one of those things. I think I've done pretty well to get to my 50th year and never had any photo inside any property I've ever owned. It's nobody else's business. I just find it an intrusion. To be honest, I can't think that I've ever read a feature in a magazine about someone's home. Maybe I've occasionally flicked through an interior design magazine, normally if my sister shows me something, and I'd think, that might be a nice idea if I ever wanted to do that. But I wouldn't do it because that's what Robbie Williams' kitchen looks like. I have bought the odd bits and pieces. I like the auction house in Lots Road; Sunday afternoon with friends. I have some nice pieces that have followed me around, a fairly eccentric mix of stuff, old and new.

When I go to someone's home I look at their books and music. That tells you a lot about somebody. I have a large jazz collection. I tend to like quite neutral colors, but I don't have a template in my mind for what a room has to look like. I do like a room to have personal qualities and not look like something out of a catalog. I have a lot of good friends that I stay with in other countries—Australia, Switzerland—but I've never wanted anybody else's house, actually. I've never sat there thinking that I'd rather be there, than where I live. I could live in other countries, though. That would never be a problem for me. I've lived for good chunks of my life outside the UK while I was training—in Chicago, Florida, Rome, Melbourne—so I would be quite comfortable living even for an extended period overseas. I would always like to feel that I could come back to the UK. When I first started in sport, the accommodation used to be a bit spartan. During the Oslo track meet, it was a sort of student hostel that we stayed in, with a communal canteen. No menu, just some photographs of the food above the counter. In fact there was probably more nutritional value if you ate the photographs rather than the food. You can imagine the Soviet Union in 1980: the facilities were very basic. As soon as the games moved on, the Olympic village became the living quarters for some Moscovite car workers. But then, toward the end of my career we were staying in five-star hotels. The only thing I do have a problem with—even in a really warm climate—is air conditioning. I loathe it. Any athlete will tell you, the last thing you want to do before a race is to be sleeping in air conditioning. It dries out your throat and leaves you more susceptible to infections. I tend to fling open the windows— even if it means traffic noise.

In terms of the London Olympics, I am chairman of the local organizing committee, which is the group that stages the games, so all those details are within my group. The size and scale and scope of the Olympic village, the shape and design of the rooms, the transport arrangements—that's all very much part of my job now. The first important thing is that the Olympic village is going to be in the Olympic park, which means that the athletes are within walking distance of their venues. You want athletes to come to your city as competitors, not commuters. To make a modern Olympic Games work, you need a proper legacy once the athletes have gone. We want houses that have an afterlife, so we will be taking into consideration what the housing need in that part of London is going to be after the games. I know what athletes will want and we had an athletes commission that signed off on all of the plans in our candidate file. We know that there will be 10 thousand athletes and that 99 percent of them will be eating in the village, so the houses will only need basic food-preparation facilities. One of the early designs for the village came back with carpeting. No athlete wants carpet. First of all, there are all sorts of issues with allergies, and second, it isn't strictly necessary. Recognizing that the world is connected, most athletes will arrive with laptops and computer games and all sorts of things, so you need all the right wiring. There is a connectivity in the world now that simply didn't exist when I was competing. Back in 1948, when the last Olympics were held in London, there were six athletes to a Nissan hut.

For me it's the last lap of my own Olympic odyssey. I've competed in the games. I've become a commission member of the IOC. I'm on the council of an Olympic sport. I've written about it, broadcast it, and now I've been lucky enough to have been part of a team that's brought it back to my own country. There's not much more that I can do— other than make sure that we get it all done in time for the opening ceremony.

RIGHT

About the only thing that I do collect is security accreditations. I have one from the Moscow Olympics, the Los Angeles Olympics, all the European championships I've raced in; then latterly of course, as a member of parliament, for party conferences; and then for the International Olympic Committee of the bid to London 2012. They are a permanent reminder going back nearly 30 years. The spikes are the ones I wore when I broke the world records for 800m, 1500m, and one mile in 1979—three world records in the space of 41 days.

My house is a nest; it's where I come back to from my expeditions, where I can write my books and put my experiences—my adventures—to bed. But it's also my launch pad. It's immensely cozy; I love the slight sense of decay and disorder. The house is as you find it. Inside, the disorder is mine; outside, it has a weathered sense of permanence. I bought it seven years ago. Up to then, I'd been living in various people's spare bedrooms. Finally I thought, oh dear, at last I'm going to have to buy a house. I took an enormous gamble, but I have managed to stay here and keep up the mortgage payments. Finally all my books that had been following me about were unloaded, along with my objects: the fossils I'd collected as a child. I'm very lucky—I know that once there were ten people living in this London house—but nonetheless, I do feel I sometimes need to stretch. I would like a bit more access to living, breathing *things;* a bit of rough ground. I miss a place to grow vegetables and a bit of jungly garden.

As a child, we were always moving around. My father was a test pilot, which meant living near different airfields around Britain. He was flying a lot, he used to test aircraft in the tropics. Then later, he became a civil airline pilot for Zambia Airways and would bring back exciting things from Africa: a little baby stuffed crocodile; a tiny snake in a bottle; a Weaver bird's nest; exciting elements from far away. In a sense, he brought the outside world to *me*, and made it within reach. I had an older brother and a sister, but I was the one in the family who was immensely curious and wouldn't stop asking questions, so the more I was given these things, the more excited I got and the more questions I asked. Throughout the 1960s and '70s my father brought back things from Zambia—fossils and things; it went on and on, till my bedroom was filled with things, even maps on the walls. I realized that my father's world was too far away for me, but I could still create my own world by collecting fossils. They were objects of mystery and magic, and eventually I converted the shed at the end of the garden into a fossil museum, which no one ever came to, but I had thousands. To me they were everything. My local dentist was very nice and gave me some worn out dental tools, and I picked away at these sharks' teeth and shells and

ammonites, things from another age, and gradually I revealed them.

At boarding school, I really began dreaming of my own adventures and I thought it was inevitable that I was going to be away in some other world. Then at university I read environmental science, which was almost the perfect degree as far as I was concerned: meteorology, ecology, geology, archaeology—everything around me. It was the preparation for my life as an explorer. This feeling welled up in me, until in my final year I went on three expeditions, one to Costa Rica, one to Brunei, and one to Iceland. But they were all scientific exercises; the romance wasn't there and I thought, I just want to go on a quest. I was now 22 and time was ticking by, when I thought of this idea that there were people living out in the Amazon and Borneo, and they didn't have any money—and I didn't have any money—but if they're really nice to me, they might teach me how to survive and live in places like that. The Amazon appealed to me just because it was the land of El Dorado, the land of the gold that Sir Walter Raleigh had failed to find, somewhere between the Orinoco and the Amazon mouth. I knew that I wouldn't really find it, but this was going to be *my* quest, and after that, I would have to settle down to some career.

I've now done 15 big journeys, but that first one defined the rest, because I sort of found a way of exploring by learning from the local people, and that meant traveling alone so that I could sink in among them and find a new home. It also meant learning from scratch, almost like a child. Time and time again, I am plunked with the children, by the Orinoco Indians and the Amazon Indians and, later on, the Borneo Iban. To them I had no skills, and I began to realize how little I knew and how much there was to learn. Anyway, that expedition was almost a disaster. I was attacked by gold miners. I ran off into the forest, and ended up eating my dog to survive, and had this trauma, spending a couple of weeks walking in the forest and getting malaria, but surviving. After that, I couldn't go back to the Amazon —it was too traumatic. So I went to New Guinea and I immersed myself in a community that had found a way of coping with living in the rain forest, by adopting the role model of a crocodile. I found myself going through this initiation ceremony that involved being hidden away in a crocodile "nest," a big arena, where you're beaten every day and your chest is cut with bamboo blades to give you sort of crocodile markings, and so on. The purpose was to make a man as strong as a crocodile, but I suspect for me that this was all part of a desire to somehow come to terms with the rain forest, to somehow find a better home in it, somehow find a way of looking at that forest eye to eye. Man doesn't belong in the rain forest and everything else does—the frogs, the mosquitoes, the snakes, and these people did—and they acted as a window into this world.

I've tried to leave everything behind—not taking a satellite phone, not communicating with my world. I am living in this other world, then feeling at last, by definition, that when I've found a home there it's time to leave. I never quite land myself into a community open ended. There will be a physical objective, which I prepare for with the help of the local people, and then I feel it's time to come home. I've always had a very strong sense of home, and I couldn't have survived this long if I hadn't had a command of who I am and where I belong.

It took me ten years to be able to go back to the Amazon. My plan was to cross the Amazon Basin at its widest point, an expedition of five thousand, six hundred miles that took me seven and a half months. After endless dramas—including being shot at by drug barons—I came across these people called the Matses. Instead of the crocodile, they had adopted the jaguar as their icon. They had stripes tattooed across their faces, spikes in their nose, like whiskers; but above all was their philosophy of life. They were very quiet and solitary, especially when they hunted, and they seemed to be trying to take on something of the intelligence, the agility, the strength of the jaguar. Very different from the raw aggression of the crocodile. These people were so good to me, they were as close as I've ever found to the *perfect* people, and I'm loath to use that phrase. Nonetheless, I couldn't help but feel that they were who I'd like to be. They were listeners, observant, artistically aware. As usual, they dumped me with the children, and I met this ten-year-old girl called Lucy. Through her I saw the forest as her home and, gradually, as my home

too, in that I could keep on walking through the rain forest without looking over my shoulder wondering when help was coming, and I could survive the rest of the five-hundred-mile journey pretty well alone. For the first time I could see the jungle as nothing exotic, simply as shelter and food and a medicine cabinet. I sort of felt, at last, that I'd found a *place* in the world. After that, I started looking at deserts, which are harder to survive in and, as it turned out, I found them much more exciting. But it took time to discover that. After that I went to the Arctic, which is the hardest environment of all.

PREVIOUS PAGE

I have never thought I want to come back from a journey with something. What I have come back with is that experience, and a few token little things I have used: a wooden bowl that was given to me with water in it by the Mongolians when I walked across the Mongolian desert by myself; bows and arrows that I've hunted with. In my drawing room I have an old family desk where I've written all my books. On the right is a collection of arrows from New Guinea and on the left, one of two war shields that were given to me in Western New Guinea to settle local fighting. On the table is an Iban head and a hunter's shield, the stool is from Papua New Guinea and the rug is Turkish. I still have all my fossils in a broken cabinet on the left of the desk.

RIGHT

In my bedroom I have a wall cabinet filled with some of the half a dozen hats that I've worn on different expeditions. They were with me day and night—I slept against them; there is a bond. I've also kept some of the things my father brought back to me when I was a little boy: the red mask is from Central Africa, the drum was from Kenya and I still have the snake in a jar and the tiny stuffed crocodile. The binoculars survived the First World War; my mother gave me the brandy flask to "keep me going" when I left on my first journey; the champagne glass was a present for my coming of age at 18. To the left on that shelf is a Gabbra Nomad's water gourd and a vessel they use for camel's milk. Below the cabinet on the right, a Shaman's box of "magical objects" rests on a painted chest that was given to my great-grandfather by Rudyard Kipling's father.

I was born a very long time ago, so my memory of those early days is hazy. I remember the villa that we lived in at Istenhegyi út in Budapest. It was in a beautiful old park overlooking the city that was laid out 50 years before by the Hungarian city gardener. It had a very large vineyard and we made wine, which we stored in the basement. I remember there was a small swimming pool, and below it, cut into the side of the hill, was a grotto. The water fell in two streams into ponds further down. There was a hothouse that I later made into my studio. The main house was very old. It had first of all a long room when you came in, and I remember that the wallpaper had French landscapes. Then you went on one side into another very large room with a dining table and a lamp that was partly electricity and partly candles—just in case the power went off. Beyond that was the entrance to a little glass-enclosed area with a piano, where we would gather to sing Christmas songs. Then off the dining room, there were two rooms; one was my mother's salon, and the other was my father's "gentleman's room." In the kitchen I remember there was a place where they kneaded bread before taking it, twice a week, to the bakery to be baked. We had a cook and two maids to clean the house. My mother never cooked. She was an intellectual. I had a brother a year older, and another much younger.

I was five or six when we moved to Vienna. I think it was a nice elegant apartment. I think we stayed about six years —I am not sure. At some point we moved back to Hungary.

When I was young I was a painter, but my mother said, "If you don't want to starve in a garret, you must learn a craft to support yourself." So I apprenticed myself for six months to a potter who was part of the Hungarian Guild of Chimney Sweeps, Oven Makers, Roof Tilers, Well Diggers and Potters in Budapest. It was interesting because for the first time I acquainted myself with people outside my own social stratum. I suddenly saw how people lived in another world. Part of my job was to take the clay when it arrived, and trample it with my bare feet before we could use it. The master would fire the kiln, so I had to stay there overnight to keep it alight. I took it for granted that an apprentice has to do these things. Twice a week a man took the pitchers we had made, in a cart, to the local fair to sell. After that I put an advertisement in the paper offering myself as a craftsman potter. That was in 1926. I was 19. Then I got a job in a shop in Hamburg but it was in very bad surroundings. I was supposed to throw pottery pieces that were all the same, but whether they told me or not, everything I did had some sort of character. They were going to fire me, but decided to

keep me on as a designer. I had rented a room that had a little kitchenette and I enjoyed being at a distance from my own home. My next jobs were in a series of factories, one in Schramberg in the Black Forest. In Berlin I set up a studio where I designed pieces for several factories, including Carstens. Being freelance was not so unusual at that time. I had an apartment downstairs that I shared with my brother and I remember we had large parties in the studio. This was the time of modernism, but I had nothing to do with the Bauhaus.

I was invited by a friend to visit him in Moscow and, after that, I stayed in Russia working for many factories. When I became art director of the Russian Porcelain and Glass Industry, my first task was to go and visit the Russian factories, one after another. I remember arriving at one factory in the provinces and on each of the work tables was a red rose for me. At another factory I went, not to the john, but to the place where the women went pee-pee over a hole in the ground. Suddenly all the women gathered around to see what I was going to produce, because I was an outsider and an interesting person to them. Later I created a very large experimental shop at the Dulevo factory, where all of the activities of the factory were demonstrated. We did everything there except the firing. So I had a very good job, and my own apartment, and one morning, very early, some people came to my home and said they wanted to look at my papers and my photographs. After they had looked at these things, they said "You should come with us—we want to ask you some more questions." They did not look like police, just regular people. I remember it was very bad weather and in the garden where they had parked their car, there were some flowering bushes, which they picked. So we went in this open car with these flowering bushes to Lubyanka prison, where I was photographed from the front and from the side, just like they do with criminals. They told me that the charge was that I had prepared a successful attempt on the life of Stalin. When I said to the investigator, But he's alive—how successful can it have been?, he said, "Don't make bad jokes." There was no explanation. At the time, people were being arrested and told that unless they denounce someone, they would be shot. It appears that one of my colleagues in the factory had reported me; he was later shot. Of course it was a false accusation. This was the beginning of the so-called purges, when thousands and thousands of Russian people were arrested. I was one of the first. Many of them were kept in large cells, but mine was very small. I could walk across from one corner to the other

n six steps. The walls were painted dark green, the floor was stone, and there was one small window high up, and in front of it there were bars and a kind of screen so you could not see more than the sky. There were two beds, one on either side, but only one was open, the other was tied to the wall. Beside that, there was a metal bench coming out of the wall and a metal table. In one corner, a sink to wash and a toilet. I was kept in solitary confinement in this room—cell number four—and it was my home for nearly a year and a half. Every morning they gave me a wooden spoon and then they put some sugar onto that wooden spoon and then they poured some hot water into a metal cup. I also got a kilo of hard black bread for all day long, and then in the evening, fish soup. Every third day I was taken to a courtyard where I could walk around for seven minutes. I remember there was another girl, but she was on one side of the courtyard and I was on the other. After a while, I discovered that if I moved the water faucet a bit, I could talk through the pipe to my neighbor. On the other side, I knocked on the wall in a kind of alphabet code that I'd seen in an old Russian movie. I taught it to her at night, one letter at a time, but it was very dangerous. I did not think that I would ever get out. It seemed like a very long time but then, one day, they brought me out into an office and I don't quite remember what they said, but I was released. After that, they took me with a military escort to the border, and from there to Poland, and finally to Vienna. Eventually I went back to pottery, too, but there was much time in between. When Hitler came to power, I fled to England where I got married, and then finally reestablished myself in New York City.

In 1941 we all settled into an apartment building on Riverside Drive. We were on the fifth floor with grand views of the Hudson river. My parents took the apartment adjacent to us and filled it with the furniture they'd had shipped over from Budapest. I had a studio in the basement with a small display area, but I never sold things from there and I never wanted my own shop. Upstairs we were surrounded by an extraordinary assortment of tenants. Next door lived a family of card-carrying Communists who held actual cell meetings. Also on that floor was a family with no money at all. The father was a retired Episcopalian minister. They had eight children and were poverty stricken beyond belief. Whenever there was a new baby, other people in the building would give them baby clothes, and the younger kids were all sent out to shine shoes. However, their father taught them all Greek and Latin, so they got full scholarships to Andover, Harvard, Yale and so on—and they all became professors. Below us lived a lady who wore a big sequined beret and lots of makeup. As a journalist, she had once interviewed Bernard Shaw. Gustave Becker, the American composer, lived next door to her, and on his wall was a photograph dedicated to him by Brahms.

My brother had bought a house in the woods near New City outside New York City, and insisted that I buy a farmhouse nearby so our children could grow up together—which I did in 1952. It cost 12 thousand dollars and it had one big room that had been a singing studio. Above it I put my workshop and we all live here in the summer. In the early days it was a sort of artists' community, with Lotte Lenya nearby and the playwright Maxwell Anderson, along with various painters and cartoonists. But nowadays nobody talks to his neighbor, whom you might not see for 20 years. My house is filled with antiques, most of which I've bought at auctions. I would often buy pieces that other people weren't interested in. I have an Elizabethan chest that I bought for 10 dollars in the 1960s. I could not be held back from going to auctions. I often bought material from buildings that were being torn down. I got old metal fire escapes from Harlem, and wood, marble, and slate, and factory windows. If I see a chair I like, I buy it. Now I guess I have too many chairs. I've also designed some furniture, mostly tables.

Last November 13th (2005), I was 99.

I still design pottery in my studio. I am happy to do commissions, but I don't wait for people to ask me; if I think of something I want to make, I do it. If I have an idea in the middle of the night I write it down or I draw it. During most of the year, I am in the large apartment near Columbia University which has been in our family since 1940 (a block from our old Riverside Drive home). I like being surrounded by my beautiful Biedermeier antiques, many from those days in Budapest, as well as some of the furniture, woodware, and glassware that I have designed, and also my beautiful and useful pottery.

PREVIOUS PAGE
An 18th-century cabinet containing my Hyalin set, used on special occasions.
LEFT
My studio where I work with my design assistant, Olivia, surrounded by samples of my designs.
OVERLEAF
The big living room (30 by 40 feet), added on as a singing studio in the 1930s, was furnished mostly by auctions.

When I went to design school in Paris 20 years ago, there was not the same interest among young people—in their home—as there is now. Things have changed a lot. Twenty-year-olds were not that involved in decoration at that time. Even now, I see many people who do interesting things, but they're not that involved in what they have in their own apartment, actually. It's the same with what they wear. Just because you are an industrial designer, it doesn't mean that you are involved with your clothes. I don't understand this, because everything goes together. Anyway, at that time there was only Habitat, and that was it. We're talking about the middle of the 1980s. It was before the new culture of quite cheap objects, but still very modern, very good. The flea market was providing good things, and the Salvation Army and places like that. Everyone started being very interested in the 1950s and Formica and that kind of thing.

I didn't get my own place until quite recently; at that time, my boyfriend's place was my apartment, I guess, but we did nothing to it except looking in the garbage and picking up things in the street that we found. We had no money, but it was fun. We got a lot of chairs, and lamps, some I still have actually. We were in the neighborhood where all the craftsmen making jewelry worked, and they had a lot of technical pieces of furniture—cabinets with little drawers. My office now is full of these things. In Paris, we have these big green containers that the city put in certain streets for a week, and everybody puts their junk in them. So we managed to get the schedule of where the containers would be each week and we went out especially to look in them. That apartment was a really good one; it was on the roof of the building. Actually, it became full of mess because of the containers. Nice things, but maybe you can have too many nice things after a while.

My parents' apartment was very messy too and it still is, with many treasures everywhere. We lived in the 16th arrondissement in front of the Bois de Boulogne. I remember lots of big, big black insects flying about—dragonflies—very sweet, very nice. It was a modern apartment with a balcony and big windows. It was not that big, one hundred square meters, but it had one huge space rather than many little rooms. I think they bought the apartment before it was built so maybe they asked for some changes, less walls and things like that. At that time—the mid '50s—you had a choice

between old pieces of furniture from your family, or nothing. They were looking for some help from a decorator and they asked Charlotte Perriand, but she said, "I can't, I have too much work in Japan," so then they hired some students of hers. It was a very avant-garde thing to do. My father was a shoe designer, so he led the way, but my mother was happy; she liked to be different and to show off with new things that other people didn't have. My grandfather had been quite a terrible character in that he was running a very avant-garde ladies' shoe shop in rue du Faubourg Saint-Honoré. He hired Salvador Dali to do his window displays before the artist became famous. My father was also quite adventurous. My parents quickly became friends with the architects, so they did it more or less together. This was before I was born, but I know they had very many ideas themselves. There were no fights, they agreed.

My parents always slept in the living room. I remember there were a lot of plumbing problems too—mostly because we were forgetting that the bath was overflowing—and so I had some opportunities to check the other apartments and I was so shocked. There was such a different mood: old carpets, curtains, bourgeois pieces of furniture. So quite early on, I noticed that my friends' parents' apartments were very different from ours, and I was almost ashamed. I wasn't sure if ours was better or not. I didn't know. When I was 16, I was dreaming of having a very neo-romantic atmosphere: small, dark, and completely different from my parents, with old sofas and old drapes and a little dusty. Not modern at all. They only changed the apartment once, in 1989. That means they'd been there almost 40 years in the same way. After my two sisters and I had all left, they remade it. They removed the wall of my sister's room and incorporated that space into the one huge L-shaped room—a combined salon, living room, and bedroom. They still sleep in the living room but now the dining table is further from the bed.

I lived at home until I was 25, but I spent part of my time at my boyfriend Christophe's place. Eventually we got married and our rooftop apartment got too small so we found one opposite the Folies Bergère that was very big—one room was 70 square meters. But the neighbors were traditional and horrible and we stayed only a very short while, then we got divorced. After that, I moved with my new boyfriend to a very bourgeois apartment with many rooms, wooden floors, very old-fashioned. A big difference. We stayed there for a year, but the apartment wasn't the only reason I was depressed. My boyfriend died in a motorcycle accident. The thing I remember the most was the mice. Tons of mice. There was a bakery downstairs, so I think they were having a lot of fun. I was living with mice in the kitchen, running on the bed, like a nightmare.

Around this time I had started my own design agency, called Tse & Tse, designing objects: vases, lamps, tableware, and things like that. We still are, actually. My business partner, Sigolene Prebois, and I had studied in the design school together and, of course, when we left we couldn't get a job. In fact, we didn't even feel like getting one, so we got a workshop and just locked ourselves in that place wondering, what shall we do? As soon as we had a few things ready, we met the owner of an old design store called Sentou who was just starting to get more modern. They loved our work and we were free to display it the way we wanted and to make exhibitions when we felt like it. We never needed to open our own shop. It was the beginning of the '90s, and the Baroque style of Garouste and Bonetti and people like that was very fashionable. Lots of gold and red. On the other hand, you had Habitat and Ikea, but there was nothing in between. So our work filled that gap. It was very minimalist and very different from the rest and that's why people appreciated it.

Anyway, after a year I felt strong enough to finally move to my own apartment. I completely focused on that for two years. I worked on it every weekend. It was like a big game, like therapy. I was able to breathe. Up until then, I'd always done things with men, so they had their say. Now I could do only what I wanted to do. I thought I wouldn't stay long, so I made all sorts of experiments with color because it didn't matter. It was done step by step. By instinct. I really managed to say something about myself. My ambition is to find a new big apartment which I will buy, as close as possible to where I am now. I'd let my boyfriend do what *he* wants in the next apartment. For me, I've said what I wanted to say. Now, I'm much more relaxed.

If I moved to anywhere else, it would be to India. The first thing is to have a really good base in Paris, then rent something in New Delhi or somewhere. I want to live in two places. I love travel. It's very

necessary inspiration, not only for my work, but inspiration for life. The first time I went to India—in '96—it was a big shock. I just loved it: the energy, and the way the people are so strong. It's very good to see that people live differently and with different things in mind, actually.

Now I think that there are many more people getting involved in decorating their apartments. The market in France has become huge. Ten years ago, there were maybe three decorating magazines; now there are tons, and every fashion magazine has a few pages about decoration. On television too (I forgot about that, because I have no television). We never had television at home, it's another world to me. I find it frightening. The politics and the news. I think people are too horrible to watch, and the entertainment drives me crazy. I like the theater, I prefer live things.

OVERLEAF
You could see this room as the culmination of my years of searching the Paris streets for green containers, though some of the folding metal and wood garden chairs came from flea markets. The enormous table was used to display and sell rolls of fabrics at my aunt and uncle's jersey-fabric showroom, La Soie de Paris. The fairground-style lights along the ceiling have a variety of different colored and shaped bulbs from India, and the boxes and cabinets on the wall contain Christmas balls of all sizes and colors. In the corner, the paper lamp is one of the 1950s Araki light sculptures by Isamu Noguchi, the Japanese-American sculptor who studied in Paris in 1927 under Constantin Brancusi.

FOLLOWING PAGES LEFT
The wall between the living room and the kitchen was removed and replaced by a red painted column, and all of the cabinets have open backs; I like seeing the shapes of the cooking equipment. Along the counter-top is a flower container that we designed, which you can display any way you want, straight or round.

FOLLOWING PAGES RIGHT
My bedroom is short of storage space, so some of my clothes are kept on a high shelf, in giant shopping bags from India that I like as much for their patterns as for their flexibility. The boxes on the wall are feta cheese containers given by the next-door Greek grocery, and the fabric on the bed is one of dozens that I have brought back from Asia.

I was lucky with my first home in London. I lived in it and loved it for 30 years. At the heart of my happiness was the house itself. Light and reflective of light, much of it was paneled in ancient curved, soft pine. The house was rustic in the basement, cottagey on the top floor, and the paneling on the middle floors was so old and had been so often painted during its three-hundred-year life that it had taken on a character far removed from its original, intended, formality. It was worn and rounded and conveyed the patina of comfort and time. I have lived since then in an unsoftened plaster house and made my "home" in the garden.

Home is the place where one can cast off one's layers of other selves and rest in one's own skin. For all that, what reminds me or speaks of home most are perhaps the comfortable chairs (the chair is the lap of the room); the sight of a cup, especially the hand-painted ancient Quimper cups from Brocante holidays in Brittany; drinking morning coffee from David Garland's beautiful shaped cups; filling my favorite bluey-gray, yew-fired glaze beaker with this week's flowers from the garden—any week will do; clean sheets; my bed. Collections of inherited, lent, worn furniture; cloth—old French market cloth, Collier Campbell cloth, embroidered samples; a collection of seedpods, and all the good memories of journeys they hold; colored walls; harmonies; paintings in seemingly accidental colors—some sinking in to the wall color, some making themselves clear and separate; all these spell home for me.

The act of sharing at home, of putting shiny glasses on a table and choosing a special tablecloth, is a pleasure. It says we are at home and ready to eat together, to talk, laugh, cry, elbows on the table.

I was born in Manchester, where we lived in a newly built crescent. When I went back to see the house much later I appreciated its modernity: it had very long windows which let in lots of light. I still absolutely love light, more than anything else probably. Most of what I remember from the time is running to visit our many remarkable and intriguing neighbors, all refugees who had fled from Hitler. Later, when I went to my school friends' houses, I noticed that their front rooms were always clean and neat. Nobody seemed to go into them and I gradually realized that they were being saved for best. We had no such thing in our house; everything was for every day. Yet that was not because my parents didn't care about their home: actually they minded very much about their surroundings and valued their possessions and the space that these occupied. Over the years they commissioned pieces of furniture, including a desk that my sister has and the oak table that is now in my kitchen. My father was an academic, a scientist, and later a pharmacologist in commerce. He was interested in poetry, writing, and the theater,

but above all he was interested in nature and nutrition. Before I was born, he'd worked in Belfast and had done research into the Irish famine. He wrote a paper suggesting there were so many cattle in Ireland that if the Irish had drunk a pint of milk every day and not relied so heavily on potatoes, there would have been no malnutrition. My mother was an actress. She was working on many evenings, and was hugely well organized. Every Sunday she made lists—on lined blocks of paper—of menus for the week ahead, and wrote out everybody's daily timetables! My mother had a good eye for, and was very moved by, color. Her purchase of the John Piper sitting-room drapes seemed the major focus of our home. As she needed each new thing for the room, she would take cuttings of the fabric up to London so that she could harmonize the colors and textures of her purchases with John Piper—she allowed him to rule the roost. On one occasion when we went on a choosing expedition, we got on the bus and my mother realized that she had forgotten her pile of cuttings. "Never mind," she said, "'you'll remember the colors." And of course I could remember the colors. I didn't know that was particular to me, but she did. She must have been aware of, and sensitive to, my feeling for color early on; when she was planning to give me a small table and chair for Christmas when I was about three, she asked me what color I would like them to be. I said red and yellow, and I admire her because she went ahead and painted them in those colors, never suggesting that I might like different ones. It was my mother who introduced me to painting. She bought me powder paints and drawer-lining paper to paint on. I made her mix the paints to get the colors as I wanted them, but then wouldn't let her into the room where I was painting until I was finished. Later, I drew cartoons too; I could capture the mood of people, rather as my mother did as an actress. I drew ladies in patterned dresses, trying to see how many different patterns looked good on one dress. Painting and drawing was an expected pastime, in the same way that going for walks with my father to look at insects, birds' nests, and animals was. The seasons, chalk, and fossils—he alerted us to these and to the magnificent, abundant patterns in nature. We spent hours looking at the patterns on butterflies' wings, for example.

We moved to Liverpool during the Second World War. The house was far too big so we had lodgers upstairs, but what I most associate with that house is my lifelong friendship with Matisse. Among the bookshelves was a book about him. It had a cover of oatmeal-colored linen with the title "Matisse" printed in fantastic, special blue ink. I climbed up and got that book down almost every day of my life. I think it was Matisse who said that when a person got up from looking at one of his paintings, it should be like getting up from a really comfortable chair. That's certainly how I felt, and feel. I associate that house with poetry too, because my father began to teach me how to read it there; and with the garden. My father was a keen gardener and the space was filled with vegetables and fruit, ducks and chickens, but also a massive chestnut tree with my swing. Later we moved to the south of England, to Hertfordshire, where my sister Sarah was born. There the garden had enough room to learn how to do long jump; it also taught me something about the concept of using color in the garden. One year my mother planted an enormous amount of wallflowers. I remember being very struck by the fact that you could choose to have such wonderful colors and couldn't understand why everybody didn't do it. When I was about nine, I went to stay with my paternal grandmother. Her home was very different from ours: she had black-stained oak furniture; she made special food that was particularly wholesome; and she had views about cloth. She would only wear the colors of country landscapes—the greens and browns of fields and trees. She had absolutely no time for the vulgarities of other colors, like pink. She wore creamy-colored satin collars next to her skin. She made all her own clothes, became a couturière, and taught me to sew.

What I really wanted to do was to become a painter, and yet I knew I wasn't Matisse. I could make clothes quite well, and one day, when looking for dress fabrics at Derry and Toms department store, I found the fabrics were absolutely hideous, and I thought to myself, I know what I could do—I could paint for textiles. The conviction came just like that. At the same time I was liberated from not being able to paint to being able. I was politically motivated to produce beautiful cloth for the mass market. I didn't believe in an elite. When I first came upon William Morris designs, I found his patterns repellent, his renditions of nature seemed so stifling. It was an echo of the time, long before, when my parents commissioned a local artist to handprint our bedroom drapes; I'd found the results terribly disappointing—they looked so plonkity-plonk, with no mystery in where and how the pattern repeated. I thought it would be far more wondrous and glorious to make a painting that would disguise the essential systematic repeat of the printing process. I wanted the design in textile to offer respite, to encourage the eye to trace subtle movement; find stopping places and spaces; free the soul; take the spirit on a sort of wandering journey, free of thought. I loved that sensation and I still love it. In the early 1960s manufacturers bought their patterns from freelance designers, and when I approached Liberty's in 1961, I decided that if they bought two designs, I would become a textile designer. In fact they bought six. When I left their office, a man called Gustav Weiner followed me out with the additional comment, "By the way, you can draw so you can come back." I didn't know it then, but what he understood was painting for textile. He commissioned many designs by telephone. On one occasion when I asked him, what sort of size flowers do you want?, he replied, "The size fairies can go into." We both knew what size that was. I treasure that memory, because it tells you that a textile designer needs to work with a good producer. When I married and had two babies, my sister Sarah, who was at school, began to help me at weekends. I find it touching and amazing that I expected her to do exactly what I needed; she went on to art school and studied painting and became an absolutely marvelous designer in her own right and my lifelong partner in pattern-making.

I can now almost only draw and paint in a pattern-repeat size. I love all the magical things that color does, whether it's printed or woven. The thing about a color is that it isn't that color until it's surrounded by other colors. Colors that may not be sympathetic to one another can be made to become utterly sympathetic by juggling with their weight, softness, shroudedness, or sharpness. I find experimenting a never-ending delight. A design, if it's good, can be made fantastic with different color emphasis. The same design can be turned this way and that, when produced in different colorways. Creating a collection of designs in all their colors takes between a year and a half and two years. This process is like a long journey and it's amazing how much one learns along the way.

Like art, poetry, and music, design is an attempt to bridge the changing internal and external worlds, and despite the time lag between the initial paintings and the arrival of the bolts of fabric in the shop, there is a synchronicity between the impact which the designer feels when that bridge is formed, and which people feel when they buy the fabric much later. We run a series of workshops and ask participants to bring in their favorite pieces of cloth. When they speak about them, it is clear that what is in the fabric is not only the designers' narrative but also the participants' memories and imagination. I have complete faith that if we can feel it, we can paint it. If we can paint it, then the recipient will feel it too; and as experience and vitality, life is shared.

PREVIOUS PAGE AND RIGHT
The best description I have of my garden is in *The Good Gardens Guide 2006*: "A garden of secrecy and surprise, created by an artist for whom gardening and textile design are mutually inspiring. The conservatory, with its pretty frame of blue and red stained glass, looks across to a winding path almost submerged under a wash of vibrant, scented, or textural perennials."

From the time that I was a proper sentient being, I noticed people's houses. I noticed the smell of a house and I could relate houses to the people in them and the way they lived. I'm interested in all the "who" questions. Who is it? What sort of person is this house speaking for? Some homes I like more than others. From the 1980s on, I just thought, bloody hell, what a lot of money they've spent, sometimes to absolutely ghastly effect. I just noticed the degree to which people at every level started changing things and regarding home as a style statement or a status symbol, so that houses were much less "organic" than they used to be as they got very consciously "fixed" all over, all at one go. I can remember in the early 1980's seeing my first newly acquired, newly done loft on the Thames, on which a great deal of money had been spent, thinking, oh this is absolutely fantastic—a new way of life—I want it, for several minutes running, before completely going off them. I'm trying to remember what my first place of my own was like. I think I spent about two and six on it. It was completely basic. It was in Bayswater—a bed-sitter. Almost Notting Hill, which wasn't smart and expensive then. I wasn't bursting to get away from old stuff, or to avoid new stuff. Nobody talked about "eclectic" then. You had what you had and some of it you liked. You couldn't just throw things away. My parents thought that if you wanted a chest of drawers for a spare room, you didn't go to a new shop, you went to Portobello Road, bought something Victorian, painted it white and maybe changed the handles.

One of my earliest memories of my parents' place in Hampstead is of two chairs that, to very small me, seemed huge, absolutely throne-like. I didn't know what they were, but of course I've got those chairs now, and I also know all the fancy fogy words to describe them. One is an early 17th-century Wainscot chair from somewhere in the country, and the other is a Restoration chair, as in restoration of Charles Two. Very crudely carved, it has fat cherubs holding a crown. We lived in this part of north London because of my grandmother's frustrations. She was a talented musician who went to the Paris Conservatoire. Lizzy Whittington won lots of medals, but as a woman then she wasn't allowed to perform in public. Eventually she was bundled off to South Africa where she met and married my grandfather, also a runaway, and started making babies. Back in Sussex, what should these babies do in a more permissive world, but become serious musicians, and move—as most artistic types did in the 30's and 40's—to Hampstead. So when I was a child it was almost a commune, with my grandmother and her musician daughters and my parents all living in the same street. Our house was the larger chunk of a very large, and externally, quite hideous Victorian house—the rooms inside were OK. I've inherited my musician maiden aunts' house and one day I'll probably live there. when I was very small I had a crone—not a smart nanny—who made me tiny lunches, which I'd usually sick up, and later on au pairs. No brothers or sisters. My mother loved furnishing the house and there were really only three sources of "things." My parents haunted the cheaper auction

rooms—not Christie's, King Street—and Portobello Road. Then there was stuff they'd got from my grandmother; and finally—the holy grail of right-thinking Hampstead middle-class types, and the absolute source of political and aesthetic correctness in all things—Heal's, in Tottenham Court Road. I've got a lot of their stuff now—I cherry picked it. But curiously when they died, and I looked through everything, somehow most of those desirable-again Scandy-modern things had vanished. Worn out, perhaps, or been consciously edited out as my parents reverted to brown furniture. That perky 60s' stuff had gone. There was constant gentle evolution, new drapes, things recovered, pictures always moving around. My dad was a civil engineer, so we had a lot of architecture books and books on, you know, bridges and Powerful Buildings.

After that first bed-sitter, I had a series of apartments and then I bought a house in Queens Park and that was really a bloody nice Edwardian house. The man I sold it to keeps on telling me how much it's worth now. The area has become tremendously fashionable. I was a pioneer! It's fascinating how things move on. People are much more ambitious and they do more now. He's done all the things that I only *thought* about like opening up the loft, and converting the second bedroom into a big en-suite bathroom. I'd thought, that's such a waste of a whole bedroom. But I did make it quite nice and I enjoyed it there for ages.

Now I write for the *Independent* newspaper twice, sometimes three times a week, as well as being a consultant to businesses and organizations like the British Council. One thing I look at is design fads which will end in tears, because Brits have gone for house makeovers in such a big way. Some friends of mine spent 99 pounds on a kitchen knife—a *knife!* I think a knife should cost around five quid. How can you possibly spend that much? The answer is, when you think it's either a professional instrument or a piece of sculpture. The terrible thing is, of course, that I'm complicit to some extent in this. The likes of me and other management consultants have taught businesses how to add value to things. This isn't a faucet, it's a sculpture by a known designer. Its a modern classic. Therefore it's a completely different pricing proposition.

The home now has become fashion-ized. People are prepared to do absolutely anything, even to change the basic structure. But amazingly enough, given all the information, the ambition, and the resources that people have, the results are often completely horrible. And they're horrible in a certain way. Some of the most expensive houses in the universe, ones you see in smart real estate agent's glossies look so illiterate and so awful. It's a style that's not really modern so much as bleak. No character; no expression; no art; absolutely no commitment. It's wipe-clean life. If I ever thought I liked that, I now know that I don't.

RIGHT

The staircase is practically the first thing you see when you enter my house, which was built in 1813. The dining room is through the doorway on the right, and the kitchen is at the far end of the hall.

The idea for my first lamp came when I was staying with my first wife in a very cheap pensione in Venice in 1966. We were lying on the bed with the only light in the room a dangling bulb, you know? That was the moment that I fell in love with the light bulb. It was like a sensual experience. I realized that the traditional light bulb, invented by Thomas Alva Edison in 1879, is the most beautiful symbiosis between poetry and industrial innovation. I drew my design on the spot—the way I could see it—and later I went to a glassblower to get it made. The metal part I made back in Munich, and I called it "Bulb." I showed it to a few people who said, "Can I have one?." When I started to design lamps I had no idea who Castiglioni or Magistretti were, but I soon learned, and of course they became my heroes and, later, my friends. At first I was crazy about form, but soon I recognized that the *type* of light was more important than the shape.

Growing up on the tiny island of Reichenau in Lake Constance in Germany, on the border of Switzerland, I was always aware of the quality of light on the water, of reflections, of light in the trees. Poplar trees have leaves of two different colors, dark on top and light underneath, and when the wind blows, it was like a kind of impressionist painting—very light and very cheerful. I was surprised that when I started to work with light and to think about light in more depth, all these things were still there in my mind. When I designed the light for Issey Miyake's shop in Savile Row in London—it was a big cloud with three thousand silver braided leaves on a steel spring, which moved with ventilators—it came straight from my observation of those poplar trees. When you see bits of paper caught up in a little whirlwind spiral, when paper dances on the street, I'm very hot on moments like this, but I can't say that it was the inspiration for my Zettel'z light. Paper is one of my favorite materials because it's soft; however, I think it's always nice when the yin and yang qualities are there: soft but also strong. I've also done lamps that were inspired by Rigatoni and by tea strainers.

My earliest memory is as a child, sitting with my brothers and sisters—there were five of us—on the sofa listening to my mother read fairytale books, or singing. It wasn't a grand house, there were five rooms and the furniture was quite beat up, inherited pieces. We had poor people's wallpaper, that means the wall was painted and then the pattern was put on with a rubber roller; you chose between abstract or flower patterns. I remember my mother painting it with my eldest brother. Life was difficult for my parents for many reasons. It was wartime, my father was very into Buddhism at that time and he was very strict with us. We were only 60 kilometers away from Zurich, but we couldn't go into Switzerland. Actually Zurich, when I did go, it was my first big step into the world; being exposed to the paintings of Matisse and Picasso and these artists. I never finished high school; my father died in 1946 and my oldest brother, who was 21, said "Look, you have to learn a profession." I had a choice of typographer or a furrier and I chose type. I rode my bicycle 14 kilometers each way every day and became an apprentice at a printer who produced newspapers and books. It was a job; when you are 15 years old you are very focused on work, but most of all sex is on your mind. I'm very glad that I had typography as a base, as a trade, because you are forced to look at how letters are done, how to space them, and to be very precise, and besides, we could read wonderful books that we printed. We had deadlines too—oh, the masters were tough with us; we worked 52 hours a week.

I didn't move away from home until I was 19. I wanted to move into the big wide world. I had been on some little vacations: I'd been to Italy, to France, to England, and to Scotland, all by hitchhiking. I looked mostly at history, and at people. Human beings are, for me, the most important thing in my life. I had a fantastic shock when I went to England and I found that it was so colorful; all those brightly colored front doors. I noticed that they had houses that were totally different, there was daylight coming in from both sides, north and south or east and west. In Paris I was impressed by how much attention the French paid to what they ate and what they shopped for; the richness of what I saw in the markets. I also got to see people's homes; hitchhiking through the country, I would be given a lift by farmers who asked me to come and have lunch or dinner, and then later they'd put me back on the road. This was the 1950s. I couldn't speak very good English, but I found the British very friendly and they made me feel really welcome. The French less so, because when I got in the automobile they'd say, "Where are you from?," and when I said Germany they'd stop and kick me out.

Back in Munich, I studied design, commercial art let's say, at art school for three years, but I knew I wanted to move out of Germany as soon as I could. As often as possible, we students would hitchhike to Paris for three or four days to get the rub off from the flair that Paris had at that time. But the focus for me was the United States and finally, when I was 27, I was able to emigrate. I headed for New York, of course, and for the first three weeks I was just with big, wide open eyes, but I had the feeling that I had to go west, so after a few months that's what I did, to San Francisco, where my girlfriend, who had been studying in Paris, joined me. We got a one-room apartment with a little kitchenette, and people would say, "Are you married?" "Yes, of course we are," because at that time it was illegal. We had no money; we furnished it ourselves with secondhand things from the Salvation Army. We had one of those beds which you fold out;

the springs were so strong that when you pulled it down you had to jump on it immediately or it would fold up again. We got married, but my wife was pushing at that time to go back to Europe, not to Germany but to England. I wanted to stay on for a while as I had a good job. To live in London was our dream, but when we got there, the immigration restrictions were so tough that we had to go back to Germany. My wife was pregnant by then and she wanted to be near her mother. So somehow we got stuck, having been away for three years; those first few months back were very tough for me but somehow I managed. I was doing graphic design projects, but I was getting a bit tired of clients who would say, "Why can't I have purple instead of green?" (I couldn't stand purple); or "My wife says we should do it like this." That's when I saw the light bulb.

In the beginning, I knew that I couldn't make the turnover I needed with just my so-called modern line, so I had to invent next to it some more conservative lamps with lampshades, a little bit of nouveau riche taste. Those things sold very well and brought in some money. At the same time, I could employ eight women doing nothing but lampshades, so I started to try to help people in need; women who had been divorced, with children, all this sort of thing. I became aware of how people live, and how difficult it is for some people to make ends meet. I had a list of the top interiors stores in Germany and I drove around and got orders, then I had the problem of producing them. Some designs I had no idea how I was going to make, but that didn't limit my imagination. If you have an idea, there's always a way to realize it. Today I have just been to see a big company who are doing really incredible research into new lighting techniques. I am really attached to working with new techniques and to making things that are, let us say, smaller or touch-sensitive, things like that. These are definitely the greatest influence on lighting. When I first came up with my system called YaYaHo in 1984 it really changed everything. With the use of a transformer, two or more low-voltage cables were stretched across the room, and a variety of small halogen fittings were suspended from it. What I really liked is that people could make their own arrangement of the components, the way they liked it. I don't like to be a dictator; I like to have people join me in the creative process. Now it has been so badly copied by so many companies, but it had a big influence. Since those early days I've done spontaneously what I feel. I never do market research. I'm not involved in trends, or interior fashions—not that I'm conscious of; I follow my instinct, what I feel I have to do. Sometimes it is difficult to fight with my team who say "OK, but you should do *this*"; sometimes I listen but most of the time I don't. After all, it's my own risk, and I think that risk is so important, in all levels of life. I'm still taking

risks. I had no shop ever, except in the last six years I have had a showroom in New York showing our products, examples of our projects and one-offs. Retailing is a totally different thing and I'm not good at it, but I have a good helper, and New York is the window to the world; a lot of people come and see what we do, it's amazing. I think at this moment, there are a lot of lights out there, but they're done without considering the power of magic light has. People really neglect the mysterious part of light. They look at it only as a function. They choose by the shape and not the effect. Sometimes when I go to restaurants I wear a baseball cap to avoid the glare, it can be very painful. Mind you, there are wonderful restaurants too, where the light is done very carefully. I hate those places where you see just the light beams —downlighters—but have nothing to look at, nothing for the imagination, I'm fed up with it.

When I go to someone's house, I do look at their books, but mostly I look at the people who live there, and of course I see light too. Sometimes I cannot bear it and I make a remark or I move their lights. No wonder you're not happy with this dreary light, I say, come, let's try different things, take that lamp and put it on the floor and see the reflection and its effect. What I would like to say to people is that if they find a light atmosphere in a restaurant or in a hotel that they feel well and pleasant in, they should try to recreate it. Most of all, however, I come back to the simple naked light bulb. Have a few of them on a wire and place them high or low, below eye level. Don't just have one or two light sources, have more and turn them on depending on your mood. Dimmers are important too. It will take a few years, but in the future there are definitely things in research that will make our light world very, very exciting. I've never used my own home as a showplace; I live in a "tree house," I live more like a freak, it's chaos. I use a lot of prototypes here, I experiment, I look at a design and I say, no, it could be better, and so on. I do have some nice pieces in my home, but I'm not particularly *well furnished*. Already a picture hanging on a wall is a problem for me; I'd rather have it standing on the floor, leaning.

OVERLEAF

I live on the outskirts of Munich. On the third and top floor, the kitchen is connected to the living room, part of one big, open space. I cook and I invite people here less often than I used to, since I'm away a lot. Also, as you see, not only the bookcase, but also the dining table is full of books and other things. Because we were tight for space, I designed the staircase so that the bottom three steps can be pulled away to give access to a kind of closet or storage room behind, but in fact you can just climb over it. It's not very comfortable but it works all right.

When I started in publishing, I didn't want to write about decorating, I wanted to write serious things, but the publisher persuaded me to do a decorating issue at *Philadelphia* magazine. I said, I don't want to tell people how to decorate with a staple gun. This was the 1960s, before Martha Stewart. What a fool I was!

So I started doing some very amusing stories. I always say that the home is a tremendously sensitive subject, because there's so many things you can tell about people from their homes. Whenever I interview people now, for beauty, I ask if I can see their house. When I interviewed Sophia Loren I said, I really don't know a person until I see their house. So I went to see her home and I discovered that everything was so voluptuous, all the lamps were like big boobs and big buttocks. I wrote about interiors from 1969 to 1980. One of the big things I used to see was the "rope across the living room" syndrome: when the house was all fancy and there was a room in the back that they lived in, watched TV, read the newspapers, and they never lived in the beautiful rooms. Maybe you could say that about this place, though I don't have that room in the back.

One of my earliest memories is of my parents fighting over the furniture arrangements. My father was always pushing my mother to redecorate, so I had this major decorating fetish in the family. I guess that you would call my parents upwardly mobile; my father always wanted to have a beautiful home, he was always hiring decorators. When I was very young, my mother's best friend was a decorator, and my father would be arranging the furniture and saying, "Should we get this new?" One day he'd come home with gorgeous satin quilts. His parents were poor, he never went to college, but in the home he fancied himself knowing more than my mother, which I think was unusual for the 1930s. My mother was very insecure about her taste, but she knew about quality—her parents were upholsterers. Both my parents were born in America, but their parents were immigrants from Hungary and Austria. My father was artistic in some sense. He was in the wholesale paper business and sold a lot of decorative papers that were used to line trunks, boxes, shoes, and whatnot. Beautiful patterned papers. At the time, I wanted to be a dress designer and I made a whole scrapbook of clothes made from those papers—paper dolls' clothes. We were always entertaining. My parents were constantly having parties, parties, parties. They had loads of friends.

When I was born we lived in Forest Hills, a part of New York City very close to the 1939 World's Fair, which was also in Queens just two train stops away. I don't know how many times I went through the "World of Tomorrow" exhibit. It was the most spectacular thing a child could ever do. You sat in these moving chairs, like little trains, and were taken through. All around you were panoramas of the future. That was all I did at the World's Fair. That was why I got so interested in modern design. Then when I was 11, we moved to Great Neck—a modernish house that we rented from, I think, a celebrity gossip columnist. It was a terrific house but, again, the decorating was always an issue. There was nothing meant to "last for life" in my family; it was beautiful "for the moment." The house was almost art deco. I went back to see it some years ago, and it definitely had a lot of art-deco influences. There was a glass-brick wall, and in the living room my parents installed this fantastic marble fireplace with animals carved on it and whatnot. It was a big purchase and they were very excited, but they were putting it into a house we only lived in for two years, we didn't own.

Then we moved to Riverside Drive in Manhattan when I was 13, and they hired B. Altman to do the house; a lot of famous decorators started there, including Mario Buatta. I remember our dining room had hand-painted chinese wallpaper and I can still picture the drapes—the most beautiful shade of peach; sheer but not too sheer, with apple-green satin swags on top. They were gorgeous. Then in the living room it was all dark green—that was very popular in those days—and we had a baby grand piano, which they wanted me to play. At around this time, my parents hired William Pahlmann, the famous decorator, to do my bedroom and my brother's bedroom, and I can tell you everything that was in my room: I had a chartreuse bouclé headboard, a plaid taffeta dust ruffle, and I think probably a bedspread with plaid pink and blue and chartreuse. There was also a "real" dressing table with a plaid skirt, and the wallpaper—I think my mother chose that —it had bunches of roses all over the walls and the ceiling. I remember I used to count the bunches to go to sleep.

When I got to college all the students, my friends doing architecture, were designing the lobbies of modern office buildings. Later my friend Sunny worked on the UN (United Nations) building. At Yale, I was in drama school studying theatrical design, but through Sunny I became very interested in architecture. Not in decorators. I've never hired a decorator. In fact, I worked as a decorator for a while when I got married. The only people that I thought were better than me were architects. But I became very minimalist. When I finally became engaged and I was moving to Philadelphia, I had to choose my silver, my china, and my glass for wedding presents. I had to register. So my mother and I started going shopping and we were fighting the whole way. She wanted me to be traditional. I wanted a Jens Risom sofa, then I had Herman Miller, a Saarinen chair, Vladimir Kagan. I chose the most beautiful silver, which I still have; it was totally plain H. Nils silver. I was extremely rigid, I wanted to be everything my mother was not. I was the bride; the bride wins! My husband didn't care. He was a doctor, he didn't know. He thought I walked on water.

My first apartment was written up in a magazine—I was the most modern person in Philadelphia when I moved there in 1950. Everyone came and swooned over my apartment because it was so modern. Later, we moved to this huge townhouse in Philadelphia, but with not a lot of money left to redecorate or renovate it. I built this fantastic dressing table using old pear crates. I was very creative. Then I decided I'd have our bedroom done by an architect so I asked Bob Venturi; he was a friend of mine. He designed this hysterical bedroom for us, which we never built. The architects looked at this couple—Sam and Joan Kron—and they drew a line down this huge long room and they put the bed in the middle and they divided the bedspread in half in two different colors. They put long closets on both walls, and in 12-foot-high letters they put "Sam," and on the other side, "Joan." They saw us as split. We never built it, but their sketches were great, so clever. We got divorced instead.

Then I married Jerry and we moved to New York. We were both divorced and both poor, so I did something very clever using metal cabinets that cost only 20 dollars each from an office supply company. That was the beginning of resourcefulness in decorating, and one of the seeds of High Tech. Later, with my friend Suzanne Slesin, we did a book about that whole design ethic. We still live in that same apartment. At first we had it all white tiles and platforms, very 1970s. Then about six or seven years ago, I ripped it all out. I have gone through many redecorations. I've had a rich decorating life in all of my houses. Everything was always photographed and written up. Because of High Tech, I always felt obliged to live that sort of life, and then one day I said, look, there's another side of you that loves really frou-frou things. I'm going to express myself, my total self; not only will I be modern, but I'll be eclectic. That's when I was able to finally put up all the flea-market finds from my trips to Paris over the years. Now I feel that I don't have to prove anything to anybody. I used to say that my son Daniel

was going to be an architect. I would take him to the library and we'd take out books on Le Corbusier and Frank Lloyd Wright. He's six years old, and I'm reading him architecture books. I'd tell people, he's the only kid in Philadelphia who knows what a cantilever is. He turned out to be a photographer. He has great taste. He's turned into me. He says he's so rigid in his taste that there's no comfortable place to sit in his house. You can just see how life repeats itself. He is such a purist. So I say, I can't sit down in those chairs that are so low and hard to get out of. Can't you buy a sofa for your mother?

OVERLEAF

This is my eclectic living room. For the longest time I had been looking high and low for a chair for myself, and eventually it became my obsession. I wanted something that was showy but not overscaled; something glamorous and very comfortable. Then I found this chair in a furniture showroom. It was in gold leaf and black leather, and I thought this is it. I wanted to cover it in black satin, but my friend Mario Buatta said, "No, you're going to have stripes." So I got swatches of every striped satin that there was in New York and I spread them all out, and he came over and we chose one. In the '60s, I was very pop arty, putting on art exhibitions in Philadelphia. At the same time, my mother was doing needlepoint and she wanted to make me pillows, so I said, let's do a pop-art collection all in black and white. She thought I was out of my mind. She always thought that.

POSTSCRIPT

Since I first talked about the apartment it has gone through one more remarkable transformation, and now, alas, there is a new end to my story. Jerry, my husband, died after a long illness, and the last week of his life we turned our master bedroom into a hospital room; our bed went into storage and the home-hospice people sent in a hospital bed and an oxygen machine. We got nurses around the clock. It was sad but beautiful to die at home. Even he said, "This is the way to go—at home, surrounded by your family."

For many young designers, the first piece you do is often the best you can do, because it is so natural, so evident. It's you. Every day we see thousands of things that we record in our mind and this is the basis of our personality and also of our universe: all you see, all you hear, the people you meet. And so this world—your world—is coming into the object you design. So when you do your first piece, it's the best result of your world. It's like when you make coffee, the first cup is the best.

When I was young I always rejected authority and it was the same when I went to art school in Brussels in 1988 to study interior design. It was not a very open school, you had to do the projects that the teachers told you to do. There was not a lot of freedom, but in the second year I was already making furniture and I did a screen I called Paradoxe Mobile as an end-of-year project. It was the first piece that I did in metal by welding tubes and so on. Although it was a school project, in fact I did it with the help of friends—one had a garage to repair automobiles, other friends were making some theater decor—so it was made in three different workshops. After some time they got bored and didn't want to help me any more so I had to find somewhere else. It wasn't a very commercial piece but I showed it in a gallery in Brussels a few years later and it was bought by Ralph Lauren. That was very motivating; it was a good start. Even ten years later, people ask me about this screen and I still show it on my website.

The house of my parents was built in 1969 when I was in the belly of my mother. It was a very modern house, a little bit like Mies van der Rohe. It had a flat roof and windows from the floor to the ceiling, very nice architecture, but the furniture was not at all modern. My parents did a lot of traveling to England and at that time things were very cheap for Belgian people, especially antiques. That was their interest, so the house was furnished with a lot of antiques. They were absolutely not interested in modern or contemporary furniture. It was a very good contrast and I still believe that it's the best way to have an interesting space. It's what I'm doing myself these days, except the opposite. I have an old house and I

put only contemporary furniture inside. Maybe it's because I lived in that house that I'm finally doing this job; it's possible.

My parents never encouraged me to draw or paint, but my brother and I, when we saw something nice in the street, would bring it back home. It was a big house and there was plenty of room to store things. Also we were keen on automobiles, so we had some old ones that we would repair. At first I did bricolage projects, making shelves and things, and then I began to make some assemblage: lamps with feet, and furniture that was a collage of old pieces. The basis of my work was not coming from the material, it was from philosophy or concept; like sculpture but with functionality. Most of it was for my personal use. Later, when I left art school, it coincided with my parents moving to France to live. They had problems selling their house—I don't know why but it took three years—so I was living there with my grandmother. That was a very free period; I wasn't obliged to do anything so I began to make prototypes for myself. I hired a welding machine and started to make furniture, using all the material that my brother and I had collected. The important thing is that after school, I always thought to do things that were reproducible in serial, not things that are unique and you can never do again. It's more linked to life. Also you're working for average people in a positive way; it's interesting to touch many people, to make life better or nicer. Today when I do things for a private client, I always try to design all the pieces so they can be reproduced afterward. I think that one of the definitions of design is to be produced in a series, otherwise it is art or sculpture.

Anyway, that house of my parents, when all the antiques went out, became a perfect space to make an exhibition. I had already made ten different pieces: a bed that I still use today, the screen, some lamps; everything in metal. There were some paintings by a friend of mine as well. I was surprised that about one thousand people came. It was incredible, but I didn't sell anything. After that, I completely forgot that I had to move out of the house almost immediately, and I had no money of course. At that time Brussels was like a ghost city, you know; there were a lot of empty buildings. Everyone wanted to live outside the city. I never understood this; it's completely stupid. So I thought I could find an industrial building that I could live in for free while I repaired and took care of it, since I was an architect. Eventually someone offered me a place and I'm still here ten years later. You cannot believe what it was like; people had stolen everything, even the pipes. I was camping, but I was 23 so it wasn't a problem. I renovated it myself with friends, it's still in progress. On the first floor there was an old café that I made into my atelier and for years I made furniture there by myself, as well as interior design for various shops, offices, a model agency. The thing was not to earn money by building things, but to make experiments. I needed to see, to touch, to judge it, and then to go further. Now I collaborate with an atelier in Liege, 100 kilometers from Brussels, and they make all of my pieces for De Padova, MDF Italia, Extremis and so on. But I still like to do things with my hands. Now I want to move; I've always dreamt of having a huge horizontal space, 300 meters square. I think it's important for my job to have space, to make a distance to see the pieces. I want to make larger pieces too.

Meantime, my girlfriend has bought a beautiful house here in Brussels, on three or four levels, so when I want to make some impressive meetings I can take clients there. When people come to my office, the effect is not so good; it's reality. To tell you the truth, I think I've never bought myself a new piece of furniture. I have so many prototypes everywhere here; I don't know where to put them. There are so many things that are not designed yet. People always say that if it's any good it's already been done, but I prefer in my work to find something that is really evident, but has not been done before, but which seems clear that it has to exist, you know? The people who are talking the best about design at the moment are the Italians, especially in Milan. In Italy it is really in the culture, they've lived with design for 50 years. In the 1950s Magistretti, Castiglioni, all these people were like superstars.

Everyone knew them. In France, in Belgium, and also in England, I believe, there are very few people who know what design is. Most prefer antiques or rustic furniture.

At this time, I'm more interested to do public spaces or spaces that are not for one person only, like hotels or offices. I'm just finishing a library for one of the commune de Watermael-Boitsfort in Brussels and the Belgian Consulate in Montreal. I'm more interested in that than in houses; maybe if it's somebody I know or that I'd really like to work for. What is very hard is to work with clients who know nothing about architecture and design because in that case, my job is not to give ideas, it's more to make marketing of myself, you know? I think it's two different jobs.

People often ask me what is my inspiration. Isn't it a stupid question? They want me to say, oh yes, I love Philippe Starck, or something. I tell them that the best inspiration I can have is from a nice talk with somebody. It gives me some reference points; a lot of information.

It also gives me energy.

OVERLEAF

In our living room, we've mixed a number of different styles and periods, with prototypes of some of my design pieces. The TETRA dining table, which I designed for Driade Aleph in 2003, has a painted bent-steel frame with a glass top that has been lacquered on the underside; beside it are some old French chairs that came from my girlfriend's grandmother. The frames were in oak but I refinished them in black. In the mirror, which I called Vice Versa because it swivels on a vertical axis to allow hanging for clothes on the back, you can see a glimpse of the kitchen counter and the Jamaica stool designed by Pepe Cortes that is produced by Amat. The screen is the second edition of the piece that I produced originally at art school, but this one has a light zinced-steel fabric fixed on the tube frame. Beyond that you can just see the doors to the garden and, on the wall, a piece representing an alphabet by the Belgian painters Rambouts & Droost.

JOHN PAWSON

When people come to my house they always open a cupboard. They can't resist. When Janet Street-Porter came, she insisted that she can always tell people from what's in their cupboards. But I especially hate them looking in the bathroom cupboard, I hate seeing people's medicines, it's almost rude. So I had cleared everything out. During dinner, she went to the bathroom, and on her return other guests asked her what she'd learned. "Absolutely bloody nothing."

I love order, but I'm hopeless at achieving it. That's probably why I like to have as little as possible. I tend to lose things, no matter how beautiful they are. I never even had any books until just recently. I have had objects that I thought were really beautiful, but got rid of them. When my father died, he had pared down until all he had was in a small tin box. My best filing cabinet is in my brain. I think that's where my inspiration comes from. That's why the written word is always the nicest way to describe a building or a space.

In architecture terms, the house is the most complex single thing that you can do. I find it much easier to design a shop or a museum or a skyscraper than a home, because of its very single function. There are so many things happening, and clients bring so much baggage to the project. They think that I need tons of information about their likes and dislikes, but we're all the same; I don't really need to know too much. Having said that, it is a team thing, and there are many decisions that a client needs to make. Most of my clients want to design the house themselves and they think they are going to get exactly what they want. But, inevitably, they don't know what they want. I used to be more insistent about certain things than I am now, but you have to listen. I would encourage them to have a shower rather than wash in their own dirt. Inevitably if you provide them with a decent piece of architecture, that will change the way they live anyway.

One day I might build my own house, but I have already designed 20 houses that I think of as mine. I could live in all of them. That's the only way I can design. I couldn't give the client something that I didn't agree with. I could live in some of the shops I've designed too. I feel that I have ownership up until the time the client moves in. The thing I find most difficult is the furnishing of the space after it's built. That's why I'm so in awe of decorators, who can produce different furnishing schemes again and again. It's so complex. People underestimate how difficult it is to create new furniture designs. I can't come up with a suitable sofa design. I can do variations on tables, but to make a thing look fresh and new each time is very difficult. Certain objects get to a stage where you can't improve on them. People often think that the sofa is the easiest thing of all to choose; it's a big blob in the middle of the room. For me, there is no such thing as a sofa that is light, elegant, and comfortable, and that doesn't change the space radically. Even the traditional ones I find tricky. Clients think that I'm bonkers. At the same time, I can see that people do need somewhere to loll, drape, flop, or sleep, and they also write or eat on them. To me, the only ones that look good date from a time before sofas became upholstered. I like the formal upright style of Schindler, but to make it comfortable you need to add a lot of cushions and still you can't flop too much.

At home when I was young, my father's idea was that every person in our family had their own "club" armchair, a side table, and a reading lamp. I grew up in Yorkshire in an incredible mansion outside Halifax, part Norman and part 17th-century. I had four sisters, and my parents loved entertaining. My mother cooked, I played music, and my father was always changing things. We had painters and carpenters almost nonstop, and an architect called Geoffrey Cash, who my father directed. He was such a regular that he often stayed for dinner. My room began as a tiny cell-like space which I loved—only just big enough to walk down one side of the bed—but as my sisters grew older and went off to school or got married, my father would knock down a wall, making my room progressively larger. By the time I was 16 my room was huge, but I still kept the same three pieces of furniture.

My room was at the top of the stairs that led directly from the kitchen, so I would be woken to the smell of bacon frying. Eventually I moved out into a cottage in the garden, which my father had decorated, but in the end I couldn't bear it and stripped it all out. He thought I was mad, but I felt better in a sparse room.

From a very early age I had a strong drive to have where I lived as I wanted it, and I wanted it at almost any cost. When I was teaching in Japan from 1974 to 1977, I was given a university apartment in a very posh mansion block, very traditionally decorated in a European way. Eventually I couldn't stand it any longer, so I bought some paint and recklessly, without really thinking about the consequences, I painted it all white—even the fabric-covered walls. I just needed some neutrality, a space that was lighter and airier. I wanted to control the environment I was in because I couldn't control what was going on elsewhere; to create physical rationality out of mental bedlam. I wasn't interested in what anyone else felt, but when the university found out, they were totally shocked. They said, "One of our teachers has had a temporary aberration," and it was all glossed over. The trouble was, I put the second coat on too quickly, while the undercoat was still wet, so it never totally dried.

After that I had a tiny flat in Tokyo with a view of Mount Fuji. Standing in the center, I could almost touch both sides. The only piece of furniture was a low table in the center, so we always sat around that. No matter how many people came, we were still all around that table; even if there were three dozen or so, they sat in two circles and even three. In my current home, I am interested that our life is still centered around the kitchen table. This seems to be the hub of the house. When guests arrive, they go past the living room to the kitchen. It's where we eat and read and spend most time. In my design of houses, I strive very hard to make every room special. Even moving up and down the staircase should be a special experience. My houses seem to have a very sensual quality. The people who are most comfortable tend to be those who are most comfortable within themselves. Certainly my sons and their friends feel totally free. They can impose their own aesthetic on the space, get their stuff out and colonize it for themselves. I wouldn't expect either of them to have the same sort of house as mine, but you never know.

PREVIOUS PAGE

This is the entrance hall of a family house we finished in 2005. Artificial light bathes the Donald Judd bench set in an alcove. From here stairs lead up to the bedrooms and down to the family kitchen and living area.

LEFT

One of my most interesting home projects in 2005 was this house in the Setagaya district of Tokyo, for Yumiko and Katsuhiko Tetsuka. The main living quarters on the first floor occupy a large open space facing onto a double-height courtyard. A stone bench that originates indoors extends the full depth of the house. Nature is represented in accordance with Japanese architectural conventions, as an isolated element—in this case, a maple tree—rather than as landscape.

OVERLEAF

The vacation home for the photographer Fabien Baron is located in a wheat field in southern Sweden. Large windows with concealed aluminum framing allow sharply defined views out, to read as part of the actual fabric of the interior—to the extent that a different location would make a materially different house. In the kitchen/dining area, a six-meter oiled oak island work surface dominates the space. Poured concrete floors and white plaster walls keep internal color to a minimum.

Though I trained as an architect in Torino, I've never really wanted to build my own house. I only do architecture when it is part of another project—when I have to rebuild or restore an old building because I need a good "box" to do the interior; to provide a nice environment for the project—a house or a shop or whatever it is.

The first real home I had—nicely designed, nicely planned— was when I was living in Hong Kong. At first, finding a place was a nightmare. It's very easy in Hong Kong to find a house, because you decide the price and the square meters you want, and they show you 25 houses practically all the same. I was so romantic— I said, why can't we find an old house? One day I was in a taxi with the real estate agent and I saw a beautiful house with a garden, and I said, why can't we find an apartment in a house like that? The lady looked at me and laughed. "This is the Governor's house." It was where Chris Patten lived. Eventually we found an area very near the old airport, a little street with small houses from the 1940s and '50s, and we bought an apartment on the top floor of a three-story building with a garden that had two lychee trees. It was very beautiful. The windows had nice old brass handles and everything had been very well kept, which is very strange for Hong Kong, where the weather destroys everything and people are careless. At that time Claudio and I were living part of the year in Milan and part of the time there, while he had work in China and I had a project in the Philippines, so I was shipping furniture and materials from everywhere. It was easy to find local craftsmen: they work very fast and they are very bad. There's no quality at all. We lived there for eight years but it was never "finished." It had the character of a colonial house, which now is totally lost in Hong Kong. At that time I began to be much more concerned with the home than I had been before.

My earliest memory of home wasn't really a home at all. When my sister and I were very small, we used to go every weekend to an area in the mountains called Valle d'Aosta, and every little mountain or valley had one of these small medieval churches made in rough gray stone. They were usually empty and sometimes there were steps up to a gallery where you could look down into the church. To me, because they were small, I thought of them as houses, and I said to my father, why don't we rent that house instead of staying in the other one?, which I liked less. My father was in the construction business, and when I was very young we moved into a new house that he'd had designed by a well-known architect friend of his. I don't remember anything unusual about that process, because builders and architects were always coming and going. It was in a very nice area of Torino between the river and the hill, where there were a lot of nice houses with big gardens. I don't remember who chose the

furniture, but it was very modern: an Albini table, a leather sofa by Vico Magistretti. At the time I didn't realize any of this, but now I do. My parents never changed anything or moved anything around. They lived there all their lives; my mother is still there. I used to have a grandmother who lived nearby and who was completely crazy for food. The big fun for her was buy food, cook food, give away food. This was her hobby and also her full-time work. She was doing it all the time, all the time, all the time. We were accepting and eating these miracles in food—escargot and things like that—but also giving it away because we couldn't eat it all. I suppose my mother never really had to cook much and now she has zero curiosity for food, not even cooking *one* potato. My grandmother said that she was very lucky in her life, because when she was young you had to marry somebody that your family chose for you. But she didn't like that man, and when he died she told me, "I said to myself, nobody will tell me what to do any more." She had a fun life, always cooking.

I remember that when I was seven or eight, one of the magazines, maybe it was *Abitare*, published a series of three square posters. The first was a beautiful picture of a Dogon village in Africa, from very far away; the second poster was the same village but from much closer; and the third was a detail of a Dogon door. I had these on the wall of my room for many, many years and I would say to myself, I want to go there, to see how things really are. Since then, I've been to Africa a lot, but not to that area. There was no encouragement of creativity at home and I really hated school from day one, so I tend to forget everything about that. I didn't know what I wanted to do, but I systematically did the opposite to what they told me to do. Eventually I ended up doing architecture, but they would have preferred me to do something more technical—more serious—maybe engineering. You have to remember that at that time there were no design schools. More girls used to go to architecture school than engineering courses, which were almost exclusively men. One of the things I will always remember was toward the end of the five years, attending one of the last lectures by Carlo Mollino in the university. He was teaching perspective drawing (there were no computers then of course). He was facing the blackboard—his back to the students—and he was drawing with both hands, like the conductor of an orchestra. Both hands were drawing in a completely symmetrical and independent way. For me it was one of the most impressive performances I ever saw done by a human being. Later I discovered that he had sometimes been working with my father but I didn't know that then. At the end of the course I left and went to central Africa. An ethnologist who was working there on a project connected to the university had advertised for one photographer and one person able to design small houses for the local people, so I told him I'd come. There was no pay. I was maybe 22 and I spent two years there—very happy. Everything was so leisurely, we were working to African time, a completely different concept of time. That was when I got very curious about other people's systems of mind; that a way of living is also an expression of a way of thinking. I found those houses very interesting and very inspiring. In fact, after that I decided to go to China. Back in Torino I had a phone call early one morning from Alessandro Mendini who at that time was the director of a magazine called *Casabella*. He had read a thesis I'd done at college about radical architecture—those strange groups like Body Art, Archigram, Soleri, UFO, Archizoom, and so forth, who were working at the time and with whom I had become fascinated. Mendini asked me to work for his publishing group in Milan and to develop the project into a book. So I went. Doing more research and being a part of the magazine, I began to discover people working in design and in factories, and I found a world I liked. At the time a company called Abet Laminati were offering bursaries to encourage designers to work on the decoration of surfaces. I did so much on that project, very crazy, very funny, and very nice ideas; they were so impressed that they gave me my first freelance job. Then other jobs followed and in fact I'm still working for them, all these years later.

During that period I was very lucky because I lived in a beautiful little Amsterdam-style house with four friends—two couples. They were very good designers so the house was really fantastic. I had no ambition to get my own place. Then one night at a dinner with a friend, I met Claudio. He was living and working in China and he had been inviting everybody to come, but at the last minute nobody wanted to go. I was very curious. Mao Tse Tung was alive and everybody was talking about China a lot at that time. So I said I'd come. He lived in Beijing and when I got there it was fantastic. There was a feeling like being in a theater. The spaces were huge, the roads so wide, with millions of bicycles. Sometimes there would be one automobile crossing this river of bicycles. It was impossible to go to houses, or even to talk to people, but from the aesthetic point of view we *loved* that China very much. It was severe, but it was really beautiful and there was apparently no poverty. After that I wanted to work in Asia, but of course I couldn't find a private client because the factories are not rich enough to pay for a consultant. So I worked through the big international agencies like the EEC and the World Bank, who gave me a brief to work with local manufacturing skills and traditional crafts and techniques in these countries, to produce products for the home that were contemporary and suitable for the European market. At first I worked in the Philippines, but then it developed to Thailand, Indonesia,

Malaysia, and Vietnam. I would spend each year 50/50 between Milan and Asia, spending five to six weeks at a time based in Hong Kong. This work wasn't something I learned how to do at school, it came little by little. Now we have schools that are oriented to teach people who want to learn how to design objects, to design interiors, to design fashion shows. Then, we really didn't have all this information. We had to discover everything for ourselves.

Eventually I had to find another place to live in Milan, and one day, by accident, a friend of mine told me they were selling this building where I am now. I came to see it and in five minutes I decided to buy it. It was so ugly, not appealing at all, but I decided that I could turn it into something nice. When Claudio saw it he thought I was mad. I don't really enjoy the process of doing up a place, but I like to think about what can be done. I always love the project that is not yet finished. When the process is complete, that's it, I lose interest immediately. I don't have a special love for one chair or one spoon or one ashtray. I just look forward to doing something else. I have a small design company now and employ ten people, across three divisions: one designs objects and furniture, one does interiors and exhibitions, and one researches trends, materials, and so forth. A few years ago we worked on the concept for the Armani Casa project.

I would like to work in public spaces: hotels and maybe restaurants. I travel so much that I think I know what you want to have when you go around the world. Traveling today is much less interesting than in the past. Too many nice hotels look the same. Eventually we sold the place in Hong Kong, and Claudio now lives in Shanghai. Meanwhile, I've just bought an apartment in Paris which I'm redoing. When I go to someone else's house I don't really *look*. I'm like a cat; I *feel*. Chinese people talk about good feng shui or bad feng shui. I really don't like to analyze in a systematic way. I look around and decide if I feel comfortable or not, and then little by little, I discover things.

In the living room of this house, OVERLEAF, that I converted for clients in Tuscany, I restored the original farm buildings, but then introduced new colors and materials. To humanize the gigantic proportions of the space, I used a small number of large elements in pairs and moved the sofas away from the walls. In the same house, the dramatic effect of the bathroom, FOLLOWING PAGES, comes from my use of color as well as the size and proportions of the room. In the kitchen, NEXT PAGE LEFT, all the elements are traditional, but I have reinterpreted them with a contemporary point of view. In my own kitchen in Milan, NEXT PAGE RIGHT, similar elements create a totally different effect. I love finding everyday things that are beautifully designed, and I often have them on display.

When I was growing up with my two sisters, none of us was very artistic, but there was a *huge* encouragement to write. My father was the writer Idris Shah and he wrote about Sufis. So, as children, the one thing we heard day and night was the sound of a typewriter. He was very prolific and he wrote a few stories for us, which have been made into books that I now read to *my* children. The house was full of stories. So it gave me the sense that writing a book is just like any other process, it's not very difficult, you just have to sit down in a chair for quite a long time and crank it out. So that's what I do now. I never saw my father struggling with writing. If there's one thing that he instilled in us children, it was that in your life, be productive. Produce, produce, produce. If you're weaving baskets, weave a lot of baskets. If you're knitting sweaters, knit a lot. At the same time you have to put in a lot of effort before you start reaping the rewards. I'm a huge believer in the apprenticeship process—starting at the bottom and working your way up. Sooner or later all the competition starts to fall away. If you keep going, you break through.

We lived in a very beautiful Georgian house called Langton House, in a village called Langton Green, near Tunbridge Wells in Kent, and I lived there from soon after I was born—in 1967—until I was 23. Consequently, I've got very strong memories of this very secure, wonderful childhood home, and now that I have two children, I find myself thinking about it a lot. The house was always packed with interesting people, so although it was in a very quiet English village, it was a crucible for all kinds of writers and artists, but also many other people as well—from bricklayers to lawyers. Sometimes there would be as many as 30 people staying for the weekend, and listening to my father ranting on as he liked to do. Much of the intellectual chat was lost on me as a child; it was only later that I realized who those people were. Doris Lessing, the writer, was often there; also J. D. Salinger was a good friend. At the same time, my father's writings attracted a lot of hippies that he was always trying to get rid of. Most of them were stoned out of their minds. Gosh, yes—I remember all that hippy environment. I should say as well that my father was from Afghanistan and he had always wanted to take us there when we were small, but it was too dangerous. So he would take us to Morocco instead. Neither of my parents could drive, so the gardener, a very sweet old guy called Jamie, would drive us from Tunbridge Wells, through France and Spain, to Morocco, where we would stay for a couple of months each year. Some of my earliest memories are of the blue men and the desert and Fez; the smell and sounds of that country; the thrill of leaving Gibraltar by boat; seeing Europe disappear and Africa emerge; arriving in Tangier as the sound of muezzin calling the people to prayer is echoing over the city. It's a very magical thing, and I guess it planted a seed in my head that, later, I wanted my children to have this boost of cultural color. My mother is half English and half Indian, so she has a great sense of color and design, and because my parents never had much money in the '60s, she thought she could decorate the house quite inexpensively by bringing fabrics and rugs and brassware and all kinds of trappings from Afghanistan. Those Georgian houses were usually quite formal, but ours was rather bohemian. There was always new stuff—new clutter being acquired from our trips—but the house stayed very much as it was. When I was 13 I was sent away to boarding school, but I was very sad—I felt almost *betrayed*, because I wasn't in this place that I absolutely adored. There were no pictures of football players or rock stars in my bedroom, it had a Moroccan painted bed and brass lamps and Afghan rugs. It was only later that I realized there were other ways to live.

When I was 17 I started traveling on my own, first to the United States and then to East Africa, where I studied political science (African dictatorships) at university. After that, during my 20s, I traveled a lot. Japan, India, most of the African countries, all over the Far East. In India, I met Rachana, who is now my wife, and we lived in New York for a year. But eventually I realized that I had to begin a more serious, a more organized life. My father died and I inherited just enough money to buy a tiny house in the East End of London—Whitechapel. Built in the 1780s, it was a very sweet early Georgian four-story house that had been renovated by a yuppie guy, but the rooms were only as big as postage stamps. I felt a bit like a fox in its lair. Then when our daughter Ariane was born I felt wracked with shame that I was bringing her up in such a tiny place. The wonderful thing about my childhood was that we were always outside playing in the woods, or down in the swamp in the mud. That was very important to me and I didn't want my children to grow up *inside*. To me, *inside* is a place to go if it's dark or if there's torrential rain. After three or four years, we started thinking of moving out of London, but wherever we looked the houses I liked were too grand, too expensive. So then I began thinking about Spain, maybe Granada. In the mid '90s what happened was, for someone like me—I don't have to turn up at the office—with the internet, I can write anywhere. I could be in Shanghai now for all you know. I thought that if I could be productive and write original stuff then I'd get commissions and that would mean I could live anywhere, and that's how it worked out.

Someone I met said, "What are you going on about Spain for—why don't you go to Morocco?" Suddenly I realized what a brilliant idea it was. In my mind it was a place of syrupy, yellow memories of my childhood. I was so down in the dumps that I got the feeling that this might be my savior. It was just a question of when and where. At first I went there about 15 times in one year—a few days at a time—looking at property. In Marrakech I looked at maybe 70 riads—which are very trendy now—but they were just too expensive. Then I started to look at Fez, which is an unbelievable Arab city, exactly like something out of the *Arabian Nights*. Then back in London, I got a phone call from the mother of an old school friend, whom I hadn't talked to in years. She had heard on the grapevine that I was looking for a house in Morocco and she owned one in Casablanca that she wanted to sell. "Go and see it," she said. I flew out there the next day, and I found something out of a dream. It was a very large house—maybe 30 or 35 rooms including bathrooms, and it had four or five courtyards with pools and fountains. But the house had been boarded up for nine years and it was in the middle of a shanty town—all around was this incredible vibrant tin-shack community, which to me was quite mesmerizing. It's real Morocco. Having said that, it was a very posh part of Casablanca, just five minutes' walk from the ocean, so my fear was that I wouldn't be able to afford it. But the owner knew that if she sold it to someone else, they would almost certainly destroy it and build apartment blocks on the land. She knew that I would renovate the house with traditional crafts and that I would fill it with children and with life.

It's traditional in Morocco to employ people to keep an eye on your house—look after your garden and so forth—so the house came with three guardians, who in nine years had almost never entered the building. In fact they were astonished that someone had bought it—fearful for us moving in, especially that we had two small children. There was no electricity and no water, and the house, they said, had jinn. All Muslims believe that overlapping our world is a world of spirits—jinn—who can be both good or bad. They are supposed to be created by smokeless fire. Muslims believe that if your house is boarded up for a long time, whereas in London you might get squatters, here you will get jinn. So we set about this quite painful journey of renovation.

There was an architect that turned out to be a disaster and it's a very long story, which I have since written a book about, but eventually I realized that if I could find the master craftsmen, then I could renovate this house. For example, even if you have a house that is five hundred years old, you can still find the great great great grandchildren of the craftsmen who did the original floors or the mosaics to come and restore it in the same way. To keep the guardians happy, we eventually had to hold a huge exorcism. Imagine in London trying to find an exorcist, but here it took only about five minutes. Twenty-three men and one woman, between the ages of 17 and 50 and wearing red and white

robes, arrived; and for the next four days there was chanting and drumming, there were trances and writhing on the ground. They killed a goat and nailed up its gall bladder and drank its blood and drank their own blood and killed chickens. The house was full of black smoke and incense and noise—a very shrill sort of bugle instrument. Jinn hate blood and milk and salt, so that was thrown everywhere. They worked mostly during the night, resting during the day, until eventually they said that they had *sucked* all of the jinn from the walls and swallowed them whole. Taking their money, the exorcists ran off into the mountains again—they had certainly worked hard for it. To me the house just felt the same, but the guardians were very happy and the maid was very *very* happy. The renovation after that took about two years. If you have work done on a house in Morocco, it's very different from in Europe. You have to source and buy absolutely everything yourself. Every bag of cement, every nail, every screw. The other great thing is that all the work is done by hand. For a year we had 40 or 50 workmen living in the house. They would come from villages or from Fez and they didn't have anywhere to live, so we just put them up here. During that time, I never saw a power cable or an electric drill. For example, the guy who did all the mosaics—which is a serious work of art—would turn up each morning with only a white scarf folded over with his lunch in it, and his hammer in the other hand. That's all he needs.

Now that it's all finished, I've never been so happy. I'm still traveling and writing about it—in fact I just came back yesterday from Afghanistan. For me the great thing in my writing is the idea of the huge quest. For example, I once went in search of King Solomon's mines in Ethiopia and wrote about it. It's not so important if I find the thing or not. But to me—more than ever now that I've got children—the greatest moment of the journey, is arriving back home.

OVERLEAF

We bought or had made, a lot of the furniture in India and that style works very well here in Morocco. It's all part of the same Arab/Oriental culture which swept into India because of the Moguls. The house otherwise, is decorated very very simply, with the emphasis on the materials and the craftsmanship.

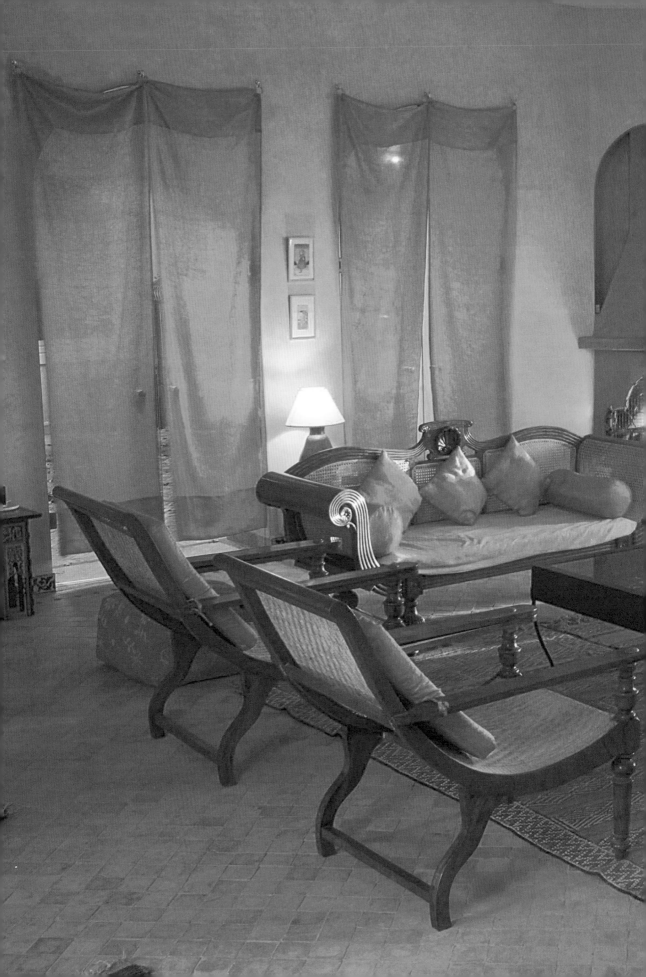

During the year that I worked on this investigation into what people think about HOME, I contacted nearly two hundred people, from Brad Pitt to Helen Clark, The Prime Minister of New Zealand. Sometimes I reached them, sometimes I didn't. Sometimes—via their agents, their PAs, their PRs, or their publicists—the message got through, sometimes it didn't. Sometimes I got the impression that the subject was too private to talk about, sometimes too unimportant. Several said that it was too important to talk about on the telephone. Sometimes they sent me a generous reply:

Dear Stafford Cliff
I'm afraid Alan Bennett isn't able to contribute. He thanks you for thinking of him but has simply too much on his plate at the moment. He wishes you all the best. Yours sincerely LL. 25.5.05

Dear Stafford Cliff
Thanks for your email, which I passed to Baroness James. I'm afraid writing commitments and other constraints on her time mean she can't agree to be interviewed for HOME—but she asked me to wish you good luck with the project.
Sorry to be disappointing.
Best wishes, WF.19.5.05

Hi Stafford,
I have approached Nicole (Farhi) re this and unfortunately she has decided not to get involved. She isn't very comfortable discussing her home and is also rushed off her feet at the moment as she doesn't have an assistant.....Thank you for thinking of us and best of luck with the book,
Best regards, KM 3.5.05

Hello Stafford
Thank you for your Ewan McGregor request. Sorry for the delay in replying. Unfortunately due to Ewan's heavy schedule at the moment he is only doing project specific publicity. However I will keep your details on file if anything changes—and the best of luck with the project. Many thanks, TC 13.4.05

Dear Stanford
Thank you for your e-mail. I'm sorry, but Michael Palin will be unable to contribute to your book—he has an extremely busy schedule already. Thanks for asking him. Regards, PB 11.4..05

Dear Stafford,
Thank you so much for sending the information below. I have managed to talk to Matthew Williamson and he is very sorry but he feels that with his heavy work load at the moment that he cannot be involved in any further projects at this time, We wish you well with your book, C. 29.3.05

Dear Stafford,
Thank-you for your e-mail. Unfortunately, due to an already over exhaustive schedule Vivienne Westwood is unable to commit to any further projects / interviews at present
Best Regards, TCG.18.3.05

Hi Stanford,
Many thanks for your email requesting an INterview with Ellen MacArthur for your new book. I am afraid that due to Ellen's schedule she will not be available for your request at this time. I am sorry that we will not be able to help you on this occasion. Best regard, LH. TeamEllen 17.3 05

Dear Stafford,
Thank you for your e-mail. i have spoken with Don McCullin, and I am afraid he is not interested in contributing to your book. He wishes you good luck and success with the project. Cheers, MG. 10.6.05

Hi Clare
re; Nigella Lawson I'll run it by her but I don't think it'll be one for her. Best wishes MH 19.7.05

Hello Stafford
I did get a reply from Terry Gilliam asking me to let you know that he's not available to participate in your project. Best wishes, LD 14.6.05

Dear Stafford Cliff
Our apologies for the lateness of this reply. It is a busy time at OMA but we are endeavouring to answer all correspondence and requests as soon as possible. Thank you for your kind invitation for Mr Koolhaas to participate in the "HOME" book, however, Mr Koolhaas will unfortunately not be able to participate. Thank you once again for the invitation and we wish you all the best with the publication DL. Public Relations. 22.6.05

Dear Stafford,
I had another chat with Emma about your project and, sadly, she has to decline on account of the level of other commitments she has professionally and through all her charity involvement. She sends huge apologies and wishes you much success with the book. Best wishes, MG.
Assistant to Emma Thompson 4.7.05

Dear Stafford,
Thank you very much for your email regarding David (Schwimmer) and the possibility of him being included in your book, however I am afraid that due to existing schedule commitments he is unable to participate in this.
Kind Regards AH 5.7.05

Dear Stafford,
Thank you for your email regarding Sam Taylor-Wood. Unfortunately the artist wishes to decline your offer to participate in the publication outlined below. I am sorry that on this accasion we were unable to assist. If I can be of further assistance do not hesitate to contact me.
Regards, Sara. White Cube 11.7.05

Dear Stafford,
Thank you for your email. Unfortunately, although the artists are flattered by your request, Gilbert & George would like to decline the offer to be featured in your publication. I am sorry that on this occasion we were unable to assist. If I can be of further assistance do not hesitate to contact me.
Regards, Sara. White Cube 11.7.05

Stafford,
I believe that you have been in touch with James's PA, Helen. I am very sorry that I have not called you since we last spoke. Unfortunately the answer, again is no to James being able to do the interview with you. I am sorry if I have not been totally clear with you, but as I said, James does not tend to talk about this subject now. He generally likes to talk about engineering, R&D, patents and design and technology within schools. His time is also just so busy at the moment and he spends most of his day in the labs with the engineers. He is also spending an increasing amount of time in the US too. I hope that your book goes well and I do look forward to seeing it when it comes out. Please let me know and I will make sure I get a copy. Maybe James can do something in the future with you. Kind regards, CB.Dyson.14.7.05

I am afraid this is not possible Hugh (Jackman) leaves London next week for Canada for the next film and he is filming here at the moment and has no spare time.
Kind regards, LC 22.7.05

Stafford,
We met with Terrance years ago! I have accepted telephone interviews for papers & polls but feel books too important.
So is HOME! Jack Lenor Larsen 22.7.05

Dear Stafford,
I hope you are well.Unfortunately Mr Klein has chosen to decline this opportunity but he thanks you for

thinking of him. Good luck with the book.
Best Regards, Malcolm. 5.8.05

I understand you initially put your request through David Collins' office, however shortly afterwards we were brought on board to handle David's PR. All outstanding requests were sent to us, most of which we declined on his behalf and this was one of them. Our main role is to manage his time as he has very little of it as he has so may projects that he is working on at the moment. I'm so sorry to let you down, it's just that right now he has no time to do this.
With best wishes JH. Camron 5.8.05

Dear Stafford
I am Kate's assistant at Sputnik. She is still on holiday at the moment but she told me that she had said no directly to your request to interview the Duchess (of York) when she last spoke to you? Apologies for the misunderstanding.
Kind regards KC 8.8.05

Dear Stafford,
I would like to thank you for your kind offer to be involved in your current HOME book project. It sounds like a very interesting concept. At this time, I am committed to my own book project so I am not able to accept your offer to be interviewed. Thank you so much for thinking of me. I wish you success with your new book venture.
All the best, Ricky Lauren Oct 19, 2005

Dear Stafford Cliff,
Many thanks for your letter. I am sorry to be the bearer of bad news, but there is no way that Judi could meet with you before the end of December. Judi sends her regrets that she is unable to help after all, but she wishes you well with the project.
Yours sincerely, S. J.
Personal Assistant to Dame Judi Dench, C.H., D.B.E. 28 November 2005

Dear Stafford,
You are not bothering me at all! Project of HOME Book is really interesting. I´m sorry to say, however that Pedro (Almodovar) won't be able to form part of your book. His schedule for 2006 is full and during this year he needs to focus on his own projects. I hope you´ll understand his decision. But please do inform us about your further projects. I wish you good luck with Home book. Yours sincearly, Liliana. Dec 20 2005

Thanks for your request however I am very sorry but we will need to decline as Baz (Luhrmann) is not currently doing any non-project publicity at the moment and he is travelling overseas while you are in Sydney as he is in pre-production for his next feature project. See you soon- M. Jan 18 2006

I've asked Martha (Stewart) about this several times now in hopes of getting a positive response but she is simply too overwhelmed with the demands of shooting a daily television show and running the many facets of her business as well, so I fear we have not been successful. She thinks that it is an interesting concept but right now it isn't going to be possible to have her cooperate at the pace that you need, so I think I am doing you a favor by saying it's best to move on. So sorry as I had greater hopes but wish you the best and look forward to the outcome. Susan. Jan 23. 06

Dear Stafford,
I've heard back from Alain (de Botton) and unfortunately he's not going to be able to take part in the project as he's off on tour in New Zealand and Australia. Thanks for thinking of him though. best Anna 17.4.06

Dear Stafford,
My schedule unfortunately does not allow yet, but soon. I will be in touch.
Cordially, Ian (Schrager) Feb 28 2006